understanding the
MALAYSIAN WORKFORCE

Guidelines for Managers
Revised Edition

Edited by
Asma Abdullah & Aric H M Low

Malaysian Institute of Management

Published by
MALAYSIAN INSTITUTE OF MANAGEMENT
Institut Pengurusan Malaysia (22978-D)
227 Jalan Ampang
50450 Kuala Lumpur
Malaysia
Tel: 03-2164 5255/242 5255
Fax: 03-2164 3224
http://www.mim.edu

ISBN 983–9065–12–2

First Published January 2001

Printed by Kinta Enterprise
Kuala Lumpur

FOREWORD

The primary determinant of an organization's prosperity is the quality of its workforce. Therefore, for most organizations a critical success factor is the motivation, productivity, resourcefulness and skills of its employees.

The Malaysian workforce is influenced and shaped by multicultural forces which make it unique and quite different from workforces in other countries. Understanding the distinctiveness of the Malaysian workforce, therefore, is crucial for managers, both local and foreign, if optimum productivity and performance is expected. It is also a prerequisite for the enhancement and maintenance of good industrial relations and harmony.

The Malaysian Institute of Management should be congratulated for publishing **Understanding the Malaysian Workforce: Guidelines for Managers**. The book is particularly welcomed in the context of human resource development as the key driver in fulfilling Vision 2020 and the creation of new Malaysia through k-economy.

I also congratulate the editors, Asma Abdullah and Aric Low, for putting together the contributions of the many Malaysian experts into a cohesive and readable form.

Datuk Dr. Fong Chan Onn
Minister of Human Resource
Malaysia

Pejabat Menteri Sumber Manusia, Aras 2, Blok B (Utara), Pusat Bandar Damansara, 50530 Kuala Lumpur.
Tel: 03 - 2557220, Fax: 03 - 2554700

PREFACE

The passage from the 20th to the 21st century is a watershed in economic history. In crossing the century, we leave behind an old economy made up of bricks and mortars and distinguished by a dominance of the national state. With globalization and digitalization, we make way for the new economy and the emergence of a universal market unrestrained by national boundaries. The movement from the old to the new economy will require us to embrace the new technology and, with it, a new paradigm of doing and managing business.

To be competitive, we have no choice but to use the best tools available. If e-commerce is to be the high potential for wealth creation opportunity, we should reach out and master the new game. It is a game that will keep changing frequently as the world's attention is caught by a global mania to create, innovate and push the frontiers of technological possibilities.

As we keep pace with change, it falls on managers to manage the change process. It is in this area of managing change that professional management will be severely tested. How do we cope, reorganize, restructure, realign and reengineer our work and our relationships to best exploit the new technology? Much of the change process will depend on the given cultural dimensions of the organization.

Malaysia has a plural workforce which is still strongly influenced by ethnic, religious and cultural backgrounds. We need to understand these dimensions so that we can more intelligently manage our human resource. As we anticipate much more change to be introduced in the coming years, we need to be more adept at managing the change at ground level. This means that our understanding about the behaviour of our workforce, what motivates them and how to assemble them into a force of one, is a prerequisite to transforming our organizations from the old to the new economy.

This revised edition of *Understanding the Malaysian Workforce* describes the behavioural characteristics of Malaysians. Effective management of the Malaysian workforce should, therefore, benefit from a clear understanding of the appropriate way of relating to Malaysians in specific business situations.

The Malaysian Institute of Management is grateful for the contributions of many experts in the production of this publication. Special thanks go to Asma Abdullah and Aric Low for editing the book and to Karen Yue for her tireless effort to produce the publication.

DR TARCISIUS CHIN
Chief Executive
Malaysian Institute of Management

INTRODUCTION

This is a practical "hands-on" book for managers who want to know more about the influence of ethnic values on managerial practices in Malaysia. Its main purpose is to sensitize both local and foreign managers and professionals to the different ways of interacting with and managing Malaysians who come from many different ethnic groups.

Background

The idea for a revised edition of the original 1992 publication of *Understanding the Malaysian Workforce* (reprinted thrice: 1994, 1995 and 1996) was triggered at a forum held in late 1997. As a result of the meeting and more sharing of perspectives and insights about the Malaysian workforce, we have added three new chapters in this revised edition.

The first edition was published by the Malaysian Institute of Management (MIM) with support from the Konrad Adenauer Foundation and in collaboration with the Foundation for Asian Management Development, Japan. We are pleased to note that the book is now widely used – both as a guide and reference for local and foreign managers and working professionals – on how to get along with Malaysians. Students of management in both local and foreign universities have also used it as a basic text to learn more about the hidden dimensions of managing people.

We hope this timely revision with its new insights will continue to expand our knowledge and understanding of the Malaysian workforce. We have also added to each chapter a new segment on issues and challenges that are distinctively Malaysian and which managers in Malaysia would face at the workplace.

The thoughts and views compiled in this book are based on the collective experiences, observations – or shall I say "wisdom" – of a team comprising seasoned managers, consultants, academicians and trainers who are themselves multicultural in composition. Except for one *Orang putih* Whiteman, the rest of the team are Malaysians of different ethnic origins – born, bred and working here but who have had exposure to numerous foreign cultures in their social interactions here and during their stints abroad whether for education, work or social visits.

As mentioned in the earlier version, work in this area of interest started in late 1989 with workshops on intercultural and cross-cultural management. Many speakers, including Geertz Hofstede, Robert Westwood, Hari Bedi and several others in the field were invited to share their views and research. A national survey on managerial values was also conducted and at the end of the project, the book writing team met to discuss how to organize the content around a central focus (i.e. how values and culture influence behaviour at the workplace). The initial book records some key observations, guidelines and a summary of Malaysian values relating to a number of managerial practices made by the contributing authors as they interacted with fellow Malaysians.

Our contributions then and now are as much from the "heart" as from the "head". The findings therefore are a blend of empirical studies, shared day-to-day experiences and observations made at workshops and conferences. In addition, discussions with national and international experts, researchers and consultants in the field of culture and management were also conducted.

Rationale

The nineties in Malaysia was clearly a post-colonial era. Yet despite this, the colonial yoke has not been fully removed. Deeply ingrained and still perpetuating is this view that a good education, especially in management invariably means Western education. In addition, even the image of a manager is that he must be like the *tuan besar* speaking and behaving like one. Every Malaysian manager, for fear of being labelled as *kolot* old fashioned and not up-to-date, wants to be identified as modern and progressive. As a result, he looks to the West for a recipe of knowledge that seemingly has all the instant answers and solutions to his managerial problems.

Malaysians, brought up with their set of unique cultural values, tend to carry them into the workplace to influence the way they think and act. These values cannot be dismissed and have to be understood by managers who naturally have a tendency to view managerial practices from a Western paradigm. They have to examine the meaning of these local values and wherever possible, use them to serve as a bond to form the basis of shared practices observed at the Malaysian workplace.

In the recent past we have seen a proliferation of management classics and popular best sellers such as *In Search of Excellence, The One Minute Manager, Covey Principle Centered Leadership, Grid Management, Quality Control Circles, Winning Teams*, etc. Thus, in many training and boardrooms, the popular concepts promulgated are all too often referred to without prior critical review of their appropriateness to the local context and organizational settings.

Our contention is that while these ideas from the West provide well-tested principles and techniques in management, they may not all be so culturally relevant when applied across borders. Behaviour has no meaning until and unless it is understood in the cultural context where it is learned and displayed. The local context has to be addressed, especially in the area of people management. It is only by incorporating the local nuances, values and beliefs that there can be a uniquely Malaysian management style that is a synergistic blend of the best of both worlds – East and West.

A great deal of soul searching, research, writing, discussions and debates went into the production of this book. We feel that the materials we have included are important to Malaysians as they strive to live and work together harmoniously, synergistically and productively. Hopefully, it will enable managers in Malaysia to better interact with a diverse workforce whose values are deeply rooted in ancient Asian history and traditions.

In writing this book, we too have become more aware of our own ethnic values and the need to be more sensitive to those with whom we live, work and study together. Learning about our own values has been a challenge and an enriching experience for all of us who have been exposed to a predominantly Western management education. It must be remembered that as Malaysians, we are open to many foreign management practices in every field of people management. However, merely adopting managerial practices and techniques originating in other cultures may only generate "symbolic conformity" but not really meaningful shared behaviours among the workforce.

So, eight years later (after we first published the first edition) we can safely say that one's cultural programming tends to have a major influence in the way we think, feel and act if we want to be accurate in our assessment of others. The current and future workplace will see people from a diversity of tastes, educational exposures, and orientations. We can no longer adhere to the concept of universality in management constructs, recipes and "one size fits all" theories on human motivation and people development.

The new globalized scenario, while making it easier for us to share the similarities we have with one another, will also help to promote and celebrate differences. The notions of "the global and the local" and "the universal and the particular" will become part of the way we work regardless of where we are. Therefore, understanding and not just respecting and tolerating local values and practices may have to become part of a manager's repertoire of skills.

With the dawning of the new millennium comes an increasingly interconnected workplace where managers are expected to strike a right balance between what is necessary to be globally responsive and what is locally appropriate. Malaysians will have to explore their own strengths from within – in the spirit of *Malaysia Boleh* – so that the Malaysian management style is strongly anchored in local "soil", i.e. core values that are distinctively part of our national identity. This will provide greater confidence to all of us on selecting what contextually will or will not work, and by so doing, enable us to be culturally literate when working in different settings.

Structure

There are 15 chapters in this Revised Edition. For ease of reading, attempts have been made to arrange the chapters in an integrated and logical sequence, yet each chapter can be read as a standalone on an area of managerial practice.

The book is divided into three main parts, namely, Foundation Concepts, Managerial Interactions and Special Applications. However, a common theme in all chapters is the repeated emphasis in each chapter on key Malaysian values of building harmony, maintaining relationships, showing respect for elders and those more senior, projecting concerns for face, and exhibiting humility, which are manifested in different ways as Malaysians interact with others at the workplace. Repetition of these values by a number of authors in their respective chapters indicates their importance at the Malaysian workplace. Being sensitive to these values may enable managers to get that "extra mile" from their workforce. Each chapter concludes with some guidelines on what to do and what not to do when interacting at the workplace.

Part 1 outlines some basic fundamental concepts relating to the influence of ethnic values in the areas of communicating, leading, motivating and building a multicultural work team.

Part 2 focuses on the need to be sensitive to some of the key values which influence managers in their day-to-day interactions as they make decisions, recruit and orientate new employees and manage conflict at the workplace.

Part 3 discusses specific applications which are peculiar to the Malaysian workplace: managing meetings, dealing with government agencies, working with Malaysians and expats, managing change and the future outlook.

Acknowledgements

As a coordinator of the book project, I (Asma) have been fortunate to enrol Aric H M Low in assisting with the revised edition as he brings in a fresh new perspective in reviewing all the chapters in this edition. Once again, we wish to thank the writers and contributors for their continuing support in this revised and updated edition. Most of them were involved right from the start when we held a forum on the subject in December 1997 with sponsorship from the Konrad Adenauer Foundation. In particular, we thank the presenters of papers and participants including Dr Hamzah Kassim, Prim Kumar, Lim Hian Boon (who departed on 24 November 1999) as well as Dr Ezhar Tamam, Dr Zainal Ahmad and Dr Roselina Ahmad Saufi. We also wish to acknowledge the authors of the original edition who are not involved in this revision but whose original contribution we have retained as much as we could, and they are Ong Siok Beng and Chong Sheau Ching. Special thanks also go to Karen P S Yue for her untiring efforts in providing editorial support and production supervision to get the revised edition to the printers on time.

Selamat membaca.

Asma Abdullah
asmaabd@pop.jaring.my

Aric H M Low
aric@pc.jaring.my

CONTRIBUTING AUTHORS

ASMA ABDULLAH, *MSc (Ed) (US), MEd (Counselling) (Malaya), BA (Anthropology) (Aust), DipEd (Aust)*
Asma is a human resource development specialist in a large US multinational organization based in Kuala Lumpur. In the last 10 years she has been writing, speaking and conducting seminars on the influence of culture on management in both foreign and local based organizations. She is the author of *Going Glocal: Cultural Dimensions in Malaysian Management* and editor of *Understanding the Malaysian Workforce: Guidelines for Managers*, both published by MIM.

ARIC H M LOW, *MBA (Bath), ICSA (UK), AAdm, AMIM*
Aric is a Chartered Secretary and serves as a director on the boards of a number of companies. He advises corporate and business bodies on company and statutory matters. He also serves on the council of the Malaysian Association of Accounting Administrators (MAAA) and as financial advisor and administrator to a world relief and development agency. He regularly trains business students and conducts courses in a range of management areas including Managing Change, Organizational Development and Business Organization.

A KHALIQ AHMAD, *PhD (Alig.), MCom (Alig.), MPhil (Alig.), Chartered Marketer (CIM) (UK), AMIM, MCIM*
Dr Khaliq is an Assistant Professor at the Department of Business Administration, Faculty of Economics and Management Sciences, International Islamic University Malaysia. He is Deputy Dean, Research Centre, IIUM and has many years' experience in teaching and research. Currently, he is a member of the local council of the Chartered Institute of Marketing (CIM). He has published five books and over a dozen articles in leading journals.

BIEN MEI NIEN, *MBA (HRD), BA, CdipAF (UK), Hon D Ed (RGU, UK)*
Mei Nien is the Managing Director and Principal of Professional Advancement Achievement Centre (PAAC), a private educational institution of higher learning that she established in 1984. She edited MIM's publications, *Malaysian Management Cases* Volumes 1 and 2, and contributed to *Case Writing – A Guide, Malaysian Entrepreneurs* as well as the first edition of this book. She sits on a number of committees including

being the current President of the National Association of Women Entrepreneurs in Malaysia.

EZHAR TAMAM, *PhD (Oklahoma), MA (Michigan)*
Ezhar Tamam earned his doctorate from the University of Oklahoma at Norman, and masters degree from Michigan State University at East Lansing. He is currently head of the Department of Communication at Universiti Putra Malaysia. He teaches courses and directs graduate theses in the area of cultural influence on communication. His current research centres on strategies in managing intercultural communication challenges attributed to cultural differences.

MANO MANIAM, *MA (Vermont), BA (Malaya)*
Mano's professional career includes being a General Manager, Executive Director, teacher, lecturer, trainer, researcher, writer, environmentalist, actor and director in theatre and films. At MIM, he headed the three-year research project in Intercultural Management Studies which led to the initial publication of this book. He is a founder member and Deputy President of the Case Writers Association of Malaysia (CWAM).

NORMA MANSOR, *PhD (Liverpool), MPA (Liverpool), B Econs (Hons) (Malaya)*
Dr Norma is currently Professor and Head of Department of Administrative Studies and Politics at the Faculty of Economics and Administration, Universiti Malaya. She has co-written books as well as published articles in journals in the areas of organizational behaviour and management, culture in leadership, and conflict management.

ONG ENG ENG, *BEd (Counselling & TESL), Cert Ed (Maths), Cert Zipopo Moral Leadership*
Ong Eng Eng is the Director of Creative Personnel Skills Services Sdn Bhd. She is a qualified counsellor and training consultant in areas of soft skills, personal development, family enrichment, corporate management and development. She is also a UNIFEM facilitator for the Advancement of Women and a certified trainer for Zipopo Moral Leadership. Her services extend all over Asia. Some of her notable contributions were in Beijing as the SEA Coordinator for the 4th World Conference on Women.

PETER SHEPHARD, *PhD (Columbia, USA)*
Dr Shephard is the Managing Director of Brain Dominance Technologies, a subsidiary of People Potential Sdn Bhd. He also teaches on several MBA and Doctoral programmes in areas of Organizational Behaviour and Human Resource. He has been a management consultant for over 28 years (23 in Malaysia) and trains and consults to a wide range of clients throughout Southeast Asia, especially several large well-known multinationals on Human Resource Management, Organization Development and Training.

SARAN KAUR GILL, *PhD (London), MEd (TESL) (Malaya), BA (Hons) (Malaya), Dip Ed (Malaya), Dip in Applied Linguistics (RLC, Singapore)*

Dr Saran, an associate professor specializing in Language and Communication in the Workplace, is presently the Head of Academic Training at the Centre for Academic Advancement at the Chancellery, Unversiti Kebangsaan Malaysia. She has successfully bridged the gap between academia and industry through training programmes that focus on business communications, assertive communication skills and business presentation skills. She is presently researching in the area of women, leadership and intercultural communication. A highlight of her career has been as module writer, chief trainer and coordinator of the Volunteer Orientation/Cross-cultural Communication Programme for 10,000 Malaysian volunteers for the 16th Commonwealth Games.

SHARIFAH MARIA ALFAH, *MM (AIM, Philippines)*

Sharifah Maria Alfah is now training consultant and facilitator for Usulinc Sdn Bhd. She is also specializing as executive coach and mentor and has developed programmes in Leadership Management and Coaching. Her experience in Human Resource spans a period of 27 years, working for both public and private organizations and the last job in the corporate world was as Vice President and Country Manager of HR for Seagate Technology. She is also the Chairman of MIHRM, Northern Branch and teaches Organizational Behaviour and HR for DIHRM programme.

SURJIT SINGH, *AMN*

Surjit is the Managing Director of JITS Management and Training Consults Sdn Bhd. He has 40 years of experience as a teacher, executive-officer, administrator, trainer, author and consultant. He has served as the Malaysian representative on the panel of contributors for the Asean Training of Trainers Manual. He is also a founder member of the Case Writers Association of Malaysia and presently serves as a Vice President, Training and Education, in the Malaysian Society for Training and Development. He recently co-authored *Human Resource Development in Organisations*. He was also presented the Lifetime Achievement Award in the field of HRD by the MSTD.

TARCISIUS CHIN, *PhD (Manchester), MBA (British Columbia), BA (Hons) (Malaya), Hon D Bus (RMIT), FMIM*

Dr Chin is the Chief Executive Officer of the Malaysian Institute of Management. He has previous experience both as an academic at Universiti Malaya and as a practitioner at Cycle and Carriage Bintang Berhad. He is the Director of Studies of MIM's degree programmes and is currently an Adjunct Professor of the RMIT University, Melbourne. He is the editor of MIM's journal, *Malaysian Management Review*. He writes regularly for the fortnightly column "MIM Speaks" in the *Sunday Star* and is a contributing author of *Management in Malaysia,* an MIM publication.

OTHER AUTHORS OF THE FIRST EDITION

ONG SIOK BENG is a training consultant specializing in Business Communication Skills. She recently retired from government service as Head of the English department in a leading teachers' training college in Kuala Lumpur.

CHONG SHEAU CHING has worked in development projects in several Asian countries. She was involved in development projects in Malaysia which required her to deal extensively with all levels of the Government in Malaysia. She currently writes for a column in *The Star.* She holds a Masters degree in International Administration.

CONTENTS

PART 3 – SPECIAL APPLICATIONS

1

INFLUENCE OF ETHNIC VALUES AT THE MALAYSIAN WORKPLACE

ASMA ABDULLAH

INTRODUCTION

Managers work with people, and effective managers take into consideration such factors as attitudes and assumptions, personal beliefs, values and aspirations, and the interpersonal relationships of subordinates. All these factors impact on how Malaysians function at the workplace to drive business actions.

Malaysia, with an expected workforce of 9.3 million by 2000 (Seventh Malaysia Plan, 1996-2000), has often been described as a "minefield of multicultural sensitivities" due to its diverse racial and ethnic composition. Like its population composition, each workplace comprises, in varying proportions, the different races and ethnic groups – Bumiputra (comprising the Malays, Dayaks, Ibans, Kadazans, and Muruts), Chinese, Indian and other smaller racial groups.

Each ethnic group has a rich and distinct culture based on age-old beliefs, traditions and practices rooted in the Asian heritage. Therefore, the Malaysian work scenario is culturally diverse. Yet, in this diversity, Malaysians work in apparent harmony and unity brought about by a few unifying factors, the most

1

important of which are values that have withstood the test of time and are common to all the ethnic groups.

The influence of cultural values on the way work is done in Malaysia can be seen in employees' behaviours. Employees bring with them cultural values acquired from their home environment and schools. These influence the way they relate with one another and perform their daily work. Ultimately, the way work is organized and performed is an expression of what they consider important.

Therefore, these values have to be recognized and understood by managers when they interact with employees in their day-to-day work. To bring out the best in the workforce, managers have to be sensitive to different cultural nuances, beliefs and traditions and harness them into common bonds of solidarity. When these are upheld through shared practices, a unique Malaysian work culture can evolve to support the goals and objectives of the organization.

OBJECTIVES OF THIS CHAPTER

This chapter aims to provide an overview of the common values that bind Malaysians of all ethnic origins, and how they are manifested at the workplace through shared practices. It begins by identifying key issues and challenges at the Malaysian workplace and how managers need to recognize these values when solving problems and making decisions. The workplace may portray an intracultural and homogeneous setting, an intercultural and diverse setting, and a cross-cultural setting with foreign nationals.

The chapter also attempts to define culture and its key elements of symbols, rituals, heroes, values and underlying assumptions, and describe the differences between the two types of underlying assumptions (Western and Eastern/Asian traditions) which tend to give rise to differences in values between them. Some typical observations made by others on the more significant characteristics of Malaysians at work will also be shared.

In addition, the chapter will highlight the findings from a recent survey of Malaysian managers from the three main ethnic groups on a number of statements relating to their cultural values and their work orientations. These findings will be compared with a small sample of Anglo Saxon managers currently working in the country.

A summary of core values will be given, and the chapter will conclude with some general guidelines that both local and foreign managers may want to consider when managing the different ethnic groups in Malaysia.

ISSUES AND CHALLENGES

A distinctive management identity which can be considered indigenously Malaysian has yet to evolve. As a result, the study of management has largely depended on concepts and practices that have originated in foreign soil – be it American, Australian, Japanese, British or Canadian. Hence, there are a number of issues and challenges which managers in Malaysia face in their daily work and these are:

- **Sensitivities and hidden nuances**

The diversity of the Malaysian workforce requires managers to be familiar with the core values of all the ethnic groups in the country. While a manager is familiar with the values of members of his* own ethnic group, he may not be altogether comfortable when he manages a subordinate or relate with those from another ethnic group. There are often sensitivities and hidden nuances of members of his workforce which are often unstated and not clearly defined and explained to others. These sensitivities become more apparent at the time of decision-making, especially when an action taken is not congruent with the values of a particular ethnic group.

- **Curriculum on local culture**

The study of local values and how they are interpreted at the workplace has yet to be included as an academic subject in management schools in the country. Most human resource development professionals take this area of study for granted as the emphasis on harmony and understanding tends to make it difficult to accentuate differences among the diverse groups. As a result, most Malaysians grow up in their own ethnic enclaves without a deeper understanding of what is beyond symbols and rituals of each other's culture as observed through religious practices, food prohibitions, dress code, and polite face-to-face interactions at the workplace. Tolerance is for the moment seen as a workable compromise in dealing with the differences, but there is little attempt to go beyond symbolic understanding.

- **Quantitative skills over-emphasized**

The culture of an organization is best described by its own employees who have internalized the unwritten values that underlie its management practices. By being "permanent residents", employees are often the best informants on how their managers and leaders interpret the values of their organizations. The current emphasis in the study of organizations is more often centred on the quantitative approach, which focuses on the work climate, compensation policies, and leadership styles. However, the findings generated through this

---

* The pronoun "he" and its other forms ("his", "him") are used throughout this book with a general meaning to include reference to the female person wherever applicable.

approach seldom offer managers concrete advice on how to deal with issues and dilemmas related to local sensitivities.

- **Ethnic orientation at the workplace**

Malaysian managers, regardless of ethnicity, education and training, are likely to bring their own cultural values to the workplace. For example, a Malay manager would tend to emphasize the values of family togetherness, harmony, relationships and "give and take" while a Chinese will regard highly the values of hard work and financial incentives. Indians, on the other hand, may prefer respect for elders and harmony. These ethnic-based values tend to pervade the workplace. Managers are expected to take them into consideration when making decisions and solving problems.

- **Western constructs received in a cultural vacuum**

There is still a tendency for local human resource development professionals to rely heavily on management and behavioural theories based on Anglo-Saxon (Western) constructs in studying organizational behaviour in Malaysian organizations. Concepts such as self-esteem, self-actualization, and empowerment, which have originated in individualistic work settings, are often used without any attempt to examine their appropriateness in a more collectivist and hierarchical setting like Malaysia and whether they have the same interpretation at all. As a result, many of these imported (Western) constructs are received in a cultural vacuum in Malaysian organizations as there is no frame of reference in the existing structure to situate them.

DEFINING CULTURE

Culture can be defined as a shared and commonly held body of general beliefs and values which define the "shoulds" and "oughts" of life of certain ethnic communities. These beliefs and values are learned at an early age in life, and one is usually unaware of their influence.

As stated by Hofstede (1991), "Culture is the collective programming of the mind which distinguishes the members of one group from another – the interactive aggregate of common characteristics that influence a human's response to the environment." In addition, culture also includes the programming of the mind, body and spirit embodying the cumulative deposit of knowledge, experience, meanings, beliefs, values, attitudes, religions, concepts of self, status, perception of time, role expectations and spatial relations acquired by a large group of people in order to adapt to the environment.

Culture manifests itself in patterns of language and thought and forms of activity and behaviour. Culture, both explicit and implicit, can be described by examining the symbols people identify themselves with, the rituals they

4

observe and the heroes or role models personifying their values. All these are based on a set of underlying assumptions about how they view nature, other people and God. While symbols, heroes and rituals are easily identifiable through observed shared practices, values and assumptions can be inferred from people's behaviour.

In describing a particular culture of an ethnic group or social organization, the following five elements can be used.

1. **Symbols** are seen words, objects, hand gestures, different forms of dress, ways of addressing people—all of which are used to enhance commitment and compliance among insiders. Some examples include the *salam* (the clasping of the hands in greeting) among Muslim Malays, the "lion dance" of the Chinese and the *pothu* on the foreheads of Indian ladies.

2. **Rituals** are systematic and programmed daily routines such as the way Malaysians of different ethnic groups perform their religious ceremonies and weddings. In the context of organizations, rituals refer to how letters and e-mail messages are written and transmitted, and how planning systems and business luncheons are organized. All these express the values of a particular group of people and indicate the strength of their adherence to a certain behavioural norm. Thus, it is important that the right activities be selected as they become traditions through time. Through ceremonies, rituals and oral traditions, values give a culture or organization its strengths and uniqueness. They are standards of decorum to enable people to know what to expect and how to behave.

3. **Heroes** serve as models for behaviour and exemplify the ideal members, managers or employees within an organization. They are often referred to and recognized by others as role models or key role players. What role models think and act often personify the values of the culture.

4. **Values** are the unseen aspects of culture and can only be inferred from people's behaviour. While values are not easily perceived, they form the heart of a culture. Values influence our thoughts, feelings and actions and, unconsciously, how we work and relate with others. More often, the values of a culture that characterize a society cannot be observed directly but must be inferred from various cultural products like people's behaviour, symbols, rituals and what heroes do through shared practices. Presumably, these cultural products and expressions reflect what members revere and want to pass on to succeeding generations through the process of socialization.

5. **The basic underlying assumptions** of a particular culture tend to prescribe the ways members perceive, believe, think and evaluate the world, self

and others. For the purpose of comparisons, the following three basic orientations will be used to compare Malaysian and American cultures:

a. **Views of Man's relationship with Nature,** including:
   - Man's control over nature and the environment versus harmony with it

b. **Views of Man's relationship with People** including:
   - Concept of self : separated and related
   - Relationships versus task
   - Hierarchy versus equality
   - Monochronic versus polychronic time orientation
   - Shame and guilt
   - Low and high context form of communication

c. **Views of Man's relationship with God** including:
   - Secular and religious
   - Revealed and acquired knowledge

These underlying assumptions need to be understood because they provide the basis for the differences in thinking and acting between Western-oriented cultures and Eastern ones. Although cultures can no longer be seen as dichotomous wholes, failure to look at these underlying assumptions can cause us to evaluate people from another culture by using our own cultural assumptions or "lens".

The following assumptions influence the values revered by members when they work and relate with others (Schneider, 1988; and Hofstede, 1984, 1990; Trompenaars, 1992):

• **Views of Man's relationship with Nature**

In Western tradition, Man is separate from Nature. He is viewed as the master who controls, exploits and harnesses the forces of Nature through technical and scientific devices to satisfy his personal and societal needs. Goodness means separating oneself from Nature and establishing mastery by looking for ways to control and manipulate it to human advantage.

In the case of the Eastern (Asian) tradition, Man is part of Nature and is more inclined to have absolute harmony with it. He has to integrate with and adapt to the environment which makes him subservient to or be in harmony with Nature. This belief tends to promote a healthy co-existence with other people and willingness to accept things the way they are. For example, the Malays are more inclined to hold ceremonies like *doa selamat* (prayers for safe ridings) while the Chinese are more inclined to believe in *feng shui* and a prayer shrine of the *datuk*. Likewise, the Indians are also more inclined to refer to astrologers prior to holding auspicious events.

- **Views of Man's relationship with People**

The Western tradition tends to focus on the individual rather than the group. He is expected to set his goals and determines through his own efforts to fulfil these goals. As an autonomous individual, he is expected to be self-reliant, have his own options, be motivated by challenges and competition, and attain fulfilment through his own personal achievements. He treats others as equals and is able to separate ability from personality in his work. Status is based on egalitarian norms and hierarchy is of less importance. Greater priority is placed on task rather than the individual and differences are resolved through face-to-face open discussion.

The "Western man" also values action (i.e. what a person does) and regards time as important and must be distinguished between time for work and time for play. As time can be measured, spent and saved, he moves quickly to keep pace with it.

The "Eastern tradition", on the other hand, views Man as a member of a family; he is dependent on others and as a result derives his identity through members of his in-group. He is related to them and so group or communal feelings supersede the incentive to excel over others. The basis of establishing contacts with other people is to initially cultivate good and friendly relationships. Members in the group believe that it is only through understanding and a "feel" for the other party that they are able to live and work smoothly with one another. For example, the slogan *KITA BOLEH* epitomizes the group-relationship value.

In addition, Asians believe that one's life is largely a matter of "fate". Personalities are reacted to in their entirety. There is a tendency to accept or reject the person completely. Relationships are hierarchical and people are treated according to their position in society. Differences or conflicts are often handled through an intermediary in order to avoid losing "face".

The "Eastern man" is also less hurried about time and as a result "doing" is not emphasized as much as "being". It is expected that man take things as they are because of the importance placed on harmonious living. What a person is, is important. Work and life are not separated and there is stress on the present. Life is lived from day to day.

- **Views of Man's relationship with God**

Some cultures, especially in the West, believe that there has to be a separation of state from religion and would therefore promote a secular approach to development. Religion is not an important factor to be considered in one's daily work as it is a personal matter.

But in some cultures, it is important to incorporate a more holistic approach which combines both religious and material (temporal) dimensions in one's outlook on life. The whole person – mind, body and spirit – has to be taken into consideration as it is important to blend spiritual and material dimensions in order to have a sense of interconnectedness with the world (environment) around him.

In the West, Truth and Knowledge are derived from facts and measurements, and the use of scientific methods of inquiry. In the East, they are determined not from objective facts alone, but by spiritual and philosophical principles as well. Malaysians, being Eastern-oriented, are therefore more inclined to bring their religious values into the workplace.

TABLE 1 shows the five key elements of culture.

TABLE 1: Key elements of culture

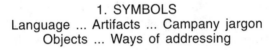

```
┌─────────────────────────────────────────────────────────────┐
│ ┌───────────────────────────────────────────────────────┐   │
│ │                    1. SYMBOLS                          │   │
│ │        Language ... Artifacts ... Campany jargon       │   │
│ │           Objects ... Ways of addressing               │   │
│ │ ┌───────────────────────────────────────────────────┐ │   │
│ │ │                 2. RITUALS                        │ │   │
│ │ │      Meetings ... Celebrations ... Ceremonies     │ │   │
│ │ │ ┌───────────────────────────────────────────────┐ │ │   │
│ │ │ │                3. HEROES                      │ │ │   │
│ │ │ │          Founders ... Role models             │ │ │   │
│ └─┴─┴───────────────────────────────────────────────┴─┴─┘   │
│ ┌───────────────────────────────────────────────────────┐   │
│ │                    4. VALUES                           │   │
│ │     Shared Practices (to demonstrate core values)      │   │
│ │        – can be inferred from behaviour                │   │
│ └───────────────────────────────────────────────────────┘   │
│            5. BASIC UNDERLYING ASSUMPTIONS                    │
│           Ways of perceiving, thinking and evaluating        │
│    – man's relationships with Nature, People and God         │
└─────────────────────────────────────────────────────────────┘
```

Based on the discussion thus far, it is evident that Malaysians take after the underlying assumptions of Eastern (Asian) cultures. For most Malaysians, the earliest and strongest source of values is the family – the most influential instruments being parents, elders, aunts, uncles or other relatives with whom there is greatest contact during the "formative" years. They are the "significant elders".

The early school environment (teachers and the types of books read) is also another strong influence. Those who are exposed to a religious upbringing – whether through the school, parents or religious literature – will tend to espouse these values in adulthood.

The third source of values comes when we mature and are able to refine our own value system. Included are college, university, social or work groups, the military (for some) and our first employers, especially managers and supervisors. By the time we enter the workforce, these primary and secondary value sources are so well integrated that they influence our own value system. It may be said that our values are often other peoples' values which we have chosen to hold or defend.

KEY OBSERVATIONS AND SURVEY FINDINGS

Malaysians, regardless of their ethnic origins, observe a set of values which are a clear and uncompromising statement about what is important to them. These values are revered and form the basis of their shared rituals which are frequently strengthened within family members and significant elders. In managing the Malaysian workforce, managers need to know and understand the significance of these values before trying to introduce any new management practices. Managers who are sensitive to the significance of these values can create a work climate that allows employees to feel appreciated and have a sense of belonging.

The following underlying values were observed to have been made by both local and foreign managers to characterize the behaviours of the Malaysian workforce based on the values they have acquired from their parents and significant elders.

* **Non-assertiveness**

    Malaysians are extremely dedicated to doing a good job. They are eager to please and find it difficult to say "no" or insist on their rights.

* **Respect for seniors and preserving face/avoiding embarrassment to others**

    Generally, subordinates will not argue with the boss, for it will be seen as a loss of face for the latter. For the same reason, a subordinate would pretend to understand instructions given to him by his superior for fear of being thought stupid. Subordinates are also reluctant to refer back or bring up any problems arising to the attention of their superiors. They usually do not ask for help when they do not understand. They tend to act with deference and obedience towards their elders.

- **Loyalty, respect for authority**

  An authoritarian style of management is still predominant and usually tolerated. Subordinates are expected to be loyal to the company and to authority. They go along with the paternal attitude that often develops between employer and employee.

- **Collectivism ("we" orientation), cooperation**

  Malaysians work extremely well in a team environment as they like to have a sense of belonging. The spirit of collectivism is more important than individualism, and this is often translated in the willingness to give priority to group interests ahead of individual concerns. Satisfaction at work comes from having opportunities to receive respect from fellow colleagues and maintaining harmonious, predictable and enjoyable friendships with subordinates and peers.

- **Harmony and face**

  Malaysians prefer compromise to confrontation, and often seek consensus and harmony in business dealings. The perspective of superior and subordinates is less likely to be in conflict. Every attempt is made to avoid damaging self-esteem or face. Open public criticism and outspokenness are avoided because they undermine harmonious relationships. Tolerance and understanding count more than legalistic and rationalistic arguments which are based on objectivity.

- **Preserving face**

  Malaysians are less forthcoming in expressing their views and opinions and are uncomfortable when critically evaluating peers and subordinates. Giving negative feedback can be awkward and difficult as indirectness is more the norm than directness. Criticisms, when given, can be taken personally and may lead to loss of face.

- **Status, good manners and courtesy**

  Malaysians are likely to engage in and tolerate elaborate forms of courtesy and standardized rituals which are calibrated according to the rank of the recipient and the formality of the occasion.

- **Respect for hierarchy**

  Social formalities are extremely important as one's social status in the community should be accorded due respect.

- **Harmony and non-aggressiveness**

  Malaysians dislike overt display of anger and aggressive behaviour. An aggressive, "go-getting" and "take charge" kind of manager may be perceived as brash, rough and insensitive. He may also threaten social harmony and cause his subordinates to be withdrawn and non-contributory.

- **Trust and relationship building**

  There is a strong preference for a relationship-oriented approach rather than a task-oriented approach when performing tasks. Developing trust and partnership understanding are far more important than the contractual obligation of getting the job done.

- **Third party and preserving face**

  There is a tendency to deal with ambiguities and uncertainties by using the indirect approach of a third party. Bad news becomes more palatable to the recipient when communicated through a respectable third party.

- **Intermediary in establishing trust and goodwill**

  The use of an intermediary to make first contact with a prospective client is important for establishing goodwill and trust. In this way, the prospective client can raise issues which otherwise would be difficult to do in the presence of the person seeking business.

- **Tolerance and respect for differences**

  Malaysian managers recognize the religious, cultural and food observances of the Malays, Chinese and Indians.

Malaysians have also been known to describe themselves as follows:

- Not as articulate and assertive as foreign peers, e.g. from Hong Kong, America and Singapore. Projecting an image of self-confidence is sometimes not in harmony with the values of humility, modesty and politeness.

- Not so candid, open and expressive in communicating feelings and ideas to others. Giving and receiving praise make them feel ill at ease. Being direct can be seen as ill mannered and may give a bad reflection of one's upbringing.

- Tend to be very cordial and polite in making their requests and conveying disappointment, especially when dealing with government authorities. May even be a little indirect for fear of being seen as too confrontational, forthright, brash and rude. If this happens, future relationships may be affected.

- Tend to be indirect when communicating disappointment for fear of hurting the feelings of the other party.

- Do not find it easy to separate professional affairs from personal life. Two good friends would be unlikely to argue openly or contradict one another at a meeting. Disagreements are seldom discussed in an open and frank manner as avoidance is the preferred mode for resolving conflict. Preserving face is important.

- Not comfortable in providing and receiving verbal feedback if they are not followed by overt actions in the form of a pay raise, lunch treat, request for advice, etc. Malaysians are not very expressive in verbal feedback for fear of being insincere or too direct.

Evidently, the observed values of Malaysians are quite different from those of Westerners. Hence, any attempt to introduce managerial practices that have evolved in a Western setting will need to consider the underlying assumptions and how members of a particular culture relate to nature, people and God.

TABLE 2 shows a list of the common values found in managers from the main ethnic groups (Bumiputras, Chinese and Indians) in Malaysia. This table was obtained from a series of conferences, workshops and seminars conducted in 1990 – 1992 by the Malaysian Institute of Management (with sponsorship from the Konrad Adenauer Foundation). For the purpose of comparison, a list of values obtained from American expatriates is also included in the table.

Based on the survey findings from 443 Malaysian and 56 Anglo Saxon managers working in Malaysia, a number of core Malaysian values are observed:

1. More group-oriented

Most Malaysians, regardless of ethnicity, are generally group-oriented (see Figure 1). The dimension of "I-We" is even more significant for the Malays, who believe that a person has no real identity unless he belongs to a collectivity or group. Hence, fulfilling obligations to family members, close relatives and even friends, is very important to maintain their sense of identity to a particular group.

The need to be part of a group is often expressed in their desire for a strong support system in the form of a "big brother" or "big sister" from whom they can seek advice and support. This network can serve as an emotional valve for employees who are not comfortable in communicating their frustrations on the job directly to their superiors. It also serves to assimilate newcomers into the workplace.

TABLE 2: List of ethnic values in Malaysia

Using qualitative approach		
A: MALAYS		
Respect for elders	Friendliness	Not aggressive
Spirituality	Politeness	Cooperation (*gotong royong*)
Humility	Harmony/peace	Good manners (*sopan-santun*)
Face	Loyalty	Faith in God (*Tawakal*)
Tact	Apologetic	Family oriented
Generosity	Formalities	Obedience
Caring	Accommodating	Fairness
Patience	Trustworthiness	Sincerity
Feelings *(rasa)*	Discipline	Courtesy
Hospitality	Teamwork	Self-respect *(hormat diri)*
Feelings	Tolerance	Non-confrontational
Honesty	Indirect	Sense of appropriateness
Rituals	Compliance	Food and ceremonies
Budi (tacit system of reciprocal obligations)		
B: CHINESE		
Food	Money	Gambling/risk taking
Hard work	Perseverance	Filial piety
Success	Harmony	Respect for hierarchy
Diligence	Face	Integrity
Education	Thrift	Modesty
Wealth	Meritocracy	Honesty
Generosity	Family oriented	Entrepreneurship
Happiness	Prosperity	Pragmatic/practical
C: INDIANS		
Fear of God	Participation	Sense of belonging
Loyalty	Hard work	Karma
Brotherhood	Security	Champion of causes
Family	Filial piety	Harmony
Modesty	Face	
D: WESTERN (mainly Americans)		
Individualism	Achievement	Independence
Success	Hard work	Freedom of speech
Punctuality	Privacy	Informality
Equality	Competition	Innovation
Assertiveness	Directness	Frankness, openness

FIGURE 1: Members' preferred orientation
(Group oriented vs Individual oriented)

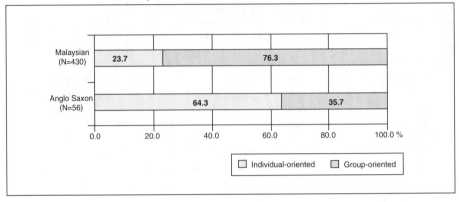

FIGURE 2: How members rank the 3 key factors in setting work climate

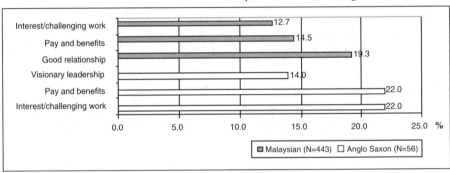

FIGURE 3: Values revered by members

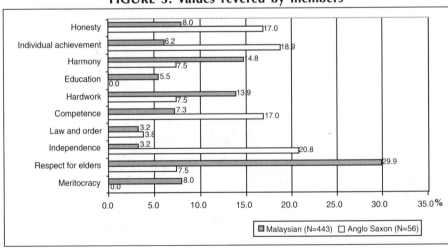

FIGURE 4: Work related values of members

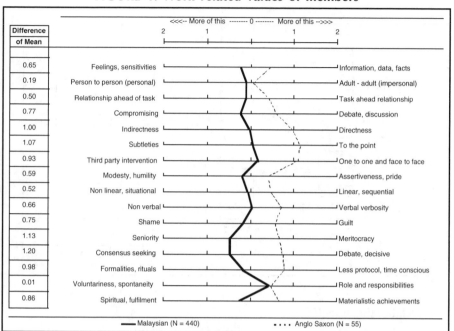

<<<-- More of this -------- 0 -------- More of this -->>>

Difference of Mean		
0.65	Feelings, sensitivities	Information, data, facts
0.19	Person to person (personal)	Adult - adult (impersonal)
0.50	Relationship ahead of task	Task ahead relationship
0.77	Compromising	Debate, discussion
1.00	Indirectness	Directness
1.07	Subtleties	To the point
0.93	Third party intervention	One to one and face to face
0.59	Modesty, humility	Assertiveness, pride
0.52	Non linear, situational	Linear, sequential
0.66	Non verbal	Verbal verbosity
0.75	Shame	Guilt
1.13	Seniority	Meritocracy
1.20	Consensus seeking	Debate, decisive
0.98	Formalities, rituals	Less protocol, time conscious
0.01	Voluntariness, spontaneity	Role and responsibilities
0.86	Spiritual, fulfilment	Materialistic achievements

—— Malaysian (N = 440)   • • • • Anglo Saxon (N = 55)

FIGURE 5: Work practices and norms of members

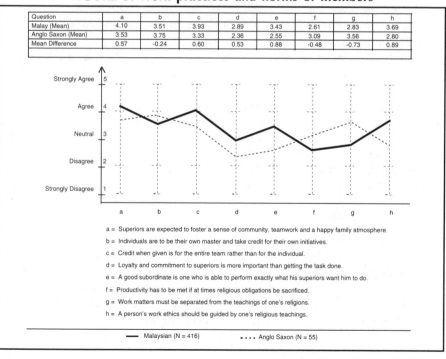

Question	a	b	c	d	e	f	g	h
Malay (Mean)	4.10	3.51	3.93	2.89	3.43	2.61	2.83	3.69
Anglo Saxon (Mean)	3.53	3.75	3.33	2.36	2.55	3.09	3.56	2.80
Mean Difference	0.57	-0.24	0.60	0.53	0.88	-0.48	-0.73	0.89

a = Superiors are expected to foster a sense of community, teamwork and a happy family atmosphere.

b = Individuals are to be their own master and take credit for their own initiatives.

c = Credit when given is for the entire team rather than for the individual.

d = Loyalty and commitment to superiors is more important than getting the task done.

e = A good subordinate is one who is able to perform exactly what his superiors want him to do.

f = Productivity has to be met if at times religious obligations be sacrificed.

g = Work matters must be separated from the teachings of one's religions.

h = A person's work ethics should be guided by one's religious teachings.

—— Malaysian (N = 416)   • • • • Anglo Saxon (N = 55)

FIGURE 6: Ways members resolve conflicts

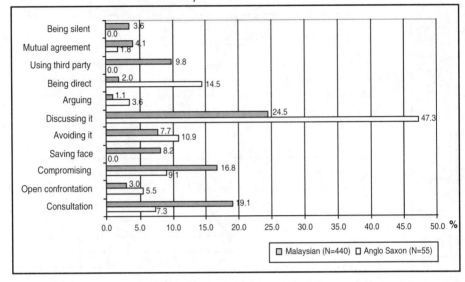

2. Relationship-oriented

Malaysians tend to focus on relationships more than the task, even in a commercially-oriented interaction (see FIGURE 2). This is shown in the findings on climate setting where most Malays especially value highly the importance of good relationships. It is therefore not easy to separate business and private lives as they are often well integrated in the social fabric of ethnic-based relationships. Direct rejection of points of view may be felt as a rejection of the person.

A person from a particular ethnic group would prefer to conduct business dealings or work with others from the same ethnic group. Often, trust is taken for granted on the part of managers towards their subordinates; in turn, the subordinates are expected to be loyal. Hence, relationships are often personalized, based on an unwritten code governing relations, differentiating peers, superiors and subordinates.

3. Respect for elders

All three main ethnic groups rated highly the value of respect for elders in the findings (see FIGURE 3). Malaysians are therefore expected to behave deferentially in their speech and manners when they relate with their elders. Leaders are often considered "wise elders" and their authority is often unquestioned in the sense that what they say is not often challenged. Very often, subordinates will show their respect by allowing the most senior and experienced staff to speak first and set the tone for the discussion.

4.   Loyalty

Another concept related to respect for elders and managers is loyalty (see FIGURE 4). This is reinforced in the statement that Malaysian managers more than Anglo Saxon managers tend to be loyal and committed to their superiors. To Malaysians, particularly the Malays, managers have a moral obligation to care for employees in return for loyalty and commitment. Very often, employees are considered members of an extended family and the employer a good parent who will protect them. Malaysians live in a complicated web of kinship ties based on the concept of mutual and traditional obligations as demonstrated in the relationship with one's family, village, state or social group. It is likely that an employee who has a good relationship with his supervisor will also be loyal to the organization. As loyalty is highly valued, employers expect their employees to be dedicated to their work and loyal to the organization.

5.   Hierarchical

Closely related to respect for elders, Malaysians are also conscious of the social hierarchy in their society. Honorifics are used for certain individuals to indicate social status, levels of authority and wealth. This is supported in the work-related values (see FIGURE 4) as most Malaysians do recognize the importance of using the appropriate forms of recognition to address their elders and high status individuals. The polite system requires one to know the correct way of salutation as this indicates good manners. Doing it rightly may enhance one's social standing and personal contacts whilst doing it wrongly may cause the other person to feel slighted. For each given status, there are definite actions through which respect can be demonstrated.

6.   Religious

Malaysians, especially Malays, identify with a particular religion – belief in a Supreme Being. For them, happiness comes from suppressing self-interests for the good of others or discovering it from within oneself through prayers and meditation. Contentment is obtained through religious and spiritual pursuits, and it is difficult for Malays to relate to self-actualization needs without taking into consideration the needs of others, especially their loved ones. This is evident in the scores given to the statements in FIGURE 5 on the influence of religion on work ethics.

A person who is individualistic may even be ostracized by his family. Because of this value, Malaysians tend to be in harmony with nature and take a stance which is likely to be considered reactive rather than proactive.

7.   Harmony

Malaysians are often happy with their work if they have harmonious, predictable and enjoyable relations with their superiors, subordinates and associates. They feel secure if others in the organization, especially their superiors, are aware of them, understand their situation, treat them fairly and assess them accurately. This is again shown in the survey findings where harmony is the second important value after respect for elders among Malaysians – regardless of ethnic groups (see FIGURE 3).

Being frank with negative opinions is often avoided as it undermines harmonious relationships and may cause employee withdrawal leading to poor performance and disloyalty towards the organization. To preserve harmony, the truth may not always be out in the open and one has to look for subtle cues to see evidence of conflict.

8.   Face-saving

Preserving face (*jaga maruah* in Malay or *lien mentzu* in Chinese) has a lot of significance at the workplace (see FIGURE 6). As relationships are personalized, face is important and needs to be preserved because of the overriding aim of maintaining social harmony and cordial relationships. Face means maintaining a person's dignity by not embarrassing or humiliating him in front of others. As the individual is part of a family or group, embarrassing him would also embarrass his family and community.

Face, therefore, prevails as a form of an ongoing sensitivity and this is expressed in the way the Chinese resolve conflict. The value of face seemed an important aspect in the way the Chinese, particularly, interact with others. Preserving another's face is part of good manners and proper civilities. Putting on a face means concealing or at least "prettying" up how one really feels. Those who want to save the face of another would demonstrate it by delaying a negative reply, not communicating negative feedback and embarrassing him.

If face is preserved, interpersonal relations will be smoothened, and harmony and respect will be maintained. Once a person loses face, he may totally withdraw from the interaction or business negotiation. Loss of face can be more painful than physical pain and this can be avoided by having contentious issues handled by a third party – a go-between.

GUIDELINES FOR MANAGERS

1.   Build relationships

Managers need to make an attempt to build relationships before getting down to task and work details. They would be wise to spend time to know their subordinates, build team spirit and show that they are concerned with their ability to work together as a strong team. In building relationships with subordinates, managers are also expected to show concern for their family members and be seen to mingle, talk and have meals together in less formal settings such as in the canteen and coffee corners. This would help to cement relationships, especially among Malays, who are more likely to "warm up" to superiors who care for their feelings, respect their religion, are polite, patient and encourage people to work together harmoniously like a happy family – with the manager as the "father/mother" figure.

For managers, their task is to ensure that work assignments are given to those who enjoy working together because of the importance attached to building good relationships. These relationships should not only be confined to the workplace but also carried into the informal setting outside of work. Most Malaysians also prefer to work with members of their own ethnic group as they are able to understand one another's values, rituals and sensitivities. It would be wise for managers to arrange work functions to accommodate this preferred arrangement.

Managers are also expected to promote activities in addition to those at the workplace that can enhance better communications and interactions. Once these relationships are in place, feedback when given will become more palatable to the recipients as it would have been given in a context of care and concern. Therefore, it is often found that teambuilding activities away from work can have a spillover effect in the workplace in terms of building cohesive relationships.

2.   Focus on the group not the individual

Malaysians consider themselves more as members of a group than as unique individuals. Focusing too much on individuals can hinder effective teamwork. This is the case especially for Malays, who are more likely to enjoy working together rather than alone. Managers may have to learn to appeal to the sense of collectivism rather than individual contribution. In seeking new ideas, they need to look for team consensus to make suggestions and implement them. By proper guidance, encouragement and patience, subordinates will be able to produce the desired results.

Therefore, a manager who tends to focus on getting more out of the individual can be a stumbling block to preserving group harmony and team spirit. What would be useful is to promote a sense of individual robustness among the team players so that they are able to think for the collective good.

3.   Respect elders and use honorifics

Because of the value of respect for elders, managers who are more senior in age and experience are often expected to take the lead, make decisions, and give directives and guidance on how a job should be done. They are expected to demonstrate behaviours that will indicate to others their experience, wisdom and caring for those who are junior in age. Subordinates are not likely to question the decisions they make as they expect the manager/leader to have the wisdom to make the right choices. They are also reluctant to question this wisdom of the superiors because it may cause the superiors to lose face. Malaysians expect their leaders to make decisions for them and they merely execute these on the assumption that these are good decisions.

Malaysian subordinates are not likely to be critical of their superiors or, at least, openly challenge their views and positions. Younger Malays are expected to show good manners in their choice of words and overt body postures when they relate with their superiors. Subordinates may be considered *kurang ajar* if they fail to display the rituals concerning showing of respect for others, especially one's elders.

However, managers must be cautious about the value of respect for elders. Carried to the extreme, it will promote a non-questioning attitude and blind loyalty, which can hamper effective communication and upward feedback. This is not consonant with or contributory to productivity.

At all times, observe decorum when relating with seniors in the organization. It is important to address the person with whom one is speaking to in the right way, according him the title or the status due to him. The use of honorifics is common when addressing a person in higher position. Therefore, it is important to find out what position the person holds, what honorific title he has been awarded, etc. The status of a *Tan Sri* or *Datuk* should therefore be addressed as such whether in written form or when speaking to him. He will be most offended if knowingly, he is not addressed as such.

4. Be sensitive to religious matters

As religious matters and spirituality are important considerations at the workplace, managers are expected to respect the sensitivities of the workforce involving religious rituals and norms. The Malays are more likely to expect their managers to allow them to observe their religious obligations while at work.

Most Malaysians hold all religious festivities, celebrations, customs and rites as sacrosanct. On festive occasions, be prepared to allow employees time off to observe and perform their religious obligations on their own or as a group.

In line with Islamic teachings, it is not necessary to shake hands with a Muslim woman if she does not extend her hand as a form of greeting. However, shaking hands is acceptable for both sexes among the Chinese, Indians and others.

5. Maintain workplace harmony

The value of harmony is important in ensuring that managers are able to obtain the long-term support and commitment from their subordinates. To preserve harmonious relationships, managers have to be able to detect and sense through unspoken words and actions, any "discontent" that can cause ill feelings and dissatisfaction among team members, and nip it in the bud.

Adopt a non-assertive and non-aggressive style when dealing with people. Avoid high-handedness, the use of coarse language and "show" of authority, aloofness and boasting. Being polite can help gain the confidence and respect of subordinates. Malaysians in general do not like to be ordered and directed loudly as this is considered *kasar* or rude and is against their culture. A manager has to cajole and use praise if he wants to get the best output from his subordinates.

Because of their nature of not wanting to question or challenge their seniors, there is a need to adopt an appropriate approach for eliciting feedback from subordinates to see if a decision is acceptable to them.

Here too, managers need to be aware that, carried to the extreme, this value may inadvertently make Malaysians tolerate mediocre standards. Feedback, criticism or creative initiatives when curbed or discouraged can dampen workplace harmony.

6. Take care of "face"

In any critical appreciation of subordinates' work, exercise care and constraint and avoid publicly humiliating them in order to preserve their "face". Malaysians generally do not like to be corrected for their actions. If need be, it should be done indirectly and conveyed in an emphatic tone. If counselling is needed, do it politely and in private in order not to cause shame. Avoid shouting, confronting in public and singling out anyone from the group, even if it is for praise and particularly for a job well done.

This is especially important among the Chinese who place a high value on preserving relationships among their own members. Reprimanding and disciplining subordinates may have to be carefully thought through so that the affected parties can receive the actions in the spirit of care and concern. Observing when to save face, give face, get face, gain face and not to lose face are important facets of the value of "face saving".

For the purpose of comparing Malaysian (Eastern) values with those found in Western management, see TABLE 3, which compares the Eastern and Western paradigms on task achievement.

TABLE 3: Summary of key ethnic values

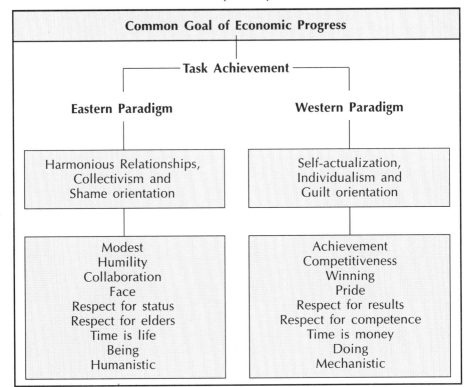

Common Goal of Economic Progress

Task Achievement

Eastern Paradigm	Western Paradigm
Harmonious Relationships, Collectivism and Shame orientation	Self-actualization, Individualism and Guilt orientation
Modest Humility Collaboration Face Respect for status Respect for elders Time is life Being Humanistic	Achievement Competitiveness Winning Pride Respect for results Respect for competence Time is money Doing Mechanistic

CONCLUSION

Managers have to understand the pervasive influence of ethnic values in Malaysia and their role in building a strong and productive workforce to face the challenges of a developed nation by the year 2020. They will have to harness the revered values of the various ethnic groups into shared practices and incorporate them in their daily behaviours to optimize work output.

With the advent of globalization, technological advancements and the demands for a skilled labour force, these values have to be preserved because they can serve to strengthen the uniqueness of the Malaysian multi-ethnic work culture. However, from time to time some of these revered values must be assessed for their relevance, applicability and impact on work processes. As noted earlier, like most things carried to the extreme, some values can be detrimental to workplace efficiency.

On the other hand, in promoting new values and work behaviours which have evolved from other cultures, managers need to ensure that there is no inherent conflict between the objectives of the organization and what the workforce wants preserved. Malaysians, in general, are willing to incorporate new work practices and habits in their daily work styles, but they are not willing to do so at the expense of their own cultural values.

For most Malaysians, the concept of development means being able to retain and preserve the richness of their ethnic heritage as well as to incorporate new work values to promote productivity at the workplace. The uniqueness of being a Malaysian lies in the ability to be flexible when interacting with people from different cultures. Being able to use appropriate behaviours at the intracultural, intercultural and cross-cultural levels will enable Malaysians to have a "rich repertoire" of behavioural approaches for preserving harmony, developing synergy and increasing understanding amongst its multicultural workforce.

Managers from all cultures seek similar goals of high productivity and economic progress for their organizations. What differentiates Asian from Western managers is the manner in which these goals are pursued. For Western managers, the task becomes the primary objective while harmonious relationships are secondary. Asian managers, on the other hand, believe the task should be achieved with the same fervour but not at the expense of harmonious relationships and loss of face. These values, along with respect for hierarchy, loyalty, tolerance for differences, harmony and humility, tend to permeate all work and business activities and have to be considered before new management values and practices are introduced.

Hence, to be effective in Malaysia, managers will need to allocate time and energy to build relationships based on trust and understanding with their subordinates. Their role as "nurturing parents", who are able to promote the growth and development of their people in the spirit of a happy family, forms the cornerstone of success in managing.

SUMMARY OF KEY VALUES UNDERLYING MANAGEMENT PRACTICES

Management Practice	Values
Communicating	Face, Politeness, Cooperation
Leading and Motivating	Humility, Face, Nurturing, Group affiliation, Relationships
Building a multicultural team	Harmony, Cooperation, Relationships
Making Decisions	Face, Respect for age, Relationships, Harmony
Recruiting, Selecting and Orientating	Humility, Modesty, Face, Relationships, Group orientation
Delegating	Relationships, Harmony, Face
Counselling	Face, Harmony, Caring
Managing Conflict	Non-confrontational, Harmony, Respect for others, Face
Managing Meetings	Respect for elders, Harmony
Dealing with Government Agencies	Harmony, Patience, Respect for others, Humility, Relationships, Loyalty, Confidentiality
Working with Malaysians	Respect for others, Harmony
Working with Foreigners	Direct, Individualistic, Task Driven
Managing Change	Relationships, Paternalistic Work Orientation, Collectivism and Hierarchy

REFERENCES

Asma Abdullah (1996). *Going Glocal: Cultural Dimensions in Malaysian Management.* Kuala Lumpur: Malaysia Institute of Management.

Hofstede, G (1984). *Culture's Consequences, International Differences in Work-Related Values* (Abridged Edition). CA: Sage Publications Beverly Hills.

Hofstede, G (1991). Managing in a Multicultural Society: The Malaysian Experience. *Malaysian Management Review.* Vol. 26. No. 1: 3-12. Kuala Lumpur: Malaysian Institute of Management.

Schneider, Susan C (1988). National vs. Corporate Culture: Implications for Human Resource Management, *Human Resource Management,* Vol. 27 No. 2.

Trompenaars, F (1994). *Riding the waves of Culture, Understanding Diversity in Global Business.* New York: Irwin Professional Publishing.

2

COMMUNICATING WITH MALAYSIANS

ASMA ABDULLAH, SURJIT SINGH and SARAN KAUR GILL[*]

INTRODUCTION

C ommunicating in the Malaysian workplace requires an understanding of the sensitivities of both the verbal and non-verbal nuances of people from different cultural backgrounds. These elements are important in Malaysia because each ethnic group attaches its own meaning and interpretation to a message. A common understanding is achieved when both the sender and the recipient of the message are able to empathize with each other and interpret the intent of the message correctly.

Generally, Malaysians have to tune in and adjust to various cultural norms and expectations when they communicate and interact with people who are from different hierarchical positions as well as linguistic and religious backgrounds. Malaysians use certain sets of communication symbols and

---

[*] The authors acknowledge ONG SIOK BENG for her contribution in the original edition of this chapter.

expected patterns of interaction when they relate with members from the same ethnic background (intracultural) and with others from different ethnic groups (intercultural), or with those from a foreign culture (cross-cultural). This flexibility in communication styles indicates that Malaysians have a strong desire to build relationships, rapport and interpersonal understanding with those whom they meet and interact.

OBJECTIVES OF THIS CHAPTER

This chapter seeks to highlight the importance of understanding some of the local values relating to communication in a multicultural and multilingual society. It aims to create an awareness of the manner in which Malaysians communicate by developing an understanding of the role of broad cultural dimensions which influence communicative behaviours. Some key observations on how Malaysians relate with others will be highlighted. The chapter concludes with a number of guidelines for effective communication at the Malaysian workplace.

DEFINING COMMUNICATION

Communication involves the sharing or exchanging of information or ideas between two or more individuals. It usually results in some action for both parties. At the workplace, executives are required to acquire a myriad of communicative skills: to exchange and share information, to offer ideas, to express agreements and disagreements, to deliver presentations, to express viewpoints, to persuade and to establish relationships.

In a multicultural society like Malaysia, effective communication extends a step further to mean the ability to understand and be sensitive to both verbal and non-verbal aspects of communication. This phenomenon is more evident when intercultural and cross-cultural communication takes place. Therefore, the way a certain language (whether English, Bahasa Malaysia, Mandarin or Tamil – the four main languages used in the country) is used, communicated and understood tends to vary, depending on who the sender and recipients are.

ISSUES AND CHALLENGES

There are a number of important issues and challenges that are found in the way Malaysians communicate with one another, and these are:

- **Cultural context and nature of interaction**

Malaysians of all ethnic groups often relate at the intracultural, intercultural and cross-cultural levels. Each of these three levels has a different set of values and behaviours which must be observed in the process of communication. Many Malaysians, because of their education, exposure and the multiracial environment of the country, are able and feel comfortable enough to use these communicative behaviours interchangeably, depending on whom they are relating with and the objective of the interaction. Regardless of an individual's dominant communicative style, it is important to use varying styles, depending on the cultural context and the nature of the interaction. More often, Malaysians tend to use a communication style of a more collectivist community – "WE" culture where the "I" is less expressed.

• Open and flexible style

Knowing just one style of communication (intracultural, intercultural and cross-cultural) can be a handicap for Malaysians in facing future challenges, especially if they want to work in multinational companies or do business with foreigners or go abroad to work where English is used. They need to be guided, when the occasion requires, to acquire a communication style where speakers are expected to be open and flexible.

• "Malaysian English"

For many, the lack of exposure and opportunity to use the English language has placed them in a position where they are not able to speak and converse in Standard English. Those who do speak resort to what is often described as "Malaysian English". While they may be able to get the message across in English, it may not be done with grammatical accuracy. This can have implications for cross-cultural communication as a request can sound "coarse" because of the form of the language that is used. For example, the phrase, "I see you tomorrow?" instead of "May I see you tomorrow?" shows a lack of understanding on the part of the sender on the finer points of English usage.

• Lack of fluency

In addition, English is perceived as a language of "prestige", having been the language of administration during the colonial era. Being fluent in both spoken and written English is often associated with social status and elitism and a criterion for entry into an intercultural or cross-cultural workplace, especially in the private sector. In other cases, it could be a prerequisite for purposes of recruitment and even promotion. In fact, being able to communicate well in English is indispensable for the manager who seeks career advancement, more so when the job requires him to relate with his foreign counterparts. In view of the general lack of fluency in the English language, especially among the present generation of local graduates, Malaysians are now encouraged to master its usage for the purpose of preparing them for e-commerce and global business.

- ## Globalization and the use of English

With increasing business globalization, Malaysians will have to be proficient when communicating and relating in the English language. The lack of fluency in and mastery of the English language among Malaysians may also affect their interactions with upper management, especially in foreign-based companies. They may be seen not to have the confidence to communicate with senior managers and be convincing in putting across their ideas in public.

KEY OBSERVATIONS RELATING TO COMMUNICATION

Following are some general observations on how ethnic values influence the way Malaysians communicate with others.

- ## Relating in three contexts

As earlier mentioned, communication is often conducted in three different contexts: the intracultural, intercultural and cross-cultural contexts where each context has its own code and symbols.

Communication at the **intracultural level** involves people from the same ethnic group. When this occurs, Malaysians who are of similar ethnic backgrounds are usually aware of the influence of certain variables governing the receptivity of the communication or message, viz. seniority, the degree of religious conviction, geographical location of origin, urban or rural outlook, etc. For example, among the educated urban Malays, a common speech pattern has emerged. When interacting, they tend to code-switch, alternating between Bahasa Malaysia and English: "Meeting time *hari ini 'dah* fix, *'tak?*" (Have you fixed the time for today's meeting?), "You *'dah* check through *sekali lagi?*" (Have you checked it through again?). Being able to code-switch seems to suggest that first of all, the use of Malay expresses cultural oneness, and secondly, the use of English establishes their commonality in being the "educated and the progressive" urban.

Communication at the **intercultural level** involves people from different ethnic groups. For example, when a Malay interacts with a Chinese, he is likely to adopt a communication code different from the one he uses to communicate with another Malay. Hence, it is common to find a Malay speak *pasar* (colloquial) Malay especially when engaged in business. For instance, when dealing with a Chinese contractor who is not competent in Bahasa Malaysia, the Malay may say: "Product *ini betul-betul* best." (This product is really the best), "*Lu tahu* boss I *'tak kira ...*" (You know that my boss doesn't mind ...). Knowing when to use English and Bahasa Malaysia, and code-switching between languages when interacting interculturally is an expression of one's attempt to build rapport and understanding with others.

Communication at the **cross-cultural level** involves Malaysians and foreigners. In settings like these, Malaysians will invariably use English as the medium of communication since they know that foreigners usually will not understand Bahasa Malaysia, Mandarin or Tamil. Malaysians are delighted when foreigners speak their local language and this can establish immediate rapport.

Hence, communication at each of the three levels described above requires one to use specific verbal and non-verbal expressions. An accepted code for functioning at one level may not be appropriate at another. For example, a soft-spoken Malay who behaves appropriately at the intracultural level will be seen as non-assertive at the cross-cultural level. Therefore, within the organizational setting, a manager has to be sensitive and use different codes of communication when he relates with his superiors, subordinates, peers, clients or consultants from different ethnic groups and cultures. Malaysians, in general, are aware of the different communication contexts and tend to adapt accordingly to them. Failure to comprehend the cultural nuances within each context can lead to the recipient's misunderstanding and misinterpreting the message.

- **Showing *budi bahasa* or the language of character**

Malaysians, whether Chinese, Malay or Indian, are generally receptive to those who display good manners in face-to-face interaction, especially when they are communicating with those from the same ethnic group. Malays, especially, are expected to demonstrate *budi bahasa* or the language of character whenever they communicate with other Malays because this indicates proper upbringing.

Some of the behaviours considered part of *budi bahasa* are:
- not being forthright, assertive or aggressive
- not responding to a request with a direct "no"
- not being too blunt or direct in expressing one's views
- not causing interpersonal conflict or "loss of face"

A person who does not demonstrate proper and refined behaviour but persists in coarse *kasar* and impolite behaviour is therefore insensitive to the dignity of others. He may even be described as insufficiently educated *kurang ajar* – a term which is very insulting to well-bred Malays.

A well-known Malay proverb says:
"Hidup di dunia biar beradat, budi bahasa bukan dijual beli."

In English, this means: "When living in the world, be disciplined; manners or politeness cannot be bought and sold." It takes a great deal of discipline to cultivate good manners, which are enduring and cannot be separated from the character of a person.

Calling seniors or elderly people by their first names (encouraged and considered an informality by Americans) may be considered ill mannered, especially when the seniors or the elders have been conferred titles and are persons of high rank and status.

The Chinese and Indians too, have the *halus* and the *kasar* aspects of communication, depending on the status of the parties in the interaction. The degree of respect for the other person would depend on whether the interaction is between equals or between supervisor and subordinate.

Indians, in their communication, are also guided by traditions which are rooted in their religious beliefs, family ties and deference to elders within the larger family unit. At the peer level, communication is more open and egalitarian. Facilitating feedback and discussions are often observed, and if there are conflicts and differences, elders play the intermediary role. There is an acknowledgement of culture, tradition, refinement of manners and values. If these are absent, it will reflect poorly upon one's family upbringing.

It is not uncommon for young Malaysians to address elders as "Uncle", "Auntie", "Brother" or "Sister". This relationship sometimes bewilders foreigners when, for example, a salesgirl addresses a foreign tourist as "Uncle" instead of "Sir".

- **The polite system**

Malaysians of Malay, Chinese and Indian origins have a polite system embodying specific codes of verbal and non-verbal expressions in their interactions with others. Because Malaysia is so culturally diverse, it is common knowledge that the Indians have a tendency to be vocal; the Chinese, preoccupied with business; and the Malays, seemingly polite and non-assertive in manner.

Within the system, there are different forms of address for the varying degrees of status differences, intimacy and deference extended to a person. Understanding the meanings of these expressions is important because the Malays are especially concerned about why someone does something (motivation) and the way in which the person does it (manner).

In speech, different forms of address are used to denote the relationship between the speaker and the recipient. Among the Malays, the pronominal form denoting the first person "I" is expressed in numerous ways to connote politeness, hierarchy and degree of closeness in a relationship. Variants of "I"

in Bahasa Malaysia are:
- (Singular forms) *saya, aku, Cik, Puan, Tuan, kak ni, dek ni,* or by own name (e.g. Din).
- (Plural forms) *kami, kita.*

The pronominal form for the second person "you" has the following variants:
- *awak, engkau, anda, tuan, saudara,* name of person *(Ahmad)* or the person's title such as *Datuk, Datin, Tan Sri,* etc.

To communicate appropriately, it is important to use the correct form. A subordinate speaking to a Malay superior would use the word *Tuan* or *Puan, Encik* or *Cik.*

In the case of a commoner's communication with members of royalty, the language of the court must be used. The commoner refers to himself as *patek* and the royalty as *Tengku, Ungku* or *Yang Mulia* and *Raja.* It would be disrespectful to address a member of royalty by name.

Similarly too, the Chinese and Indians also have numerous terms of address which denote hierarchy in a family but these are less used at the workplace. The Indians avoid calling each other by name. The elder usually addresses the younger as "younger brother" or "younger sister", while the subordinate will call the superior "Sir". In a general sense, the Indians too have a polite language among the learned and educated.

Non-verbally, the polite system requires the use of appropriate facial expressions, hand gestures and intonation as an indication of respect. Malays often use the thumb when pointing to an object or person, avoid eye contact with seniors to demonstrate respect, read non-verbal cues as to when to shake hands with members of the opposite sex and use proper salutation in words and gestures with respectable individuals.

- **Reverence to authority and status**

The whole concept of communication among the Chinese, Malays, Indians and others is based on respect for age and elders and reverence to authority and status. This cultural concept is carried over into the workplace. Hence, conversation between individuals of unequal rank (based on seniority or status) is likely to be less relaxed and more formal than between equals. For example, among the Chinese, communication with the elders and those with high social standing tends to reflect respect, face and courtesy while communication with peers reflects harmony, empathy and pragmatism. The Malays show respect and deference to elders in the way they address them in verbal and written communication and through appropriate body gestures.

Likewise, the Indians are more assertive at peer level because of their ability to speak in several languages including English. Again, among the managers themselves, the tone of language will depend on the degree of formality of the interaction. In a formal setting, the way they address superiors is generally respectful. They will not question authority unless in extenuating circumstances when they have to exculpate themselves from false accusations or blame. Indians tend to be more assertive and emotional in putting their points across during a negotiation – hence their leading roles in associations and trade unions (see FIGURES 1 and 2).

FIGURE 1: Levels of communication

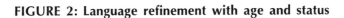

Superior

Peer — — — — | — — — — Peer

Subordinate
(relationship is unequal)

FIGURE 2: Language refinement with age and status

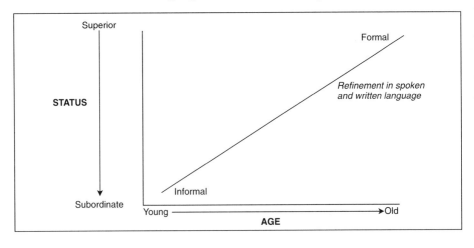

This value of respect for elders is related to one of the four cultural dimensions of power distance studied by Hofstede (1994) among employees of one multinational corporation in more than 60 countries. The dimension of power distance is defined as the extent to which the less powerful members of organizations and institutions accept and expect that power is distributed unequally. In his research, he investigated the responses of the employees to the various dimensions and their influence in their daily lives in society and the workplace. Malaysia was ranked the highest in terms of power distance. As a result, there is considerable dependence of subordinates on bosses. The emotional distance too is large and this means subordinates are unlikely to approach and contradict their bosses, who are often regarded as the patriarch with the dominant role in decision-making and whose action is not often questioned.

As a result, Malaysians tend to demonstrate a strong sense of respect for hierarchy and status at the workplace as this practice is part of their socialization process of being brought up in an Asian family setting. The findings reflect the dominant inclination towards the cultural dimensions which, in turn, influence the communicative behaviours of people of different nations. As shown in TABLE 1, there is a general trend for those from Malaysia, Singapore, Japan, Taiwan and Hong Kong to be classified as being on the left side of the continuum, i.e. the collectivist end, and those from America, Great Britain, Sweden, Germany and Australia to be classified as individualistic, being on the right side of the continuum.

Though these dimensions are both on extreme ends of the continuum, in reality, it is never an either-or situation. There are usually shades in between. However, what TABLE 1 shows is a reflection of the general cultural inclinations which exist in the various communities, specifically the influence of the cultural dimensions on communicative behaviour in the Malaysian community according to Hofstede's (1994) and Kim Min-Sun's (1995) terms.

TABLE 1: Cultural Dimensions which influence Malaysian Communicative Behaviour in Comparison with Other Communities

Malaysia, Japan Taiwan, Hong Kong		America, Great Britain Sweden, Germany, Australia
More Collectivist Cultures	⟵ ⟶	**More Individualistic Cultures**
• We (Collectivist) • Large Power Distance • **Social-relational focus** Concern for face-saving, good interpersonal relations, not hurting the feelings of others, and concern for minimizing imposition.		• I (Individualistic) • Small Power Distance • **Task-oriented focus** Concern with getting one's way (clarity) and achieving set objectives.

Source: Hofstede: 1994, pp. 23 & 49 and Kim, Min-Sun: 1995, p. 148.

In a collectivist society like Malaysia, the interest of the group takes precedence over the interest of the individual. In such societies, people from young are integrated into strong, cohesive ingroups, which throughout people's lifetime continue to protect them in exchange for unquestioning loyalty. The social manners displayed in conforming with the group's expectations are very important. Not practising or abiding by the group's communicative expectations will result in alienation and exclusion.

In individualistic societies, the interest of the individual takes precedence over that of the group. The ties between individuals are loose: everyone is expected to look after himself or herself and his or her immediate family.

In each of the above contexts, the communicative behaviours are applied to meet with the general thrust of expectations of that particular sub-community. To understand the complexity of communicative behaviours, it is necessary to understand the values of all the ethnic groups in the country and how they are expressed at the workplace.

As for the large power distance orientation found in the more collectivist cultures, its influence is also carried over into the schools, resulting in teachers being seen as authority figures who are not often questioned. Any attempt, therefore, by managers and even schools to encourage employees and students to develop a questioning attitude may need to address this ingrained dimension of power distance.

However, in small power distance countries, the relationship between subordinates and their superiors is more egalitarian and it is expected that superiors will consult their subordinates. As the emotional distance between them is small, subordinates will quite readily approach and may even be allowed to challenge the views of their superiors.

- **Non-assertiveness and indirectness**

Most Malaysians are often perceived by expatriates as subservient and timid. This may be due to their projecting the Asian virtues of humility, reserve, modesty and consensus. Interactions with the Chinese will indicate that they are modest in speech, rarely boastful and may even be self-deprecating. Being direct and revealing one's feelings to others is often thought of as signs of weakness, as it is seen as humiliating to reveal one's inner self.

As Malaysians are less likely to challenge and disagree with their superiors, they expect the manager or person in charge to provide the answers and assign them responsibilities to get the task done. There is utmost respect for the manager and his position power, especially if he is a Westerner. For example, at meetings, when Malaysians do not agree with what is being suggested, recommended or said, they will not articulate their disagreements openly. In seeking for consensus, they will look down or away and not answer.

(In this kind of situations, the unspoken word speaks louder than the spoken word.) Instead, it is more likely that the disagreements would be aired among colleagues after the formal meeting. Sometimes an accurate assessment can only be obtained by establishing relationships with a few key personnel in the organization. Hence, non-verbal signals will have to be understood, as disagreement may not always be openly expressed for fear of upsetting the feelings of the person in authority. Generally, silence and looking away is usually a sign of disagreement.

The above observations are supported by a study carried out by Jamaliah Ali (1991), who discovered the following patterns of communication in a study on indirectness as practised by Malays in business and factory environments. They are:
- the *Insya Allah* (God willing) mode to avoid saying "no" or to mean "maybe" (among other things)
- the *merajuk* (sulking) mode to convey dissatisfaction by workers
- the silent mode where silence is used to avoid conflict or confrontation
- the use of a "mediator" whereby a third party is brought in to handle delicate situations.

Malaysians are more likely to display non-assertiveness and indirectness in their communicative interactions, especially those that are problematic – for example, having to say "no", giving and receiving criticisms, and expressing dissatisfaction through a third party.

• The concept of face and expressing disagreement and criticism

Face and face saving are important cultural dimensions in a group-oriented culture denoting one's sensitivities and concern in not hurting the feelings of the recipient. "Losing face", in the sense of being humiliated, is an expression which penetrated the English language from the Chinese. Face is lost when the individual, either through his action or that of people closely related to him, fails to meet essential requirements placed upon him by virtue of the social position he occupies. (David Yau Fai Ho, 1976: 867)

The Malays too have an equivalent term, *jaga maruah*, which refers to maintaining a person's face, pride and dignity, by not embarrassing or humiliating him in front of others. As the individual is part of a family or group, embarrassing him would also include his family and community. As a result, Malaysians are not comfortable giving and receiving direct verbal criticism as this may severe harmonious relationships and cause the recipient to "lose face". When sharing ideas and views, subordinates tend to offer proposals, which are put forward in a non-threatening but conciliatory manner. Making demands and stating expectations with incentives and pressures may not be well received by their superiors.

Managers on the other hand are unlikely to be challenged or criticized by their subordinates. However, managers who make their subordinates lose face, especially in public, may be seen as arrogant or rude.

A subordinate who has been criticized or reprimanded may show his displeasure in indirect ways, such as avoiding any form of face-to-face contact with his superior. Sometimes the relationship may even be severed altogether.

• Demonstrating respect

Malaysians consider frankness and directness as out of tandem with traditional values and respect. They are often tactful and discreet when expressing positive and negative opinions. They tend to respect managers who come across as nurturing, caring and supportive elders through their emphatic tone of voice, the expressions they use and the postures they take when communicating with subordinates.

Shouting or raising one's voice is usually frowned upon and considered rude *biadab* or improper *tidak manis*. In the Malay social milieu, a person who comes across as too direct, even to the point of being terse, is often thought of as lacking proper breeding.

However, this behaviour may be perceived differently by an expatriate manager (e.g. American or Australian) whose culture stresses informality and equality. Being used to subordinates or trainees speaking up and even challenging a superior's ideas, the expatriate manager may misinterpret the Malaysian way of communicating and values of respect for rank, age and expertise as a sign of lack of confidence, non-assertiveness and subsequently lack of capability.

There is also a general tendency for Malaysians to mask their emotions with a smile or giggle or laugh when they are shy, nervous, confused or embarrassed. Some may not even establish eye contact with the person with whom they are communicating because doing so may be construed as rude or disrespectful.

• Less expressive of feelings

Most Malaysians are often indirect in responding to difficult questions. They may make a point, elaborate on it and then go off at a tangent. Westerners who are used to direct and linear communication may find Malaysians rather "circuitous" in their ways. In fact, Malaysians are aware of the direction but they prefer to take time to establish relationships with those they interact with. Rather than make a direct refusal, a Malaysian will pause for a long while, seek further clarification or invite other options before he makes a statement.

In other situations, Malaysians have a tendency not to express their feelings in a relationship as they believe their behaviour will speak for them. This is especially so when communicating with members of the opposite sex or when the person sending the message is of higher status than the recipient.

• **Being accommodating**

Because of the importance placed on harmony, Malaysians are very accommodating and will often communicate in English with their foreign colleagues because they want to be understood. At the same time, they are also eager to please and want to make foreigners feel at home in Malaysia.

In some instances, they may even adopt certain behaviours, mannerisms and even pronunciations that are more familiar to the foreigners. They are also very tolerant and understanding should foreigners touch on cultural sensitivities unknowingly.

GUIDELINES FOR COMMUNICATING WITH MALAYSIANS

In essence, managers are expected to communicate with both their "hearts and minds" as this forms the basis of sound interpersonal communication. On occasions when the values of the organization are in conflict with local values, managers need to recognize that differences should not be regarded as a liability. They need to suspend judgement and be seen to tolerate contrasting viewpoints.

Following are some guidelines for managers who want to understand and communicate effectively with Malaysians:

• **Know own culture**

A manager has to be aware that a person's set of ethnic values and underlying assumptions can affect communication norms and practices. The tendency to be ethnocentric about one's own values and not see ourselves from others' perspectives can often cause misunderstanding and miscommunication. Hence, a manager who works with many different ethnic groups has to be sensitive about the way his behaviour affects others; at all times, it would be expected of him not to use his own values to assess a person from another culture.

On the other hand, it is also important for a person to recognize his own set of values when communicating cross-culturally. This knowledge will enable Malaysians to have a sense of security and confidence about their own cultural identity. It is by knowing the roots and values of one's ethnic community that one can reach out to those from other cultures.

For those who work in a predominantly intracultural setting, there is a need to be aware that their communication codes and behaviours may appear peculiar and may not be understood by people from another culture. For example, a Malaysian should not expect an expatriate to understand the finer points of the local polite system; conversely, the expatriate manager should not expect the Malaysian to be direct and assertive in his views. Hence, there is a need for both parties to empathize with one another's communication code and be willing to adjust accordingly in order to be understood. Interactors in cross-cultural communication need to consider the values of the other party and look at things from the other party's "pair of lenses."

Being aware of our own culture and becoming sensitive about the way we communicate and how we differ from those who come from other cultures can help us see ourselves from the other person's perspective. A manager who works with a multicultural workforce has to be sensitive to the impact of his own behaviour on others. He has to learn to avoid using his own values to assess a person from another culture. To enhance effective communication in a multicultural society like ours, Malaysians need to cultivate a point of view which takes into consideration the values and feelings of all ethnic groups.

- **Establish rapport and relationships**

To increase productivity at the workplace, there is a need to build relationships between managers and employees. It is worth the time and effort as getting to know employees and their interests and aspirations can make it easier for managers to get them to go the "extra mile". A work environment based on the concept of "we-are-one-happy-family" can often boost employee morale. In fact, a benevolent authoritarian style of leadership may be tolerated provided the manager also shows respect and care for his employees.

Engaging in social pleasantries before getting down to business can facilitate a greater flow of conversation and enable both parties to assess or "size up" one another. Sharing common grounds, for instance former school, hometown and friends, can help "break the ice" for a smooth exchange of ideas.

In business, Malaysians like to know who they are working with as trust is an important consideration – so details related to the business do not often take first priority. Conversations about the family, company or current events are often used to warm up relationships and establish familiarity.

Managers too should start to build personal relationships of trust by spending time together with subordinates. While this takes time, once established, the relationship can pave the way for a manager to be more open and direct with his subordinates.

• Speak interculturally

Learning to speak interculturally by code-switching and code-mixing will enable a speaker to effectively communicate with the recipient. Being able to mix a local language with the English language – a feature among speakers in the urban areas of Malaysia – is one way of building rapport and facilitating intercultural understanding.

The ability to code-switch can also help foreigners (provided they know one of the local languages) to better relate with fellow Malaysian workers. Doing so may help them adjust to the local nuances and establish rapport quickly.

• Know pronominal forms

Managers are also expected to know how to use the correct pronominal forms in both written and oral communication, especially when relating with individuals of a higher social status. Respect is shown by the marked emphasis on politeness and decorum, especially towards elders.

When getting things done through written requests to elders, junior employees will often ask them to "consider" doing certain things and may "request" them to complete a task. Forceful imperatives (e.g. "You must", or "You are required") are considered impolite and are often substituted with a more passive and subtle style ("May we suggest ...", "We would appreciate it ...") to show respect.

A manager who is humble can help subordinates relate better to him. A low, pleasant and friendly tone of voice is often more effective when making requests than an aggressive, take-charge kind of approach, as the earlier approach denotes one's respect for the other individual. Loud oral communication is socially unacceptable and an argumentative voice and exaggerated hand gestures are frowned upon. It may be advisable to precede any requests with phrases like: "May I ask you a question?", "Please don't be angry with me if I were to comment ...", "May I say something?"

• Understand non-verbal cues

Make an attempt to understand the meaning of certain body gestures in the communication process which demonstrates one's humility and respect for the other person. Some non-verbal behaviours which are considered unbecoming are:

- placing one's legs on the table
- pointing to an object with one's foot or forefinger
- not removing one's shoes when entering a Malaysian home
- not giving recognition to an individual of high social status
- not being properly attired, especially when meeting elderly folks
- receiving things with the left hand
- calling someone "hey", "hoi" or by gesturing with the forefinger
- barging into someone's room without first announcing arrival

Non-verbally, the polite system requires the use of appropriate facial expressions, hand gestures and intonation as an indication of respect. Malays often use the thumb when pointing to an object or person, avoid eye contact with seniors to demonstrate respect, read non-verbal cues as to when to shake hands with members of the opposite sex and use proper salutation in words and gestures with respectable individuals.

It should be noted that Malay women might not want to touch the hands of members of the opposite sex in public. When greeting, it is the prerogative of the woman to put out her hand first to initiate a handshake. If she does not, just nod with a respectful bow and acknowledge her presence. Also, eye contact can be difficult for those who have been socialized to look at another person in the eye to indicate honesty. Again, Malay Muslim women are not expected to look directly into men's eyes and, therefore, tend to look away or look down.

- **Be aware of behaviours considered uncouth**

Because of the emphasis on politeness and proper decorum, there are a number of overt behaviours which are considered uncouth or *kasar*. It is expected of managers to avoid the following unless they want to be so labelled:

- Criticizing another person publicly and causing him to lose face (*hilang maruah*)
- Using bad language, e.g. vulgarities in social conversation
- Being blunt, outspoken and not diplomatic
- Addressing elders without using proper pronominals and titles
- Being insensitive to religious observances, e.g. making jokes about religious symbols and food habits

In general, Malaysians are also expected to observe different sets of behaviours at the intracultural, intercultural and cross-cultural levels of interface. Because of their upbringing and the multiracial environment of the country, they are expected to use these behaviours interchangeably depending on whom they are relating to or interacting with. TABLE 2 summarizes the three types of behaviours expected at the three levels of interaction.

TABLE 2: Behaviours Expected at the Three Interactive Levels

Level	Expected behaviours
Intracultural	Understand the key elements of the polite system for each ethnic group Be soft, gentle and unhurried
Intercultural	Learn to code-switch and code-mix Learn each other's language Use and know the meanings of ethnic body language
Cross-cultural	Speak English with a neutral accent Be clear and precise Maintain eye contact Avoid condescending behaviour

CONCLUSION

Communicating at the Malaysian workplace has to take into consideration the influence of deeply rooted Asian traditions of good manners and respect for elders. The values of harmony, face and relationships require a manager to adopt an open and friendly approach towards their subordinates. Malaysians generally prefer to associate with those who are accommodating, not argumentative and easy to get along with. Those who use a gentle tone of voice together with the appropriate gestures and a sincere desire to promote harmonious relationships will normally gain respect from their recipients. Those who come across as brash, loud and rough are often ostracized socially.

Managers are expected to understand the values and cultural sensitivities of all the ethnic groups and look for common grounds in order to build and maintain long-term relationships. While learning to function appropriately at the intracultural, intercultural and cross-cultural levels takes time, Malaysians who are able to use the skills at different levels may be able to bridge the communication gaps that exist at the Malaysian workplace.

SUMMARY OF KEY MALAYSIAN VALUES IN COMMUNICATING WITH MALAYSIANS

POLITENESS
- ○ Demonstrate good manners in verbal communication
- ○ Learn to read the meanings behind non-verbal behaviours
- ○ Speak softly and in a low tone when discussing a serious matter or when relating to lower level staff

FACE
- ○ Be indirect when communicating negative feedback
- ○ Seek the help of a respectable third party when faced with problems in communicating
- ○ Avoid open disagreement. But if unavoidable, caution the recipient and apologize after the communication

COOPERATION
- ○ Use correct pronominal forms when addressing seniors and respected elders
- ○ Maintain dignity and do not be too open with comments
- ○ Stand with head lowered as if in a slight bow when communicating with an elder to show respect

---

REFERENCES

Ho, David You-Fai (1976). On the Concept of Face, *American Journal of Sociology*, pp. 81, 867-884.

Hofstede, Geert (1994). *Cultures and Organizations: Intercultural Cooperation and Its Importance for Survival.* New York: McGraw Hill.

Jamaliah Mohd Ali (1991). Indirectness and Malay Diplomacy: with Special Reference to Business Dealings and Labour Relations. Working Paper No. 11. Goteburg, Sweden: Centre for East and Southeast Asian Studies, University of Goteburg.

Kim, Min-Sun (1995). Towards a Theory of Conversational Constraints: Focusing on Individual-Level Dimensions of Culture. In: *Intercultural Communication Theory* (Richard L Wiseman, ed.), pp. 148–169. California: Sage Publications.

3

LEADING AND MOTIVATING A MALAYSIAN WORKFORCE

A KHALIQ AHMAD and SURJIT SINGH[*]

INTRODUCTION

Managers in their leadership capacity in an organization, play an important part in shaping the motivation, commitment and predisposition of the workforce. They provide the direction, focus, meaning and inspiration to those who work for them. As architects of an organization, managers need to project themselves as role models that embody and convey in actions and words, desirable attitudes, values and beliefs of their workforce.

Managers are considered honest if they do what they decide and say, behave in ways consistent with local values, and demonstrate loyalty, honour and trustworthiness. Their competence is demonstrated through possessing the right skills for the job and being capable of achieving set targets. To employees, they are symbols of motivation to inspire the workforce to want to work.

---

[*] The authors acknowledge ASMA ABDULLAH for her contribution in the original edition of this piece of writing.

43

OBJECTIVES OF THIS CHAPTER

The aim of this chapter is to identify some of the key challenges faced by managers in the country and assess the state of management and leadership literature available in the country. Some common observations on how managers-cum-leaders from different ethnic groups demonstrate decision making, acceptable leadership and motivational behaviours will be discussed. It concludes with a list of practices related to leading and motivating based on shared values which managers should find helpful at the Malaysian workplace.

This chapter also examines the impact of cultural values of the various ethnic groups on leadership and motivation practices of companies in Malaysia. The companies selected are those which have employed Malays, Chinese, Indians and others as their workforce.

ISSUES AND CHALLENGES

There are a number of issues and challenges concerning managerial leadership in Malaysia.

• Demographic structure

Malaysian managers have to deal with a number of external factors such as the political and economic conditions, legislation and technology, besides societal and cultural values. The age distribution of a country's workforce affects its mobility, flexibility and energy. The Malaysian workforce, as in other developing countries, is considered young compared to industrialized countries such as Japan and the United States. In 1990, more than 68 per cent of the Malay workforce and 58 per cent of the Chinese workforce were under the age of 34 years (Statistics Department of Malaysia, 1993). This majority age group is found to be better educated, eager to learn new skills, expecting higher income, and more likely to relocate for better prospects. Tangible, extrinsic rewards in return for their contributions are key motivational forces to this significant section of the workforce.

• Over-reliance on Western-based concepts

Most Malaysian managers who studied management are only exposed to concepts and theories relating to how to motivate and lead others that are solely based on the experiences and research done in the West. While they are perceived as a guide in the absence of local theories and practices, the available texts do not include culture-specific techniques and skills which are contextually appropriate for managers in a multi-ethnic society like Malaysia.

44

Many of the recommended practices in the Western texts are based on the underlying values and assumptions which are alien to the Malaysian workforce. For example, some American leadership training programmes promote such practices as "challenging the process" and "laying things out on the table through open and direct confrontation", which run counter to the local cultural values of preserving face and harmonious relationships.

Geert Hofstede (1984), a pioneer in work-related values across cultures, cautioned:

> "The United States is the major exporter of modern organization theories, but its position of extreme individualism in comparison to most other countries makes the relevance of some of its theories in other cultural environments doubtful."

He maintained that the results of his 1980 research of comparing workers in 40 countries showed that national cultures explained approximately 50 per cent of the differences in these workers' attitudes and behaviour.

Malaysians, in general, are usually motivated when they are able to develop and cultivate good relationships among their bosses and subordinates. A key motivating factor at work is an atmosphere that is friendly and supportive. On the other hand, what is often proposed in management texts written in the United States is based on the values of self-esteem and self-actualization, which are often reflective of the American high-individualism dimension. The intensity and expression of these needs, particularly in terms of self-interest and self-perception, may differ across cultures.

• Multicultural backdrop

In multicultural Malaysia, there are other motivating factors, besides money and the array of other motivating factors theorized by Western theorists, which are equally, if not more, important. For instance, social factors (especially those contributing to society and the nation) are found to play a more dominant motivating role at the Malaysian workplace (Redding, 1990; Westwood, 1991; Asma, 1996).

In Malaysia, the Chinese community is traditionally trading and commercial in its outlook. The Chinese traditionally were skilled and efficient in business and therefore it was easier for them to control the entire spectrum of commerce ranging from imports and exports to distribution agencies, wholesaling and retailing. Mutual help in establishing the business of another Chinese trader is characteristic of the Chinese community. A wholesaler will easily extend help to another Chinese retailer if the latter is short of money or in debt. The recipient is bound by the Chinese custom to pay back when the time comes. In turn, he will also help a third Chinese businessman in similar difficulties.

45

It is common among the Chinese business group to accept postdated cheques for cash from a fellow shopkeeper who runs short of money. When the due date matures, the cheque will be fully settled. If the debtor defaults on the payment, he will be penalized by being isolated from the business community in the future. Word of his not keeping the promise spreads and no future help will be offered him.

Chinese businessmen tend to be concentrated in the same commercial centres. Hawkers and salesmen find that overall business in the area improves if they are grouped together. There will be competition but not at the cost of losing customers from among themselves. There are many Chinese business conventions that give the members and friends a competitive edge over others. These Chinese customs of doing business are good for a business community to survive.

Malays rarely go into business despite the encouragement and government sponsorship available to the majority of the Bumiputras. The decision to go into business is often made only much later in life – after they have retired from active service with the government, or in the corporate sector.

As a group, Malays are less likely than their Chinese counterparts to make shifts in their lifestyles. To go into business is a radical change for which they are not used to in the first place. Malays are encouraged and sometimes considerably pushed by the government agencies to go into business and seize the opportunities. Every effort is made to facilitate and assist them but the decision to start a business, however, depends upon the individual.

The third and a significant community is the Indians, who by socio-religious basis are divided into two groups. One group, the Indian Muslims, who by virtue of their Islamic faith are adapting to the Malay culture. They are comparatively aggressive in terms of commercial activities when compared to their Malay counterparts. The other group of Indians are trying hard to prove themselves in business.

The social customs and cultural norms of the Indian community – generally seen as a poverty-stricken community – are quite unique. The community has only 0.8 per cent of the economic pie of the country. The youth of the community are sometimes ignorant of various laws. Many court cases under the Women and Girls Protection Act 1973 and the Children Protection Act 1991 involved members of this community. Although the Malaysian education system offers equal opportunities to this community, including opening of Tamil schools, the dropout rate among them is still the highest.

Nevertheless, the community leaders realize the social stigma of this community and are trying hard to change their future. Recent socio-economic changes for the community include the setting up of private institutions of higher learning to provide educational and training opportunities.

*   **Finding a Malaysian identity**

The multi-ethnic society of Malaysia includes the Chinese, who are largely Buddhists or Christians, Indians, who are predominantly Hindus with some Muslims and Christians, and the majority of the Malays, who are Muslims. The state religion is Islam but other communities have freedom of worship. There is a cordial relationship at work down to the street levels among various ethnic groups. The political leadership comes from all the ethnic groups but predominantly from the Malays. Political stability is one of the most important factors for economic growth and business prosperity.

Malaysian managers have yet to evolve their own identity. While the Western manager is often described as tough, strong, powerful, single-minded, demanding, assertive and focused, managers in Malaysia tend to demonstrate a number of varied styles from autocratic to highly participative, depending on the type of organization and the ethnic breakdown of the workforce.

Again, the influence of ethnic values plays a key role in shaping their leadership behaviours. For instance, a Chinese manager may have different approaches to managing a business venture from his Malay, Kadazan, Iban or Indian counterparts. Even those who have acquired modern management skills and techniques and practise management in the Western mode, have yet to find a style which reflects a true Malaysian identity – one that embodies an appreciation of cultural diversity with the ability to have a global mindset.

This means that managers have to be sensitive to the values, needs and aspirations of the workforce, flexible in meeting the needs of people from diverse cultures, able to relate across cultures and yet remaining effective in achieving the objectives of the organization.

DEFINING LEADING AND MOTIVATING

Leading has been defined as the ability to influence or inspire others to want to do something that needs to be done. It is instilling in each employee a sense of choice of belonging and commitment towards the achievement of organizational goals and objectives. Leaders are a necessary catalyst to stimulate employees to develop their potential to the full.

An increasingly popular view of leadership today is that it is more than managing. Leadership is now seen more as an attribute - the leader must not only be competent but must also be a source of inspiration. It has to do with the sharing of common values, so that employees are inspired, empowered and committed to the vision and mission of the organization. There is a moving away from the old practice of controlling employees to one that inspires total commitment and contribution to the goals of the organization.

Related to leading is motivating, which is the willingness to achieve the above vision and mission of the organization. Leaders can motivate their employees by nurturing an environment where work is seen as enriching and fulfilling, thus encouraging employees to contribute ideas and motivating them to put in their best effort to increase productivity.

SOME KEY OBSERVATIONS

The cultural influences on the Malaysian workforce as they relate to leading and motivating can be observed as follows:

1. **On Leading**

   • **High power distance**

   A manager is often seen to maintain his power distance by the privileges he enjoys - such as a big office with expensive furniture, a big car, etc. The manager who tries too quickly to be one of the "gang" may well lose the respect of others as he may be regarded as contravening the norms of interaction among those of different status.

   • **Hierarchical society**

   Most Malaysians accept leadership as a norm of an organized hierarchical society - *Sultan* as head of state, *penghulu* as village headman, and *bapa* father as head of family. Authority is usually not questioned or challenged.

   Effective leaders in Malaysia have a vision as well as the expertise and technical competence to get the job done. Even at the national level, there has been an emphasis on a common vision (i.e. Vision 2020).

   • **Relationship oriented**

   There are a number of age-old values pervading family and social life which have been carried over into the business setting. One of these is the value Malaysians place on friendship and good relations with people. Hence, they tend to adapt and accommodate rather than confront, and prefer security and group affiliation. The obligations of communal living emphasizes the need for understanding, tolerance, respect for age, courtesy, harmony, compromise and consensus in working out rules for living together which are acceptable to all. These values are often upheld through shared practices to maintain harmony and build relationships between superiors and subordinates.

• Paternalism

Leadership is still paternalistic because of the hierarchical nature of the Malaysian society. A good superior is expected to behave like a caring "parent" who understands his subordinates' needs and concerns. A key to effective leadership is embodied in a famous Chinese saying:

"Those who care for others are forever cared for, those who respect others are forever respected."

When a leader cares for and respects his followers, the followers will be willing to go through all kinds of difficulties to achieve the objectives set by the leaders.

Similarly too, the Malays want a relationship with a leader they trust. They prefer to be led by those they feel are committed to their objectives through the words they use and actions they demonstrate. There is a moral component in the relationship between employers and employees which is similar to the relationship of a child with the extended family. There are mutual traditional obligations: employers are expected to protect their employees almost regardless of the latter's performance, and employees to give loyalty to the employer.

The father and son relationship can also be seen between a superior and a subordinate of the corporate family or small businesses among the Chinese and Indians. Employers are expected to behave like "wise elders", caring and nurturing. Values of mutual obligations again require the employer to give his employees some protection in exchange for loyalty and commitment.

• Family status

To the Chinese, the status of family is of utmost importance. Their life evolves around building the family. Hence, the head of the family is considered the leader. The hierarchical reference is clearly evident where the traditional Chinese show reverence by hanging portraits of deceased elders at praying altars. This is also evident in the customary ancestral worship among them. Besides respect for elders, the Chinese also hold in high esteem the educated and wealthy businessmen who support and help their clans through associations and guilds.

- ## Respect for personal, academic and social standing

For the Malays, an individual becomes a leader largely on the basis of the status and family into which he was born or the status subsequently conferred upon him. If the leader has been given a high rank by the organization, government or royalty, his followers and other Malays will acknowledge that rank and expect him to exercise leadership.

According to Dahlan (1991), the Malay leader is often a man of high social standing who comes from a noble family and is well versed in social conventions *(adat)* and customs of the people. He is also likely to come from the social strata of royalty *(raja)*, the leaders *(orang besar)* and the commoner *(orang kebanyakan)*. The latter group is now gaining visibility, status and influence in the political arena through education and greater social interaction and the promotion of the Islamic concept: "Allah being the all powerful and that beneath him all men are equal."

The ideal manager, in the eyes of the Malays, is one who is always seen to be calm, polite and pleasant, and his behaviour is often low keyed, compassionate and unhurried. Some of the other important attributes (Dahlan, 1991) are:

- having a large and an informal power base to enable him to achieve his goals, mainly through persuasion
- working unobtrusively and enlisting the assistance and moral support of others such as the religious leader *(Imam)*
- being devout in religious beliefs and conscientious (*warak* and *alim*) in practising traditional rites and ceremonies
- being thoroughly Malay and able to contribute to the solidarity of the group
- being sincere, humble and tactful (not pushy, which is considered offensive)
- showing concern for others' welfare
- being trustworthy, honest, just, fair, and generous

All of these qualities and attributes are well-established through the influence of *Adat Pepateh, Adat Temenggong* in the State of Negri Sembilan and the Islamic concept of leadership. As stated in the Quran: "Those in authority are to be selected from among the members of the community, on the grounds that they are capable and trustworthy" (Al-Quran: 4:58).

The Chinese, too, respect leaders who are highly educated professionally, especially those who are more qualified than their subordinates or know enough of the technical and business details to ask the right questions or to guide the followers to achieve success. For the more traditional Chinese, those who come from the same clan, village or ancestral origins in China or have the same surname, speak the same dialect, perform similar rituals and have family connections are perceived to have a better understanding of the subordinates' situation. With this "connection", they may feel more secure in the relationship and are thus more ready to trust their future in the hands of their leaders who will take good care of them.

Those who are highly respected because of their wealth, social standing and educational achievements are often well connected and known by many people. It is therefore assumed that their opinions will be well received by everyone. Since they are able to command resources to ensure that objectives are achieved, followers trust their leadership. Chinese philanthropists are often elected presidents of guilds and political associations.

Generally, these attributes also apply to the Indians, who devote much of their success to predestination or *karma* and believe that their reincarnation after death will depend very much on their conduct in the present life. Most Hindus begin their day's activities with prayers to deities; some small businesses often display pictures of deities at their work locations.

In the caste system of the Indians, there are three distinct levels of society - the rich businessmen, the professionals and the wage earners. Through education, there is now greater social interaction between the different levels of caste and class - thus narrowing the gap. However, the thread of distinction continues to be maintained by the orthodox and the less educated. An Asian idiom states: "In a family of a thousand, only one is the Master *(Karta).*"

Indians also admire leaders who set good examples and are selfless and committed to a cause. Leaders gain respect from others because of their personality traits, exemplary behaviour, bravery, moral qualities, concern and care, and the "personal" touch with their subordinates.

• Total character

Leaders are expected to possess certain admirable qualities and not just skills and competencies as what they say and do will be followed – sometimes unquestionably. The total character of the leader is often taken into consideration when assessing leadership qualities; his personal demeanour is often closely scrutinized.

The concept of righteousness and respect *Yang Mulia, Yang Berbahagia* becomes a key criterion in assessing the credibility of Malaysian leaders and the amount of respect they will receive from others. They are leaders because others admire them for their virtuous qualities. Being sensitive, caring, able to work cohesively and being polite are qualities respected by others. Those who come across as brash, loud or lacking emotional control may not be well-received.

However, some of these qualities are gradually being eroded with the emergence of the *nouveau riche* in their pursuit of economic and material wealth as evident in the Government's constant reminder for ethical and moral values in the society. But, achievement among those with humble beginnings is still respected and serves as an example and hope to society.

To summarize, the Chinese would prefer a leader whom they can trust and who in turn trusts his employees. The Malays generally prefer a socio-centric leader who is both a friend and boss while the Indians are comfortable with a boss-centred leadership provided he is fair and equitable. While these attributes may be respected by the older generation and those with traditional and conservative values and upbringing, some younger, modern or Western-educated Malaysians may not uphold them all, but would probably respect them.

2. On Motivating

While money is generally the underlying factor that drives Malaysians to work, other factors such as opportunities for self-development, contributing to the community and nation, and having good harmonious relationships are also important. The following are some observations relating to motivation:

• Group affiliation

Most Malaysians have a strong affinity for group affiliation. As they derive their identity from being part of a collectivist social order, the pursuit of self-esteem and self-actualization could be interpreted as deviant behaviours. In both the Chinese and Malay cultures, traditional communal responsibility is cherished as evident in the clan groupings and *gotong-royong* concepts. This is also evident in the "collective eating" among the Chinese – the most cherished being the family reunion dinner on the eve of each Lunar New Year celebration.

However, this traditional communal responsibility termed "collectivism" by Hofstede is not as simplistic as it looks. For example, Malaysians may be collectivist within their own clans or communities, but their level of cooperation and trust with the society at large could decrease and competitiveness increase. Sometimes, identifying too much with clans or regions may create parochial apathy and disregard for the larger community at work.

• Success symbols

Malays are motivated by their affiliations to groups, families, friends, hometown *(kampung)* and Islamic brotherhood. They measure success in terms of rapport with family, friends and associates and are attracted by tangible rewards such as a piece of land, house, building, pilgrimage to Mecca and circle of friends and influential contacts. Each has an intrinsic value. They feel secure when they are confident of receiving the respect of those they know. In corporate terms, they are also motivated if their job contributes to nation building. They respond better to efforts at productivity if they can see benefits accruing not only to the company but also to their family, the community and the nation at large.

Success among Chinese and Indian leaders is evident through their support for the family, clan or society. The Chinese will look for monetary rewards and would do their best when the needs of the family are provided for, while the Indians will be loyal towards the organization that caters for their well-being and development.

The Chinese philanthropists are highly respected especially for their donations to education and religious institutions. However, as individuals, the Chinese are often modest in demonstrating their riches. When pressed for an answer, a Chinese individual will describe his prosperity as *"so so-lah"* or *cukup makan* (enough to eat). The Chinese also believe that once success is achieved, they will be able to attain prosperity, thus ensuring a secure and happy future for the family. Success also means being able to perform filial duties well or embark on philanthropic activities that will enable them to gain "face" or "status" in the society. The extended family, clan and other affiliations similarly gain face too, thus giving the individual a good social standing in the Chinese community.

• Relationships

Given the focus on interpersonal relationships, most Malaysians are interested in building and maintaining good relationships with those they work with. They are often contented at work if they have opportunities to show and receive appropriate recognition and respect from their superiors, peers and subordinates. In fact, for a Malay, it is his relationship with his manager that most determines his motivation. Many Malays feel that: "If I have a good boss, I will work myself to death for him."

Motivation, therefore, means creating a climate where the manager shows a concern for developing and maintaining good interpersonal relationships with his subordinates. This can be demonstrated by the manager using the key elements in the local polite system when communicating with his subordinates. Managers have to generate a harmonious work climate where employees feel "valued", wanted and able to relate with colleagues in a "family-like" atmosphere.

Reciprocity, for the purpose of establishing good relationships, often takes the form of gifts, favours and even nepotism towards subordinates by superiors. However, it is wise to check that the relationship is not taken advantage of by subordinates because it may affect the effectiveness and credibility of those who lead, especially when they succumb to the generosity of helping subordinates from organizational funds. The practice of "helping our own kind" has become a common phenomenon.

GUIDELINES ON LEADING AND MOTIVATING

The act of developing desired behaviours and values through motivating and rewarding subordinates within an organization requires constant attention, commitment and consistency on the part of the leaders. In Malaysia, a manager's power base should be both personal and positional in nature.

His credibility comes from his subordinates' perception of his competence and in their demonstration of respect, admiration and desire to identify with him. His personal decorum is a prerequisite for acceptance by his subordinates, since in the Asian context, roles are modelled – not contracted – and the link between individuals and organizations is moral – not calculating. Loyalty to the organization figures prominently as employees personalize it to play a custodian role. A manager is expected to be spiritually and morally sound, inspiring, honourable and caring, yet decisive.

Tarcisius Chin (1999) succinctly sums this up by proposing that the challenge for management today in preparing managers for the future, is for the manager to maintain the IQ (intelligence quotient) drive, enhance EQ (emotional intelligence) relationships, and promote SQ (spiritual intelligence) values.

Managers should find the following guidelines helpful in their task of leading and motivating the multicultural workforce in Malaysia:

1. Spend time to build relationships

Be cordial and open when interacting with subordinates. Openness can be demonstrated by having daily interactions with staff through structured and regular social and work opportunities where managers are seen to mingle with their subordinates. Having *makan* (eating) opportunities can help reduce social and physical distance at the workplace – although one has to be alert to subordinates who may take advantage of any friendly "overtures" from their superiors.

A two-way communication process between management and employees can be enhanced by incorporating certain practices like having open cafeterias, managers walking about and spending time chatting, and sharing jokes *(berbual mesra)* with their subordinates and treating everyone as family members.

Through frequent face-to-face interactions, managers can make their subordinates develop a sense of belonging to the organization. Being seen to have a non-confrontational and compromising leadership style can help create an environment where subordinates will feel happy to come to work in.

2.   Promote feelings of togetherness

Solidify relationships between subordinates by communicating vision and targets to be achieved on a group basis. Standards, if set, must be from the group as their potential remains very much in their ability to function collectively. Encourage cooperative ventures among employees so that they learn to work and support each other on both work and non-work matters.

For the Chinese, it is important that the manager attends functions when invited by their subordinates even if it is just dropping by for a while. Otherwise, send a representative such as spouse or an adult child. A personal telephone call is encouraged. Personal visits, gifts and cards should be sent when close members of the family are hospitalized. Togetherness can be promoted by doing things such as eating together or entertaining, with the manager picking up the bill.

For Indians, a manager's understanding of his workers' religious practices and cultural ceremonies can enhance their commitment to work. Allowing time off to Indian subordinates for these events will make the subordinates feel valued and appreciated.

3.   Be humble and apologetic

Learn to be modest and humble and avoid having an elitist attitude. If there are differences in status, managers must downplay the achieved symbols (car, big office, etc.) and reduce their social and power distance from others. They have to create an atmosphere where subordinates feel comfortable to share their problems.

A humble leader is often respected by subordinates as he comes across as one who is approachable and is able to communicate in the language of dignity.

This is illustrated in the saying: *"Mengikut resmi padi makin berisi makin tunduk, bukan seperti lalang, makin tinggi makin melayang."*

In English, the above means: "Be like the padi plant, the heavier it gets, the lower it bows; be not like the hay grass, the taller it gets, the stronger it gets wafted."

The humble leader or the "small man" approach will long be remembered. Perhaps the ideal Malaysian leader is one who can incorporate the three approaches of the *towkay, tuan* and the "small man". Hence, to be accepted as a leader, a manager has to demonstrate his care and concern for his people as illustrated in the *towkay* approach, be able to use his power and influence bases as shown in the *tuan* approach and yet remain humble as suggested in the "small man" approach.

4. Understand the person

Learn to relate with the subordinate as a total human being, not as someone who only has the competence and expertise to get the job done. Rather than focusing on the task, make an effort to understand the subordinate's values and feelings *(rasa)* towards work issues and challenges. Always maintain his dignity *(maruah)* by not belittling him in any way, especially in front of others. As stated by Lao Tze: "When I yield to the workers or the person working, I encounter no resistance."

For the Chinese, it is important to remember the four principles of *Li, Yi, Lian* and *Zhe*[1] when leading others. Managers may induce others to behave properly by first role-modelling their own behaviours – if they want employees to work harder, then they should start work earlier and go home later than their employees. This is best illustrated in another ancient Chinese saying: "The bottom part of a pillar will not be straight if the upper part is crooked." Working long hours is a way of showing commitment to the goals of the organization.

5. Build trust

Cultivate a relationship of trust with subordinates based on values of caring and support for their work and personal needs. Treating employees as members of an extended family can reinforce this. Care and concern can be demonstrated through the appropriate use of words and actions. This is important because counselling and coaching are effectively carried out when there is trust between

---

[1] **LI** means good manners shown through respect, understanding and courtesy to others.
YI means righteousness in seeking justice and equity for all.
LIAN means showing restraint in personal desire, not greed.
ZHE means not engaging in acts considered illegal or against humanity, and leading effectively so as to avoid shame.

the subordinate and manager. While information, results and achievements are important, subordinates would be more receptive of any appraisal if their supervisors have taken the initiative to build rapport, trust and understanding. Issues relating to tasks are better communicated when good relations prevail and there is trust and harmony.

6.   Provide recognition and rewards

Publicize any form of recognition award, both material and spiritual in nature, to reinforce good work behaviours, at appropriate social or special events where subordinates' families are present. This can strengthen cohesiveness, loyalty and increase subordinates' self-esteem in the eyes of their loved ones.

When interacting with subordinates, demonstrate polite behaviours by using appropriate words and phrases that are part of good manners as this demonstrates the manager's respect for their subordinates and help preserve their self-respect *(hormat diri)*. At all costs, avoid making innuendos that encroach on racial sensitivities as it will make a manager appear emotional and lose his respect in front of others.

The Chinese, in general, appreciate financial incentives from the organization and higher education for themselves as well as for their children. Other attractive incentives include:

–   Allowing a father to take long leave to care for his newborn baby

–   Time off during *Ching Beng* (All Souls' Day)

–   Time off to pray and make offerings in the temples during festivals, and especially when he wants to reverse "bad fate"

–   Following rituals which are cultural prescriptions favouring good business, personal achievement and harmony

–   At social functions, having subordinates sit beside a senior manager or an influential person. It will make them feel honoured and proud. The presence of influential people in celebrations such as weddings and birthdays of elders, funerals and important private functions gives face to the recipient. Thus, the subordinate will want to behave "correctly" at work so as to maintain the liaison

–   Acknowledging long-serving subordinates' contribution through feasts, scrolls, plaques and framed calligraphy of wise sayings, etc.

–   Giving incentives to employees for religious fulfilments can enhance loyalty to the organization

–   Providing education or housing loans can ensure commitment and continuous service

An implication for management is that if a company wants to attract and retain loyal and productive workers, it may need to ensure that the reward

57

systems include both membership-based and performance-based criteria as they are vital in maintaining workforce commitment.

CONCLUSION

With the increased emphasis on the need to develop a society with high morals and good ethics, leaders and managers have to model their behaviour in line with local values. They have to be able to inspire a shared vision in terms of the values they want employees to have, and cultivate shared practices to uphold them. This can be done by incorporating the subordinates' cultural and spiritual values at the workplace and making them proud of being a member of the organization.

It is important that a "family" atmosphere be created among employees as this will instil in them a sense of commitment to the organization and contribute to national unity so vital for the success of Vision 2020.

As stated by Lao Tze, "Both get what they need if the leader has the wisdom to serve and follow, to be open and below."

Presumably, there is no distinct style of management that can be exclusively identified as Malaysian. Perhaps the colonial legacy has been instrumental in creating role models of leadership behaviour along the *tuan* approach which was effective then, but no longer appropriate today as they are incongruent with the values of a better-educated workforce.

On a positive note, it can be said that the absence of a Malaysian leadership style can help foster an openness, receptivity and a willingness on the part of managers to learn about management practices which have evolved from the various sources originating in the West and the East. The emphasis on the Look East policy in the recent past has encouraged Malaysians to incorporate the positive elements of the Japanese work ethic while the concepts and theories emanating from various business schools in the West have also influenced the thinking of our managers.

However, it has to be remembered that what fits Japan or America may not fit Malaysia. While the Japanese are a mono-ethnic and homogeneous culture, the West is driven by values of individualism and achievement. Malaysia, on the other hand, is multi-ethnic and generally collectivist. Hence, in developing her workforce, a leader or manager in Malaysia must be truly sensitive to the diversity and develop an indigenous "recipe" which is based on a synergistic blend of the best from all the races in the country.

The above discussions raise additional issues for future research and investigations. There is a need to examine whether there is a convergence of values among different ethnic groups in the Malaysian society. Periodic investigations after five to ten years to gauge the amount of social and cultural change occurring within the various ethnic groups in the Malaysian society can be done to evolve an appropriate management leadership and motivational style which is truly Malaysian.

SUMMARY OF KEY MALAYSIAN VALUES IN LEADING AND MOTIVATING

FACE
- Be polite and well-mannered when dealing with subordinates
- Do not criticize subordinates in public

NURTURING
- Show care and concern for employees and their family
- Be a "parent" figure to young subordinates
- Allow subordinates to try out new ideas under the guidance of senior team members

HUMILITY
- Be sincere in words and actions
- Listen to subordinates' views
- Apologize when mistakes are made as it is a mark of respect for the other person

GROUP AFFILIATION
- Allow subordinates to bring in friends to help with the work if work pressure mounts
- Get to know subordinate's family and friends

RELATIONSHIPS
- Build good interpersonal skills and promote harmonious relationships among team members through social events
- Be polite when interacting with subordinates

REFERENCES

Al-Quran 4: 58.

Asma, Abdullah (1996). *Going Glocal: Cultural Dimensions in Malaysian Management.* Kuala Lumpur: Malaysian Institute of Management.

Chin, Tarcisius (1999). Future Directions. In: *Management in Malaysia.* Kuala Lumpur: Malaysian Institute of Management.

Dahlan Hj Aman (1991). Local Values in Intercultural Management, *Malaysian Management Review,* Vol. 26, No. 1. Kuala Lumpur: Malaysian Institute of Management.

Hofstede, Geert (1984). The Cultural Relativity of the Quality of Life Concept, *Academy of Management Review,* 9: 389-398.

Redding, S G (1990). *The Spirit of Chinese Capitalism.* Berlin: Walter de Gruyter.

Westwood, Robert Ian (1991). Managerial Values and Practices: Convergent or Divergent Trends?, *Malaysian Management Review,* Vol. 26, No. 1, pp. 13-36. Kuala Lumpur: Malaysian Institute of Management.

4

BUILDING A MULTICULTURAL TEAM

NORMA MANSOR

INTRODUCTION

One of the key tasks of a manager is to ensure that those who work with him are able to move in unison to achieve a common goal. His performance is often measured by how well he gets each team member to render his best efforts and blend them with the effort of other team members into a well-coordinated action. This challenge is faced at every level in an organization, from the lowest level to the highest. In a sense, a manager who harnesses the combined efforts of his team members will enable the whole to be greater than the sum of its individual parts.

The need to build effective teams takes a great deal of planning and hard work on the part of managers. They have to make the values of cooperation and teamwork as part of their daily work rituals so that these values become part of their conscious behaviour. Over time, members in the team will be able to work harmoniously and generate a spirit of working together in translating a message into action.

OBJECTIVES OF THIS CHAPTER

This chapter will focus on the critical issues and challenges of building teams in the context of multicultural Malaysia. A brief definition of a team will be given, followed by some key observations of how Malaysians work together at their respective workplaces based on the values that they have internalized as part of the process of socialization into a collectivist society. This is followed by a set of guidelines for managers who want to create a climate for building teamwork among the diverse ethnic groups.

ISSUES AND CHALLENGES

The task of building a strong and effective workforce in most Malaysian companies would require managers to understand the values of the various ethnic groups that unite and differentiate them from others. Those who make an attempt to look at the inherent values which are supportive of the "working together" spirit will have much to gain from the combined efforts of their team members.

Below are some of the challenges which managers often face in promoting the spirit of working together.

• Ethnic orientation

The values of an organization may not always be readily accepted by all subordinates, who represent various ethnic groups in Malaysia. A collectivist culture tends to promote some form of exclusivity among its members and, as a result, a team may tend to comprise those from the same ethnic group because of the many similarities of language, food and religion that unite them. These similarities which are observed by most of the ethnic groups tend to create an awareness of the "differences" of who they are between racial groups. This sense of "difference" tends to make them feel more comfortable with members of their own "kind". Hence, a subordinate is more likely to support and identify with those who are from the same ethnic group. Likewise, a manager may also prefer to have subordinates from the same ethnic group.

It is a challenge to Malaysian managers to be aware of these racial-based inclinations and be able to manage without compromising on team performance and organization goals.

• Education system with vernacular schools

The Malaysian school system also tends to reinforce the awareness of differences by making it compulsory for Muslim students to study Islamic studies and non-Muslim students to undergo moral studies. In addition, Malaysia, unlike its neighbouring countries such as Thailand and Indonesia, allows alternative educational systems to co-exist with its national school system. This feature has given rise to the setting up of vernacular schools promoting Tamil, Mandarin and Arabic streams of thought separately. Malaysian parents are therefore given a choice of sending their children to these vernacular schools in addition to the national school system where the medium of instruction is Bahasa Malaysia. As a result, there is not much interchange among these various groups of schoolchildren attending vernacular schools.

- **Communal-based political system**

Again, the political system in Malaysia is also communal based. The ruling party, the National Front, is an alliance of 14 political parties representing the main ethnic groups in Malaysia. Although the focus of the party is on national unity, the component parties tend to champion issues based on ethnic concerns. Within the National Front, political decisions are made based on consensus – to minimize racial disharmony. This inclination to preserve racial harmony at all costs is often reflected at the workplace, hence representing a microcosm of the Malaysian society. At the workplace, it is common to hear that decisions are made based on racial considerations. It can be a challenge or an issue because it can be at the expense of merit.

- **Perceived discrimination arising from the NEP**

The New Economic Policy (NEP) (1970-1990) is often seen as an affirmative action to restructure the Malaysian society so that economic function would not be identified according to racial groups. This development policy and planning clearly distinguished the Malay-Bumiputras from non-Malays and non-Bumiputras. While the real intent of the NEP was for Malays to promote growth with equity based on a set of priorities and assistance to progress in the field of business and commerce, non-Malays may see it as a form of discrimination. This can give rise to misinterpretation and cause disharmony and friction among the different ethnic groups.

- **Strongholds of traditional values**

While the values of modernization and even urbanization may have influenced many managers to pay less attention to traditional cultural rites, most Malaysian parents still expect their young to show respect towards their seniors and elders, believe in a religion and show preference for doing things in groups. These values are often carried into the workplace, making teamwork more effective when there is an elderly person to take charge and lead the group.

- **Complexities and diversities of cultures**

As Malaysia is a transitional society where traditional ways co-exist with the modern industrial lifestyle, it has become doubly complicated for the manager

63

to fully comprehend the likes and dislikes of his multicultural workforce. Although Malaysia is moving into the phase of capitalistic individualism, there are some tradition-bound values such as filial piety and respect for hierarchy, which are still very strong among all the ethnic groups. A manager therefore has to demonstrate a genuine attempt to understand these complexities and capitalize on the diverse strengths of members in his team.

- **Multireligious sensitivities**

The multi-religious nature of the Malaysian society is another big challenge. For Muslims, certain things are taboo, like pork and alcohol. Some Buddhists are vegetarians and Hindus refrain from eating beef. These intercultural sensitivities are often respected but not always understood. The need to understand cultural preferences may have to go beyond tolerance as these may have an impact when members work in teams. As a result, a manager will have to understand the ethnic sensitivities and preferences, especially if his team has a heterogeneous membership.

DEFINING A TEAM

A team is defined as a group of individuals who come together to contribute their efforts in performing a certain task in a cooperative manner. Members are enthusiastic, supportive of one another, working and harmonizing with each other to reach a common goal. They work well together and enjoy doing so in order to produce a high quality result.

Teams may be formed at various levels. There are two types of teams that are easily identifiable; the first is the organization as a whole, while the second is the smaller sized task team. The latter is also more task-specific, comprising a small group of individuals coming together to do a job in a combined effort.

In the context of Malaysia, a team refers to members of different ethnic groups either from an organization or different organizations, coming together to work on a task and filling in for one another without any feelings of resentment and apprehension. This requires members to understand one another's values and sensitivities as these may have an impact on how they relate to each other.

KEY OBSERVATIONS RELATING TO BUILDING A TEAM

Malaysians are often seen to work best in teams in that they display an overt expression of willingness, spontaneity and voluntariness among members to help and cover for one another when necessary. Individualistic behaviour, often expressed by an individual in the unwillingness to work in groups, is often frowned upon and considered disruptive and often downplayed. Such individuals would consider working in a team as nebulous, as they are not given the credit for completing the task successfully on their own. Instead, the credit goes to all individuals in the group and only members who understand clearly the superordinate goal would be willing to work to achieve the objective that has been agreed upon.

Below are some common observations of the values characterizing a high performance and multicultural work team in Malaysia:

- **Ethnic tendencies**

There is a tendency for managers to prefer to delegate to those whom they can trust and in Malaysia it would often be members from the same ethnic group. Many superiors with multi-racial subordinates prefer to delegate work, especially those types that are more sensitive, to subordinates of the same racial background. This may be based on the perception that someone of the same race will be less likely to betray their trust and be more loyal. This is understandable because trust is often given to people who are more similar than different from us in terms of values and preferences. In addition, studies have shown that members in a group-orientated culture are more inclined to support the growth and development of those from a similar background. As a result, a Malay manager would depend on his Malay subordinate for things which only he can determine, while it is not uncommon to find a Chinese manager wanting to depend more on his Chinese subordinate.

- **Loyalty and pride of a team**

Malaysians value team spirit highly and managers who establish an environment where members feel comfortable of being together will be able to develop group pride and sense of belonging. The motivation to be part of the group, to give loyalty and commitment to the leader and the task in hand, tends to make Malaysians "band" together to even work beyond the call of duty. More importantly, it is the willingness of a manager to have a "give-and-take" orientation and be flexible with his team members that will cause them to contribute their best efforts to accomplish the objective of the team.

- **Tolerance for irregular hours**

Members are more likely to be willing to work irregular and even longer hours rather than follow strictly structured work schedules. In completing a specific task, members tend to expect their managers and team members to assist or empathize when emergencies or family obligations arise. A manager, therefore, often has to decide whether or not to allow his subordinates time off to meet urgent personal needs whilst making a full commitment to the team.

- ## Harmony and family feeling

Malaysians value harmony in work and in social relationships. This value can be traced back to the collectivist "we" nature of most Asian societies of Chinese, Japanese and Indian cultures where the family is the ideal social unit. The unit is further extended into the clan, group or society, making the individual almost non-existent with his larger unit. The feeling of "we" is also extended to the workplace, which is seen as a second home where members of the team have embodied the spirit of living together in harmony. There is a strong work bond resembling family ties. Hence, separating formal work and informal relationship risks breaking the dynamics of a team. Managers, therefore, tend to promote a harmonious orientation where members are expected to care for one another, especially in times of adversity. When help is needed, team members will give it willingly, as manifested in the spirit of *gotong-royong,* meaning "joining forces in carrying out a task".

- ## Learning and experimenting

Members who work in a team also do not like to follow rigid procedures. They enjoy working through experimenting and learning from one another - the younger from the older and more experienced members. As respect for elders is widely practised among Malaysians regardless of race, younger people are expected to learn to put ideas across in ways that will not affect the status and pride of their seniors.

- ## Respect for elders

Elderly members in a team are regarded as members with a moral obligation to care for junior team members. Because of the respect for family hierarchy, those in authority may therefore have to play the multiple roles of a "nurturing father", counsellor and leader in order to earn the respect of members. Although this is changing, many still hold the view that authority should be entrusted to someone based on his age, knowledge and power.

- ## Relationship

Close relationship among team members is often reflected by the familiarity members demonstrate when they interact with each other. Special or even peculiar gestures, signals or words and nicknames are often used when communicating in order to establish closeness, openness and rapport among junior and elderly members.

- ## Cooperation

When a mistake is detected, it is quickly rectified without putting the blame on one another. Instead, the whole group will work to overcome the problem. This is based on cooperation, trust and compatibility. The manager-cum-leader of the multicultural work team makes a conscious effort to promote an environment for enhancing these values. In recognizing the importance of face saving, team members often prefer not to see an individual singled out for blame, even though the blame may be justified.

- **Indirect communication**

Malaysians tend to be indirect when solving a difficult issue relating to team members. In their attempt to use an indirect mode of communication, the intent is often precluded by talking about a different issue and then carefully "steering the discussion" to focus on the issue at hand. For example, a manager will start the conversation by talking on general issues before touching on the poor performance of the team due to the "uncooperative" behaviour of the subordinate. This approach is considered more palatable to the receiver because it comes across as less threatening, saves face and does not disrupt or threaten team spirit.

- **Avoiding confrontation**

Direct open confrontation is often avoided as maintaining harmonious relationship within the team is considered more important. The political system of the different ethnic groups is based upon an incremental approach, and to avoid raising any open criticism towards another group, marginal changes are made. If there is a need to voice dissatisfaction, a less overt approach is often used so that feelings and sensitivities are not hurt. It is critical that the team works smoothly without friction and all matters are handled amicably in a friendly and family-like manner.

- **Using a third party**

Using third-party intervention is another common approach to solve problems within a team. This method is similar to solving problems at the family level where the mother speaks on behalf of the son to the father. When working in teams, the involvement of a third party becomes necessary when members do not talk to each other or when the work style of the leader is preventing the team from moving ahead. Tapping the resources and energies of a third party who is respected by both members and the leader can help relieve "strained" ties or working relationships.

GUIDELINES ON BUILDING TEAMS

To build effective multicultural work teams in Malaysia, the following suggestions are proposed for managers:

- **Preserve face**

Be sensitive when reprimanding someone for his mistake. Do so in private to avoid making the person "lose" face. Publicly embarrassing an individual can have a negative effect on the work group in terms of morale, relationships and the spirit of working together like one happy family.

- **Manage competing loyalties**

Use discretion in matters relating to team members' personal needs. Allowing them time off to attend to family emergencies may encourage greater commitment to the team as members will reciprocate by giving their personal time to attend to work obligations. Managers who are flexible and not calculative have much to gain as members will respect their sense of caring and concern for their social needs.

- **Promote a familial structure**

Be a "nurturing father or mother" or "big brother" and draw upon the familial and cultural values of team members. At all times, make an attempt to promote a cooperative atmosphere among team members by planning social activities to build team spirit with the manager-cum-leader acting as "like the head of a family". Managers may have to treat their employees as members of an extended family by providing support, coaching and advice, spending time and getting to know them to help strengthen friendly ties which can help bond people in working together. Team members in turn will give of their best towards achieving team goals.

- **Show respect**

Respect the views and opinions of team members although such input is likely to be expressed tentatively or unassertively. Be seen to be tactful, diplomatic and respectful for ideas from those who are younger. Managers who are able to incorporate ideas and suggestions will be appreciated by their subordinates in the way they seek advice and support – thus strengthening the manager-subordinate relationships.

- **Bridge ethnic gap**

Be aware of ethnic differences and sensitivities of team members so as to avoid dividing loyalties based on ethnic identification. To prevent this, the manager must ensure that team members do not perceive him to be favouring one ethnic group or certain parties. Avoid being influenced by preconceived ideas or prejudices along racial lines and strongly encourage team members to do likewise. Individuals have been employed on the basis of their particular competence; as such, any stereotyping should be abhorred for they would be seen as unfair by those from the other ethnic groups.

- **Understanding diversity**

Understand the value dynamics of the team members as each team member has been exposed to different socializing experiences in terms of family upbringing, religious beliefs and the school system. There are Malaysians who work well only on an intracultural level, but there are also those who can do well at the intercultural level[1].

• **Build trust**

Spend time to establish relationships of trust and understanding among team members before they perform the task even though it may seem to be a waste of time (since non job-related or what may appear to be "irrelevant" matters are usually discussed). Making an attempt to know the subordinate's family background, hometown or schooling is a way of reaching some common ground to help establish a bond between members. Once a relationship is built, the concept of team is easily understood as the focus on the group's task is now more important than individual accomplishments.

• **Develop "we" spirit**

Promote the spirit of collectivism as the "we" orientation allows people to define themselves in relation to a work unit or family. Team members would therefore be more concerned with fulfilling the obligations of the group rather than self-fulfilment and self-expression.

• **Focus on external objectives**

Focus on satisfying the needs and expectations of the organization's customers as this can help build a strong team. Working together to fulfil an external need gives the team members the motivation and challenge to work towards a common goal. This in itself can help "push" members to work in unison, i.e. in a cohesive manner where goal congruence is achieved. Thus, when a team performs effectively, the organization also becomes effective.

CONCLUSION

A multicultural work team can be nurtured by integrating the different aspirations and values upheld by its members. The diversity in its membership can be an asset in generating alternatives that are both varied and creative. Hence, based on the concept of synergy – where the whole is greater than the sum of its parts – a multicultural work team can develop into a hybrid team where members have a sense of achievement, affiliation and belonging. Harmony and rapport prevail, ideas and feelings are shared and the task gets done in an environment of mutual trust, respect and candour. The challenge

---

[1] For an elaboration on communicating at the intracultural and intercultural levels, see chapter 2.

for most Malaysian managers is, therefore, to extract the common values of members from different ethnic groups (Bumiputras, Chinese, Indians and others) and even people from differing cultures (Western-, Islamic- or Chinese-educated, urban or rural), and to surface them at the workplace in the form of shared practices.

In building such multicultural work teams, a manager can either impose his own methods or take into consideration the values of team members. A heterogeneous team has the potential to be more innovative and often more productive than a homogeneous team, but if it is not well-managed, the team can degenerate into a work unit with unfounded biases, stereotyping, prejudices and misperceptions on how tasks should be done.

At the Malaysian workplace, a high performance multicultural work team will invariably blend social dimensions with work dimensions. Members feel good about working together to achieve set targets. Hence, if a manager is able to harness the collective energies of the team members, a synergistic team will emerge. But if he fails, then members will tend to revert to their own enclave where ethnocentrism prevails, and this can be harmful in the long run.

SUMMARY OF KEY MALAYSIAN VALUES IN BUILDING A MULTICULTURAL TEAM

HARMONY
- Be sensitive to local beliefs and norms
- Understand and use a "give and take" approach

RELATIONSHIPS
- Promote trust and understanding
- Spend time with team members to get to know one another

COOPERATION
- Promote spontaneity, voluntariness and unity
- Get into the spirit of getting things done when there is a need

---

5

MAKING DECISIONS

PETER SHEPHARD

INTRODUCTION

Making a decision is about choosing a solution to a problem or a course of action, or arriving at an answer to a question. It involves a conscious choice after looking at the facts and information on the issue at hand. Very often, making a choice requires judgement, and whether or not this judgement is rational, creative or intuitive, an individual is required to select from a range of alternatives.

If the alternatives are already available, the rational approach may be applied but if there is a need to invent alternatives, then the creative thinking process can be used to generate alternatives before a decision is made.

A decision-making process often starts with the results to be obtained, not with the alternatives that happen to be at hand. The most important thing to remember is to clarify what should be achieved in the decision situation and what the desired or ideal outcome is. Only then can the best alternative be selected.

OBJECTIVES OF THIS CHAPTER

This chapter will examine the key cultural factors which influence decision making among Malaysians, analyse the results of a Malaysian value survey in relation to decision making and conclude with a number of guidelines for managers to consider in their day-to-day process of agreeing on a specific line of action with or "within" a multiracial workgroup.

ISSUES AND CHALLENGES

Decision making varies from culture to culture and from individual to individual. It is important therefore to examine the underlying assumptions and the values of the decision makers. A decision not to act on a perceived wrongdoing may be frowned upon by those who believe that justice must be seen to be done while another person programmed in the Malaysian culture may interpret it as an act of face saving. The saying "different strokes for different folks" is found to be just as applicable in examining how decisions are made in situations where people are from diverse cultural origins, as well as from differing personalities. For example, just as some cultures may rely more on intuitive rather than rational processes, so equally this preference may be part of an individual personality difference. Thus, when one tries to assess why an individual makes a particular decision, it is pertinent to ask: is it due more to a personality trait (nature) or a cultural influence (nurture)?

In an Anglo-Saxon culture, the process of decision making unfolds primarily through the anticipation of the consequences of alternative courses of action. However, in some other cultures, the function of the decision maker(s) is to evaluate a situation by classifying it according to pre-established categories. Whatever action ensues or whatever decisions are made will need to follow automatically from what has happened in a similar situation before.

In Malaysia, there are a number of issues and challenges in making decisions and these are as follows:

- **Perception of self**

There is a tendency for most people to think that when a decision is made, it is based on one person's thought process. However, in a group-oriented culture, this may not be the case as the decision could be made by a committee or a group who have come together to work out a solution. Hence, there are those who would feel uncomfortable when the decision does not have a clear reference to the individual.

- **Time**

While there are cultures which take pride in arriving at a quick decision, there are others which believe that a quick decision indicates hasty thinking. A manager who prides himself as a fast decision maker may be perceived by others as brash, and rather impetuous. As a result, it would be useful to gauge the average time taken to come together and make decisions that will be well-received by all concerned parties.

- **Hidden sensitivities**

Again, in Malaysia a decision is never received in the same way by all because of the multi-ethnic composition of the workforce. A decision made by a Malay manager may not always be acceptable to a Chinese and it would be advisable for him to consult his Chinese peers to give some other points of view. There could be hidden subtleties which are not clearly stated and it is the responsibility of the decision maker(s) to seek clarification before making a stand. For example, a manager in planning an event has to recognize that Malaysians may be obligated to attend to a religious or family ritual, like visiting an ancestor's grave, a temple or at prayer time

- **Global comparisons**

There is a need to understand other people's ways because such understanding will increase our own self-knowledge and objectivity. Most of us grow up with the assumption that our own way of doing things is the right way and accept our culture as "given". We are usually not aware of why we do things in a particular way. Yet, we are aware of many problems which we do not have solutions to. Knowledge of the variety of ways in which other people have met similar problems gives us new perspectives and new clues to human behaviours. Much has been written on the unique differences between American and Japanese management decision making or between English and French or Germans – but little on the Malaysian ways.

DEFINING A DECISION

When we make a decision, it can either be a rational choice among alternatives, i.e. a balance between risks and fulfilment, or an intuitive choice (based on a hunch or feeling). Either way, the decision must be able to bring about a measurable effect on the activities of the business and that it is unavoidable or impossible to postpone, without serious consequences for the business at the present time or in future.

For most managers, making fast decisions is often an expression of one's ability to get things done efficiently. It is often considered that a wrong decision is better than no decision at all. Taking risks is acceptable as one is expected to learn from them. It is possible to separate the decision from the person making it (i.e. you may make a wrong decision – but that doesn't make you less respected). This is more a Western "scientific" management paradigm than Eastern or Asian.

The consequences of a decision on the recipients, or those most affected by the decision, should be carefully weighed. A well-known social scientist, Carl Rogers (1961) observed that the effectiveness of a decision could be put as a formula or equation:

$$QT \times DA = DE$$

where QT   =   Quality of Thinking
         DA   =   Degree of Acceptance
         DE   =   Decision Effectiveness

The formula clearly shows the importance of getting commitment from members before implementing decisions.

KEY OBSERVATIONS RELATING TO MAKING DECISIONS

Several significant factors have influenced the process of decision making among Malaysians. Whether the decision is made collectively or individually, the process is strongly influenced by the social and cultural values of the decision makers.

Following are some common observations on the key factors that may have an impact on the way Malaysians make decisions:

- **The role of age**

The responsibility to make the final decision is often the prerogative of (and may even be reserved for) those in senior positions who have a larger power base (legitimate power or position authority). As they are generally respected by those in junior positions, their decisions are less likely to be challenged since doing so may be considered improper and an attack on the credibility and status of the senior members. As age is often associated with seniority and experience, those who are older are considered "wiser" and their capability and capacity to take a stance on issues may reinforce their role as competent elders.

- **Supernatural beliefs**

In most oriental and Asian cultures, supernatural beliefs and superstitions have an impact on people's lives and decisions. As these beliefs are handed down from generation to generation, Asians often acknowledge their role and may even adhere to them. Ignoring these beliefs can cause members to experience a psychological "hangover" if the decision turns out to be erroneous.

- **Feng shui**

The Chinese often consider key elements through *feng shui* when making decisions, as the concept relates to promoting "luck" or "fortune" in decision making. A *feng shui* expert is often consulted to help managers make decisions which will ensure that certain locations, dates or even names are selected carefully in order to avoid any adverse consequences like loss of profits, possibility of accidents, severed relationships with clients, etc. Hence certain events like the date for the opening of a new office or plant, or the position of the company signboard, or even entry of the company's product into the market are examples of decisions that are influenced by *feng shui*.

- **Religious rituals**

There are various rituals which are tradition-based, supernatural and religious in nature that are performed before the commencement of significant events. Among the Muslims, "religious blessings" in the form of prayers are often performed by the priest (*Imam*) before the start of an important event, launching of a ship, a pilgrimage or the opening of a new bridge, tunnel or building. For the Chinese, the lion dance often precedes the opening of new businesses or enterprises.

- **Astrological signs**

There are also Malaysians who seek the advice of palmists and soothsayers, astrological charts or fortune tellers before making a major decision. There are certain days which are more auspicious than others and these are selected to commemorate significant events and activities.

- **Harmony and goodwill**

Due to the need to maintain harmonious relationships and long-term goodwill, Malaysians are generally tolerant of colleagues observing the various rituals and ceremonies associated with each ethnic group. For example, having a prayer at the beginning of an official event or having a lion dance at the opening of a shop is a symbolic gesture of harmony and understanding in a multi-ethnic workforce.

- **Consensus**

In order to maintain consensus *mesyuarah*, harmony, status and respect for authority and old age, key players often strive for the right balance in the dynamics of group membership, relationships and decision-making processes. While small groups are usually more effective in arriving at this desired state, the presence of a senior manager often tends to reduce the level of open discussion and the free flow of views among junior officers, who are not likely to challenge the views of their seniors. In such situations, senior managers can still get the views and suggestions of junior officials by inviting them individually to give their opinions. This is because Malaysians in general are more inclined to keep their feelings to themselves unless asked.

- **Acceptance of authority**

Due to cultural conditioning and acceptance of authority, those in high status positions are often expected to contribute more in discussions and brainstorming sessions. Their views should be heard and even prevail. Dissenting views should be heard elsewhere.

- **Face**

In not wanting to let others down and cause loss of face or damage group harmony, it is easier to be general, vague or indirect about making commitments. Not being able to say "no" openly is often perceived as a form of an ongoing sensitivity to the feelings of others. There is a tendency to procrastinate in making decisions because of the emotional fear of failure or loss of face, or of relationships being damaged should the decision prove erroneous. Malays often discuss matters relating to decision making at considerable length until common consent is reached. Eventual agreement by each person means that all are satisfied and that harmonious relations among them are maintained. This may be one of the reasons why decisions take a long time to materialize.

- **Looking for precedents**

Malays tend to look for precedents and then evaluate their current situation in terms of the experience and judgement of their people in the past. To them, the one who makes a decision is responsible for the consequences. Hence, Malays consider decision making to be a burden that has to be shared, as they are not comfortable in making decisions which affect others on an individual basis. In other words, some may believe that: "It is better to make no decision and preserve the harmony than to make a wrong one and damage relationships."

GUIDELINES ON DECISION MAKING

Based on the foregoing observations on some of the key values that influence decision making, the following guidelines may be useful to consider when making managerial decisions in Malaysian organizations:

- **Be sensitive**

Look for and listen to the subtleties of ethnic or corporate cultural values and norms, as a decision which is acceptable to one ethnic group may not be acceptable to another. There is a tendency for Malaysians not to be specific and precise as it is a cultural phenomenon which is part of *halus* or refined behaviour. This is especially so when making commitments relating to time, punctuality and meeting deadlines. However, if there is a need to be specific, invite the employee to give his commitment in front of his peers.

- **Obtain views**

Try to get everyone's views before making a decision in order to create an atmosphere of harmony and commitment (realizing that some employees will not speak out in certain group situations). In some instances, it may be advisable for the manager to conveniently absent himself from the group discussion, especially when issues involving him need to be aired or when voting on a decision which is not in his favour.

- **Focus on both relationships and data**

Stress relationships and the need to make decisions that are congruent with the group's values – ahead of the facts and quantifiable data – to balance decisions and ensure objectivity. Respect the intent of the decision that needs to be made by balancing the human side of the decision process and the benefits of studying precise data, facts or figures. Using data analysis can be advantageous since by doing so, the human element is removed from the decision, thus saving everyone's face later if the decision fails to meet the desired outcome.

- **Preserve harmony**

Use secret balloting – especially when electing committee members, since the need for face saving and preserving harmonious relationships may prevent people from being frank.

- **Build support among high status allies**

Develop "connections" with people in high status positions as they play an important role in decision making in Malaysia. The cultural network, extended family, clan or contacts in places of power and influence may become vital in the decision-making process. Cultivate and nurture "strategic alliances" with individuals, especially those in high positions or with titles – such as *Tan Sri, Datuk,* General, Director, Professor, Doctor, etc. They play an important role in the decision-making network and status hierarchy.

Similarly, in the Malay community someone who has performed the *Haj* (*Haji* or *Hajjah*) and deemed religious and learned in the ways of Islam is often given more respect and deference.

- **Know the likes and dislikes of decision makers**

Get to know the likes and dislikes of the decision makers or decision influencers. In order to facilitate a favourable decision, some "intelligence work" on the background of these key people may come in useful, e.g. knowing their desire for respect, the importance of their status or title, special dietary habits, their interests and their family status.

SURVEY FINDINGS

In a national survey on 66 Managerial Values, Expectations and Practices conducted among Malaysian managers (Malaysian Institute of Management, 1991), the following ranking of values and practices (TABLE 1) was obtained:

TABLE 1: Managerial values and practices

Strong	Rank	Weak	Rank
Goal Clarity	1	Authoritativeness	66
Cooperation	2	Consultation	57
Decisiveness	3		
Commitment	4		
Consensus	15		

Based on the ranking of values, we can make several conclusions:
- In making decisions, managers need to be clear about the goals for the organization.
- To achieve these goals, managers must ensure that there is a high level of cooperation or that people are expected to cooperate in implementing decisions.
- To ensure that the decision is effectively carried out, there has to be a high degree of commitment from all involved.
- Values surrounding authority were rated lowly. "Authoritativeness" – or how authority is used – suggested that "the boss is not always right", and that "managers should not be the only ones authorized to make decisions".
- "Consensus" is seen as an important factor in the Malaysian decision-making process. Perhaps the *gotong-royong* spirit needs to be taken into consideration as a factor in decision making.

- In a culture where "collectivism" is stronger than "individualism", it would seem that group decision making is more favoured.
- "Consultation" was ranked low, which is consistent with "decisiveness" being more a function of individual status and position.

FIGURE 1 shows the core values implicated in decision making by Malaysians.

FIGURE 1: Core Values Implicated in Decision Making
(**X** indicates Malaysia's position on each continuum)

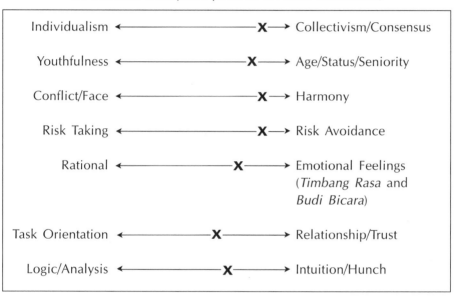

If "face" and "harmony" are central values in Malaysian management, then the use of "killer" phrases or negative criticism in public should be avoided. However, the absence of disagreement or dissenting views can give rise to a groupthink mentality among members and this can be seen to inhibit critical thinking in the long term (Janis, 1972).

CONCLUSION

Making decisions in a multicultural workforce requires that managers be sensitive and respectful of differences in the values and tradition-bound practices of their people. If these are ignored in the interests of expedience and objectivity, what tends to be expressed is a form of symbolic conformity where people accept the decision and carry it out, but they may not fully believe in it. Over time, this can erode employees' productivity, commitment and contribution towards the organization.

SUMMARY OF KEY MALAYSIAN VALUES IN MAKING DECISIONS

RESPECT FOR AGE/ELDERS
- ○ Expect the elders to take the lead in making decisions

STATUS/ AUTHORITY
- ○ Invite junior members by name to contribute

HARMONY
- ○ Know the values and beliefs of each ethnic group and how a decsion can affect others who are not of the same group
- ○ Allow each ethnic group to perform its own rituals if it means fulfilling their religious obligations

RELATIONSHIPS
- ○ Develop "connection" power with high status allies
- ○ Get to know the likes and dislikes of key role players

FACE
- ○ Communicate decisions that affect people discreetly – or indirectly – so as to maintain face, harmony and relationships

---

REFERENCES

Janis, I L (1972). *Victims of Groupthink.* Boston: Houghton Mifflin.
Malaysian Institute of Management (1991). A report on Managerial Values, Expectations and Practices.
Rogers, Carl (1961). *On Becoming a Person.* Boston: Houghton Mifflin.

6

RECRUITING, SELECTING AND ORIENTATING

INTRODUCTION

T he quality of an organization is the sum quality of its people. People are the most important and valuable resource that propels any organization to success. It is therefore imperative that an organization not only hires the right people for the right jobs but also those with potential to learn and grow and are comfortable working in a multicultural work environment, in order to meet the dynamic challenges of today's competitive business world. This clearly supports the philosophy of "people as competitive advantage" – the niche which sets organizations apart.

Beaumont (1993) highlights three important issues in relation to the importance of enhancing recruitment and selection decisions in any organization. First, demographic trends and changes in the labour market have led to a "less homogeneous workforce" which has placed an increasing pressure of fairness

The author acknowledges DR ROSELINA AHMAD SAUFI for her contribution to this chapter.

on selection. Second, the increasing demand for multi-skilled and flexible workforce who can work on their own and in teams has meant that selection decisions are also concerned with behaviour and attitudes than just with matching individuals to immediate job requirements. Third, the link between corporate strategy and human capital has led to the creation of a strategic system process that links selection decisions to the overall organizational strategy and business plans.

Responding to the needs of the industry, the Malaysian Government has reviewed the education system in order to ensure that both the internal tertiary and vocational training curricula are capable of producing a sufficient pool of well-educated and highly skilled manpower. Vocational and training programmes have been expanded, facilities improved and enrolment increased. Further, the policy on tertiary education, the domain of the Government, has changed to allow for private education institutions to provide a wider selection of academic and training programmes on a joint-venture basis with established universities – from the United Kingdom, Australia and the United States of America. The twinning arrangement complements the need for more places than are currently available in local Government universities and colleges.

OBJECTIVES OF THIS CHAPTER

This chapter will highlight some of the key challenges and unique features that one needs to be aware of when recruiting in Malaysia. It also covers some of the key observations relating to local practices in the recruitment, selection and orientation process of new employees. It will conclude with a discourse on what managers may focus on as they cover the suggested nine steps in the process of hiring Malaysians into the workforce and integrating them into the organization.

ISSUES AND CHALLENGES

The multicultural nature of the Malaysian society poses several issues and unique challenges to managers, especially the human resource personnel, who are involved in the recruitment, selection and orientation process of potential employees. Some of these issues and challenges are:

- **Adherence to Government guidelines**

Companies need to adhere to the Government's guidelines on the racial breakdown of the company's human capital such that it reflects the racial composition of the country. This requirement is in line with the "affirmative action programme" intended to increase the representation of the

Bumiputras (sons of the soil) at all levels in the organization. As a result of this requirement, there is a conscious attempt to abide by the guideline to have proper representation of each ethnic group, i.e. Malay, Chinese and Indian, in most organizations. The challenge is to meet the Bumiputra quota, especially for professional and senior executive categories for companies in urban areas like Penang and Ipoh. The Government makes subtle reference to employee statistics and racial balance when reviewing incentive programmes for foreign investors or when awarding contracts.

- **Tight and selective labour market**

Appropriate strategies and efforts have to be developed to ensure that organizations select, recruit and retain the right people. Although Malaysia's political and socio-economic climate is conducive to foreign investment, there is a tight and selective labour market. Getting skilled personnel – the right and best person for the job – has become increasingly difficult for most organizations, especially when the company is not granted any preferential status or when the salary structure is not among the industry leaders.

- **Increasingly diverse workforce**

Organizations operating across borders have to promote a global perspective and ensure that their country's human resource takes on an international flavour. This is important as more organizations now have to manage an increasingly diverse workforce, including foreign labour and expatriates from both Asian and non-Asian countries.

- **Need of multi-dimensional selection criteria**

The traditional recruiting mode has been for recruitment officers to focus on qualifications, technical knowledge, proven track records and ability as their criteria in the selection process. Personality traits that determine the candidate's ability to understand how to work and relate with people, especially from other cultures, are often ignored. For example, a new employee who is educated in a predominantly homogeneous school setting with mostly Malay pupils and who profess the Islamic religious or conservative value system may need help to make adjustments to work with others from different religious and cultural backgrounds. The ability to work at the intracultural, intercultural and cross-cultural levels is a key element to successful assimilation into a multicultural workforce. Hence, managers need to advance from the single-dimensional focus on technical knowledge and competencies as the main criteria for selection and adopt a multi-dimensional approach that incorporates the human relation competencies and cultural sensitivity savvy required in the job.

- ## Corporate culture

The orientation programme for new hires has to include the philosophy of the organization, its corporate culture, ethical standards and value system. This will provide the newcomers with an appreciation of the history and traditions of the organization. The education system tailors students towards a profession, but organizations have to orientate their new members to be effective employees. The process of "learning the ropes" has to be experienced cognitively as well as emotionally. To foster full commitment to the company, employers need to ensure that their employees, especially new hires, have a good understanding of the company's vision, goals, objectives and functional hierarchy. Companies have been known to include information on guidelines and policies in respect of religious practices, for example, on male employees attending Friday prayers and time off to attend funerals of kith and kin.

Briefly, four factors have been observed to contribute to the success of an individual's job performance in Malaysia:

- ### Technical knowledge and competence

  When accepting an appointment, a new hire has to immediately demonstrate his competence and understanding of the job. Very often, those with working experience have an advantage over fresh graduates or those lacking relevant exposure.

- ### Personality traits and relational abilities

  The challenge is in assessing these qualities during the job interview. While there are test instruments to help assess one's personality, relational abilities and work inclination, many companies are sceptical of their effectiveness or reliability as most of these originate from non-Malaysian settings.

- ### Environmental variables

  These include the climate and ethnic breakdown of the workforce, the background and supportive role of the managers, a healthy and harmonious working environment, and the availability of a support network for new hires to feel comfortable in the new work setting.

- ### Family expectations

  Immediate and even extended family needs and expectations are factors that influence the new hire's mindset. Sometimes this poses as a barrier to job relocation, especially for overseas assignments. Moreover, the values of the organization have to be congruent with those of his family's orientation.

DEFINING RECRUITMENT, SELECTION AND ORIENTATION

Recruitment is the process of identifying and attracting a pool of potential candidates. Similarly, Dowling and Schuler (1990) defined recruitment as "searching for and obtaining potential job candidates in sufficient numbers and quality so that the organization can select the most appropriate people to fill its job needs".

Selection was defined by Dowling and Schuler as "the process of gathering information for the purposes of evaluation and deciding who should be employed for a particular job".

Orientation, on the other hand, involves introduction of new employees to the organization, its functions, tasks and people.

FIGURE 1: Process of recruitment, selection and orientation

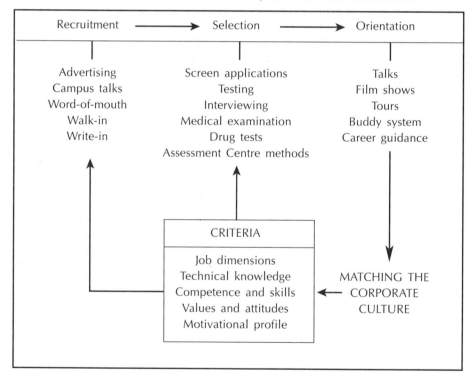

KEY OBSERVATIONS AND SURVEY FINDINGS

All organizations support a recruitment function. Some, especially multinationals, tend to have elaborate and structured recruitment processes. Others tend to use a more simplistic approach, allowing for intuitive evaluation or relying on the recommendation of friends and family members. However, consideration for a candidate's value system has been neglected, although recruiters generally show some sensitivity for this aspect, especially if recruiting a candidate of a different race and religious background from their own.

Based on the experiences and observations of Malaysian managers, there are a number of value orientations that are found at the workplace, and these include:

- **The extended-family structure**

Contrary to the practice of foreign companies, it is expected of employees in Malaysia to introduce family members or close friends with the required qualifications and experience for employment in the same organization. Its importance has been accepted by most companies, including multinationals; some even offer incentives to encourage the recommendation of relatives and friends as potential candidates, especially for floor-level jobs like production operators and administrative support staff. Often, employees who are recruited as such will feel a sense of obligation to perform well, so as not to embarrass the person who recommended them.

- **Polite system**

Malaysian managers generally do not conclude an interview abruptly or by showing the candidates to the door. The candidates can sense that the interview has ended when no questions are asked and silence and smiles set in. During the interview, most interviewers would allow some time to make their candidates feel important, even though the interviewers feel that they may be unsuitable. Being frank about the unsuitability of the candidates is considered impolite, and immediate rejection may embarrass them, especially if the candidates are of a senior management level or are more senior in age.

The normal process of rejection is with a letter or by informing the person who recommended the candidate. Sometimes a candidate can also conclude that he has not been successful when he does not hear from the company after a lapse of time. These practices may not be seen to be efficient in terms of time management and selection procedures, but they are a reflection of the Malaysian "polite system".

- **Modesty and humility**

There is a tendency for candidates to be modest and humble in terms of "packaging"" themselves during the interview process and are not inclined to "toot their own horns". Exceptions could, however, be observed among candidates who graduated from foreign universities in the West or those with work experience in multinationals, especially American owned. They are more open and forthcoming with regard to their ability and self-worth.

Interviewers who are not familiar with local values have to avoid the pitfall of gauging less vocal and assertive candidates as non-performers, especially if they avoid eye contact with them. The Malaysian society, especially the Malays, are taught that it is impolite to look at their elders or superiors "in the eyes" and women are further discouraged from making eye contact with their male superiors. Nevertheless, there are Malaysians who are more open and assertive, especially those who have been educated abroad or exposed to such similar cultures.

Stemming from this value system, Malaysians prefer to let their paper qualifications, testimonials and personal references speak for them. It is common for candidates to attend interviews with thick folders, filled with certificates, testimonials and references. An interviewer would therefore need to use an indirect questioning approach to persuade the candidates to verbalize their ability and confidence in performing the job in question.

Direct questions like "How much do you think you are worth?" or "What's your salary expectation?" will get better responses from Chinese and Indian candidates than from Malays. Most Malaysians find such questions discomforting and may just reply with "Whatever the company pays for similar job," or "So-and-so told me that the salary would be around RM1,500 per month". This may stem from the value of shying away from pinning a monetary peg on oneself. However, if the offer is below their level of expectation or market value, they may feel slighted and not bother to turn up to take on the new position, sometimes without even informing the recruiters.

Malaysian job candidates also tend to avoid asking questions or taking a confrontational stance, out of respect for the company's representative and as a sign of humility. However, being confrontational is a quality acceptable and even admired by Western employers, especially for a leadership position. Respect for the company's representative and humility determine such behaviour which needs to be understood by the interviewers. Hence, to engage in an active two-way discourse in the English language will require specific approval and encouragement from the interviewers.

- **Family orientation**

Organizations that support a family orientation philosophy tend to have special appeal for Malaysians, as they are more receptive to working in teams. A survey by Texas Instruments showed that Malaysians are generally more comfortable in a work climate with features such as:

- a family spirit of togetherness and mutual help – a *gotong-royong* approach,
- the use of terms of affinity – such as "brother", "sister", "uncle" and "aunt" – for certain individuals like supervisors and those they are close to,
- opportunities and time allocated for social interactions, for example, tea breaks or after-work activities,
- social activities like family days and having company benefits extended to family members, for example, medical and health insurance coverage.

To respond to the need for affiliation, some companies have adopted the "buddy system" or "big brother/sister" *Abang/Kakak* approach, to assist new employees assimilate into the new work culture. This "buddy", preferably a relative or friend, is paid a special allowance to help the new employee settle down. The need for a sense of belonging is also felt in jobs that are highly routine and repetitive. Therefore, opportunities for employees to interact, socialize and identify with the organization are important.

The Texas Instruments study also showed increased productivity and reduced stress levels among female production operators when they were allowed to talk to each other while working. However, there was clear understanding that such interactions should not compromise quality and productivity.

GUIDELINES FOR RECRUITING, SELECTING AND ORIENTATING

In recruiting, selecting and orientating new employees into the organization, managers may find the following nine-step approach useful to ensure the hiring of right candidates at the right time for the right job.

1. Define the scope and specifications for the job

Managers, prior to the interview, need to conduct a job analysis to ascertain and document key requirements and expectations of the job. The purpose of a job analysis is to develop clear and precise job description and job specifications. While the former describes the functions, duties, responsibilities, work conditions and other aspects of a specified job, the latter explains the job demands, authority and accountability and the kind of person who should be hired for the position.

Malaysians are generally less particular about what they get to do upon entry into the job market. However, employers are advised to have available job descriptions and job specifications that are not too limiting, in order to avoid problems should the employee be found to be inadequate or unsuitable for the job, or when the organization is unionized.

Apart from the normal content of the job description and specifications, aspects of cultural sensitivities and values should also be considered, such as:

- the background of the candidate, especially in relation to working with people from other ethnic groups in Malaysia, as well as with foreigners,
- the comfort level of the candidate, to supervise someone with more orthodox religious beliefs,
- the background of the person one has to work with,
- the demand of the job on family life,
- the need for the candidate to be assertive on the job, and
- the level of authority required and the comfort level of the candidate to assert such authority.

2. Seek applicants

When interviewing, it would be expedient to have a selection of candidates for a vacant position, for this will maximize the probability of getting the right person. There are many channels of recruitment covering both internal and external means; for example, company bulletin boards, company newsletter, website page, media advertisements, display advertisements, handbills, employment officers, private employment agencies, executive search firms, college and university placement offices, career exhibitions, word-of-mouth and specialized magazines and reviews.

The selection of the mode or the channel depends on the level of the position, the number required, the availability of candidates in the market and the urgency and confidentiality of the search. Companies requiring production operators have been known to travel far and wide to different villages in all the 14 Malaysian states to recruit young women. During these recruiting exercises, the recruiters have to work within the village *kampung* hierarchical structure by approaching the village heads or *penghulu* to seek permission and assistance.

Skill is required in writing concise and eye-catching job vacancy advertisements to ensure good response and cost effectiveness. Most companies use the services of public relation agencies to design and arrange for the printing of advertisements. Banners located at strategic places would bring in applicants for lower-level positions.

Supported by the New Economic Policy, it is acceptable to specify a preference for Bumiputra candidates in some job advertisements. However, it is not an acceptable practice to do likewise for non-Bumiputra candidates. The subtle approach has been to state language or dialect requirements, or to advertise in the various vernacular newspapers.

3.   **Screen applicants**

To ensure an applicant will provide a complete resume, a well designed application form is necessary. This will enable the recruiters to extract the relevant information required in making a judgement about the potential candidate's background and suitability for the job. In the conventional approach, the form is designed to extract the usual personal, academic, experience, knowledge and special skills information from the candidate.

However, a more effective approach to screening applicants would be to take into consideration the multi-dimensional factors (see TABLE 1) prevalent in the multicultural workplace. Therefore, in addition to the usual information sought in the form, there should also be questions on relational abilities (at the intracultural, intercultural and cross-cultural levels), family background, personal values and others – special interests, salary expectations, ability to travel and willingness to relocate. The answers and write-ups obtained will make it easier for follow-up questions or further clarification. Some companies insist on handwritten applications to evaluate the writing and language capability of candidates.

TABLE 1: Dimensions for new employees

Uni-dimensional	<ul><li>Performance</li><li>Expertise</li><li>Competencies</li></ul>
Multi-dimensional	<ul><li>Performance</li><li>Relational abilities<ul><li>– intracultural</li><li>– intercultural</li><li>– cross-cultural</li></ul></li><li>Family background</li><li>Personal values</li></ul>

4. **Conduct tests**

To evaluate the candidate's level of job proficiency, employers may want to conduct tests ranging from language dexterity, technical competencies for the job, personality profiling and evaluation of "will-do" factors. While there are quite a number of valid and tested models available in the market to assist organizations in behavioural evaluation, there are not many organizations in Malaysia which subscribe to using standard intelligence and psychological test models. Moreover, such psychological test models are often not validated with Malaysian norms, and this may prove inaccurate when assessing Malaysian candidates.

5. **Check reference**

Even though this is not a common practice, some employers do conduct reference checks, especially for jobs that are considered sensitive or "at risk", for example, positions in the human resource department, purchasing, security and senior executive positions. Reference checks are either by writing or via the telephone. Lately, there are a few professional companies that conduct reference checks for employers at reasonable fees. Some companies are also conducting verifications on qualifications of candidates, especially for professional positions.

Malaysian candidates may not give an accurate account of themselves. They either do themselves injustice by downplaying their strengths or conversely try to create a more than favourable account of themselves concerning their skills or past experiences. However, most former managers or employers of the candidates are reluctant to provide negative information on a candidate as they do not want to "throw sand in someone else's rice bowl". Malaysians, in general, are also rather indirect and less specific in volunteering information and the new employer may have to read between the lines.

It is also a common and accepted practice for candidates to bring written recommendations or testimonials from well-known persons or politicians. This may carry weight depending on the level of importance and association of the referee with the organization. Generally, reference checks are conducted with the candidates' knowledge and approval, and reference checks with the present employer are made only after the offer of employment.

6. **Conduct the interview**

A selection interview would only be held when the applications have been vetted, test results received and references made. However, there are cases where tests and reference checks are conducted after the interview. The selection interview is a critical step in the selection process and requires careful planning and execution. It is also crucial that interviewers are trained to conduct interviews. They have to understand the environment that the new hire is moving into, any immediate expectations on performance and team member orientation.

Alfred P Sloan, Jr, former chief executive of General Motors, said: "If I put a person into a job and he or she does not perform, I have made a mistake and have no business blaming that person or anyone else, no business invoking the "Peter Principle", and no business complaining. I have simply made a mistake" (Drucker, 1985).

Earlier studies on selection interviews held in organizations showed that about 90 - 95 per cent of interviewers tend not to consider the multidimensional factors prevalent in a multicultural society like Malaysia. Often, an interviewer forms an impression of the candidate, established from the candidate's appearance, mannerisms or early responses, and then slants the interview to affirm such an opinion. For example, Muslim girls wearing the religious headgear had been rejected as interviewers assumed that they cannot work late hours or with male colleagues. However, over the last few years, ever since the majority of Muslim women began donning the *tudung*, such a concern has dissipated. It may be worthwhile, therefore, to frame questions that will enable the interviewers to gauge the religious orientations of the candidate and to what extent his or her beliefs will hinder future job assignments.

In designing the interviews, four issues need to be addressed which include the degree of structure, the purpose, the content, and how to administer the actual interview sessions. Some of the interview techniques that are applicable in Malaysian organizations are panel interviews, one-to-one interviews and serialized interviews. Behavioural interview and stress interview approaches are quite rare.

To ensure that the interviewers are fair, objective and will give due consideration to cultural issues, a structured interview with properly designed questions is preferred. Interviewers have to be trained not only in skills relating to conducting interviews but also on understanding how local cultural values affect the candidate's performance in job interviews. It is also important for the interviewers to exercise "job realistic approach" and provide candidates with accurate and real information regarding the job and organization. This is to ensure that candidates are aware of the circumstances that they are going to face, which in turn would instil a greater sense of commitment and satisfaction towards the organization.

The recommended seating arrangements during interviews where the interviewers are encouraged to sit beside the candidate rather than being separated by a table, should be judiciously followed. It is not advisable for male interviewers to sit beside a female Muslim or be secluded in a closed interview room as Islam prohibits close proximity between unmarried people. It is considered not proper, *tidak manis*, and may cause the candidate to feel uncomfortable.

Similarly, although the one-to-one interview is common, the panel interview has become a more preferred process. Apart from avoiding any cultural issues, it is also seen as being expedient achieving group concordance on decisions. However, it is imperative that the interviewing process be well coordinated and panel members trained and not turn the interview process into a confrontational exercise. Besides "safety in numbers", the candidate may develop some affiliation with an interviewer – for instance, the one from the same ethnic group. Hence, most panels comprise interviewers from the three major ethnic groups.

Interviewers should have evaluation forms to complete after every interview. Observations and prognosis should cover the multi-dimensional factors as well as job dimensions.

7. Evaluate and select the best candidate

A guided interview form should be used to predict the performance potential of the candidate. Behaviour patterns that are important in most jobs are related to job tenure, work habits, tenacity, commitment, competitive spirit, planning, organizing, relational abilities and leadership qualities. The personal and work values of the interviewer will affect how he interprets the evaluation form. Ideally, there should be check and balance by having more than one interviewer or using the panel interview process.

A more systematic approach is to use a matrix of prioritized criteria, based on the job specifications and competencies model, when evaluating the candidate. It will help to compare all the candidates interviewed and pave the way for the final selection of the best candidates. Once the strengths match the demands of the jobs and the "must competencies", any gaps can later be addressed with on-the-job training and coaching. However, to prevent relational problems between the new employee and his or her superior, the safest step is not to recruit a person with perceived weaknesses that cannot be easily overcome with training.

It is important to note that selection is made to recruit the "best" candidate and only time can tell whether the candidate is the "right" one. Currently, organizations are looking for candidates with multi-skill and multi-orientation capability and mindset. This will allow for easy transfer or retraining of employees in response to reorganization or reengineering initiatives.

8. Offer appointment letter

The Employment Ordinance requires an employer to prepare a formal letter of appointment that is well written and covers all aspects of the job offer, especially the salary and benefits package. This will prevent unnecessary questions from arising. However, an offer is usually made contingent on passing a medical examination and fulfilling the terms of probation.

9. Conduct orientation

A well-designed and effectively conducted orientation programme can help reduce "first-day jitters" and enable the new employee to settle down more quickly in the organization. In general, there are two stages to an orientation programme. The first stage is known as the organizational orientation programme where new employees are introduced to the general aspects of the organization – background of the company, culture philosophy, structure of the company, general procedures and policies pertaining to employees' salaries, benefits, merit system, insurance coverage and welfare.

The second stage of the orientation programme is normally conducted at the department level. At this stage, new employees are given details about the department they are joining, the nature of work, their roles and responsibilities, the expectations from the department, and other crucial issues such as performance evaluation, importance of meeting deadlines and observing the work procedures of the department.

The study at Texas Instruments further revealed the following about new employees:

-   The first few days on the job were anxious and disturbing ones.
-   For inexperienced recruits, the working environment, coupled with uncaring peers or busy supervisors intensified anxiety.
-   Anxiety interfered with the effectiveness of the training process.
-   Turnover of newly hired employees was caused primarily by anxiety.

Employee orientation is aimed at minimizing such problems. Its purpose is to introduce new employees to the organization, help them become acquainted with their managers and work colleagues, and learn to adjust to the norms and values of the work group. It is both a socialization and acculturation process into the organizational culture.

A good orientation programme normally covers information on the organization's history, business structure, philosophy, mission and operations. It also covers information on employee compensation and benefits, personnel policies and guidelines, training and development, safety measures and regulations, and the employees' daily routine. The new employee's supervisor is often given an orientation checklist to cover areas more related to the job and work environment. This may include an "anxiety-reduction" programme in the form of seminars, a "buddy system" or orientation team (consisting of old and new employees) that can further assist the new hires assimilate into the new work culture.

To make them feel part of the "family", the orientation programme should focus more on the interpersonal relationships and the role of each employee in achieving the company's goal rather than just information and data relating to the company's history, structure and lines of reporting. It must be remembered that for new employees, getting to know an organization not only involves using the skills of the "head" but also of the "heart".

Other important considerations involved in designing and conducting orientation programmes include:

O   The orientation should be employee focused - the employer makes the new hire feel welcome by focusing on why he/she is employed and how he/she can contribute to the corporate family. Opportunities should also be created for the company to get to know the new employee.

O   The orientation should present accurate and updated information on the company. Employees will find out sooner or later if the orientation downplays or overplays the true position of the company.

O   Managers and supervisors should actively participate in the orientation sessions. This is critical in ensuring successful and early integration of new employees.

O   Long lectures and dull presentations should be avoided. Incorporating some tools like games and role-plays could enhance team dynamics.

O   Orientation should be linked to the overall integration process by providing new employees with the proper model or roadmap.

CONCLUSION

The successful integration of new employees into an organization requires time and careful planning on the part of their managers, who are the most important link in the recruitment, selection and orientation process. To do it well, managers need to have a thorough knowledge of the job demands, the competencies needed by the new employees for their jobs and the environmental variables including the quantity and quality of supervision needed and given. What is more important is the need to make new employees feel comfortable in adjusting to their environment and to feel part of the "family" with clear direction and continuous support.

SUMMARY OF KEY MALAYSIAN VALUES IN RECRUITING, SELECTING AND ORIENTATING

RELATIONSHIPS	○ Assign an experienced employee as a "buddy" to the new employee ○ Orientate new employees to the do's and don'ts in the organization ○ Candidates should feel welcome during interviews and orientation. Make them feel part of the new "family"
GROUP ORIENTATION	○ Be sensitive to the need for Malaysians to group either by race, gender or previous affiliations ○ Avoid breaking the social network that has developed along ethnic lines. However, promote activities for inter-ethnic mingling like eating together, sports events and team-building activities
HUMILITY AND MODESTY	○ Encourage candidates to talk about themselves ○ Acknowledge the fact that new employees are generally reluctant to partipate in active discussion, especially at the start of the programme, preferring to listen rather than do something. Allow time for warming up ○ Use proper icebreakers, as some introductory activities may not be well accepted by Malaysian employees, especially those involving body contact

	○ Encourage Malaysians to make formal introductions of their friends or peers as they themselves may be reluctant to talk about their own achievements ○ Take time to review paper qualifications and documented achievements
FACE	○ Be prepared with information on the organization which candidates may want to know ○ Be friendly and approachable – avoid an impersonal approach ○ Carry out rejection of candidates with cultural sensitivity ○ Prepare an appropriate list of questions to ensure all relevant information is extracted from the candidate

REFERENCES

Beaumont, P (1993). *Human Resource Management: Key Concepts & Skills.* London: Sage.

Dowling, P J and Schuler, R S (1990). *International Dimensions of Human Resource Management.* Belmont California: PWS-Kent Publishing Co.

Drucker, P (1985). How to Make People Decision, *Harvard Business Review,* July - August 1985.

7

DELEGATING

BIEN MEI NIEN

INTRODUCTION

Delegation is generally accepted as an important aspect of effective management. It is "releasing what managers like to hold on to" and giving subordinates an opportunity to do what managers do, and allowing them to show what they can do. Managers who do not delegate sufficiently become inefficient eventually and inevitably complain of being over-worked and highly stressed. The organization itself suffers because ineffective delegation prevents its managers from achieving set goals.

Managers who are effective delegators are often more successful in achieving organizational goals. Ronald Reagan, the 40th President of the United States, attributed his successful style of management to his willingness to delegate. To reaffirm this, he had a plaque on his table which read: "There's no limit to what you can do if you don't mind who gets the credit."

OBJECTIVES OF THIS CHAPTER

This chapter will look at the values underlying the process of delegation in Malaysia. Some issues and challenges on delegating, as we understand it through Western management literature, are examined and observations of how delegation is carried out among Malaysian managers are highlighted. The chapter concludes with some guidelines on what managers need to observe when delegating work to Malaysians.

ISSUES AND CHALLENGES

Delegation is a complex process. It is influenced by cultural factors found not only in the organization but also in the individual as well. Delegation is dependent on the type and degree of power extended, and the ability and willingness of the individual to assume responsibilities for assigned duties and eventual results.

Effective delegation, according to most management literature from the West, is not only a way of allocating work rationally but also a way of developing people. It is based on the underlying assumptions that a person has to be accountable for his own actions. When delegating work to a subordinate, a manager has to assume that the former is one who can be trusted to do the job. In turn, the subordinate is also confident that he can perform and deliver what he is expected to do. His ability to perform well will be a reflection on how he has been trained and guided by his manager. However, while the subordinate is expected to do what his superior wants done, there are a number of issues and challenges which managers often face in Malaysia.

- **Not questioning seniors**

When delegating a task, any attempt to query the superior may sometimes be seen as disrespectful on the part of the subordinate, as the former is of a higher status and with greater experience of life than he is. This is unlike subordinates in the West, especially the Americans, who are said to readily doubt what they are told to do and may even challenge their superiors. While they are considered to be comparatively at ease with their superiors, the Malaysian subordinates may find this to be a rather discomforting interaction. Subordinates are said to look at their superior as the father or their protector because of his rank, age, knowledge and experience and therefore are expected to be loyal and would not argue with him.

- **Accepting tasks with no questions asked**

It is also quite common for Malaysians to accept tasks delegated to them without too many questions. Sometimes the task assigned may not even be in their job description; but most of them would not feel comfortable saying "no". In accepting the delegated tasks, they will pretend to understand the instructions given to them as they do not want to be seen as rude by their superiors. It is unlikely that subordinates who disagree with their superiors would articulate their views openly. This is in sharp contrast to American managers who expect their subordinates to be forthcoming with their own independent views in completing a specific task that they may not be fully convinced that it should be done.

- **Acceptance of inequality**

In a high power distance culture like in Malaysia, inequality is accepted and subordinates are said to prefer managers who make decisions and do not off load any responsibilities to them. Malaysians also prefer to solve problems and make decisions in a group. In this way, individual weaknesses are not obvious to their superiors because of the support and guidance from elderly members in the group.

- **Tolerance of uncertainty**

Malaysians tend to take events in life more easily and treat uncertainties more casually compared to people in the West. Similarly, Malaysians differ in respect to time, unlike the people in the West, who are more fastidious in terms of their time orientation. Malaysians view time as multi-track and infinite. To most Malaysians, there is no need to hold on to time or to try to plan and control it as other social priorities are considered more important than time itself. Understanding the cultural value of time, deadlines, milestones and target dates is extremely important as it does influence the process of delegation in the Malaysian workplace.

Cultural values, which may be an obstacle to effective delegation, have to be identified as they may contribute to ineffective delegation. The work-related values of speed, accuracy of information, sharing of views, feedback and timeliness have to be clearly explained by the superior when he delegates work to his subordinates. However, the former may need to anticipate the likelihood that these values may not be fully understood and that the latter may have some potential problems in completing the assigned task.

DEFINING DELEGATION

Delegation is the process of transferring authority[1] from a superior to a subordinate, usually for the purpose of carrying out a task and holding the

---

[1] Authority is the power required to carry out the responsibilities which include the right to make decisions, to take action, to control costs and quality, and to exercise necessary discipline over the employees assigned to help carry out the responsibilities. Authority flows upward.

subordinate responsible for accomplishing the task. The delegation process stems from the manager's or superior's need to have time to plan or be involved with making decisions which reflect their responsibilities[2] in the organizational hierarchy.

The delegation process relies on three interrelated elements:

- Assigning a specific task to a subordinate, with sufficient information and resources.
- Transferring sufficient authority and responsibility.
- Creating an obligation to perform the task.

These three elements will be examined below:

- **Assigning tasks**

The prescribed suggestion is for the manager or supervisor to draw up a clearly structured job description which defines the tasks to be carried out by the subordinate. The superior, either from experience or through adequate planning, or both, has to have a clear idea of his responsibilities as well as of the areas he would have to delegate to his subordinates in order to get the job done. He is expected to be familiar with his own scope of responsibilities and be willing to assign tasks to those who report to him. This willingness depends on the degree of trust he has in his subordinates' capabilities and his acceptance of foregoing a degree of control. Charles Handy (1985), in his book *Understanding Organizations* suggests that "effective delegation is delegation with trust and with only the necessary minimum of controls". However, Handy acknowledges that it is difficult to give trust, thus resulting in the dilemma between trust and control. In the assignment of tasks, the manager will need to balance his perception of the degree of trust he has in his subordinate with his willingness to forego control.

Underlying values: Trust, Control

- **Transferring sufficient authority and responsibility**

How much authority to transfer to a subordinate will depend on the task to be performed, the superior's perception of what is necessary and the readiness of the subordinate in terms of job knowledge and skills.

---

[2] Resposibility is the obligation or duty to perform a job, e.g. checking time cards, investigating accidents, scheduling employees or keeping production records. Responsibility flows downward.

In making basic decisions on what or how much to delegate, to whom and how to delegate, a manager, especially a newly appointed manager, could be guided by the following:

-   Job description (if available) as to the areas of responsibilities of a subordinate
-   The belief and confidence that the subordinate can accomplish the assigned job or task.

There will be the assumption that the subordinate has the skills and knowledge to carry out the assignment as well as the relevant level of authority to get the job done. If these assumptions are incorrect, the manager would discover it eventually, as the task would not be completed in the manner expected. To prevent irrevocable damage, it is advisable that the manager periodically monitors the subordinate's progress and that he be kept informed should problems arise in the course of performing the task.

Underlying values: Self-confidence, Job knowledge, Appropriate skills

- **Creating an obligation to perform**

This implies accountability[3], i.e. the subordinate owes a responsibility to his superior to complete the task to an acceptable standard. The degree of obligation would vary depending on the situation but it is often assumed that the subordinate is familiar with the execution of responsibility and will be challenged by increasingly difficult tasks.

Underlying values: Challenge, Accuracy, Completeness

Based on the underlying values of trust, control, self-confidence, challenge, responsibility and a sense of achievement, it can be summarized that effective delegation will only be observed when the subordinate regards the assigned task as contributing towards his growth and pursuit of success.

The often cited problems of delegation are those related to the tendency of managers not to trust their subordinates to get the job done properly, or their unwillingness to share authority or to allow others to make mistakes. Often, subordinates are uncertain of the level of trust and confidence given to them by their superiors. On the other hand, the superiors are uncertain as to the

---

[3] Accountability is an obligation to answer for one's actions – to carry out responsibility and authority in terms of a standard of acceptable performance; an obligation to report (provide stewardship) on the work group's contribution. It requires one to answer to failures and provides an appropriate basis to recognize successes. It flows upward to the delegator.

right degree of control they should exert over their subordinates. These barriers are common enough to make them quite universal.

KEY OBSERVATIONS RELATING TO DELEGATING

The Malaysian management scene is rather unique in that there is no prevalent style or approach that can be termed "Malaysian". Malaysian managers have absorbed a great deal of theories and practices from the West as well as from Japan and other Asian countries. What, perhaps, has contributed to Malaysia's uniqueness is the cultural mix of the workforce. More than anything else, it is this peculiarity or uniqueness that makes the delegation skill demanding and challenging.

There have been many observations made about Asians, and Malaysians in particular, and some of these observations, which have an influence on the effectiveness of delegation among Malaysian managers, include:

• **Self-effacement**

This stems largely from the need to be polite and respectful, outward signs of a "cultured" upbringing. Many a successful manager or businessman would brush aside words of praise or felicitation, and attribute their "small" achievement to luck or the generosity of God rather than to his capabilities. When a subordinate seems reluctant to accept additional responsibilities, it may not be due to a lack of capability but rather, a sense of modesty. There is a tendency for subordinates to respond with "I'm not sure I can do it, but I will try" or "I have finished it, but I don't know if I have done it correctly". Very often, they say it so as not to appear brash and presumptuous. Wise managers usually wait and base their judgment of a subordinate's capability on the standard of completed tasks. This is particularly pertinent in the assignment of tasks.

• **Respect for elders**

Another cultural phenomenon is that of according respect to those who are older or of a higher rank (social, political or organizational). When a manager delegates work to an older subordinate, there is a tendency to be more courteous and patient. In some cases, the manager may politely ask for the subordinate's help to accept the task, e.g. *"Tolong saya sedikit..."* ("Please help me a little..."). Even if the manager has a strong need to hurry on with the work, his sensitivity to his subordinate's age or position (social or political) will hold him back. This sense of reverence reinforces the subordinate's response of according respect to the manager's authority. A more brash and impatient delegator may be termed *kasar* or ill-mannered.

Malaysians generally respect rank and position in organizations and society, and when this respect is abused, the respect is still given, but more reluctantly. Although some may feel that this respect for age is particularly strong among Malays, it would be advisable to apply this value when dealing with all ethnic groups because respect for age cuts across all racial boundaries.

- **Knowledge**

Subordinates, when accepting orders (especially from a superior who is younger), expect the superior to have better education, and greater knowledge and skills. A superior who does not fulfil these expectations may need to tread even more gently to gain cooperation and support. To influence subordinates more easily, the superior must be a good planner so that he appears knowledgeable. He must understand the requirements of the task delegated and give guidance if required. This will give subordinates confidence in the latter's judgment.

- **Authority**

Malaysians are probably most familiar with how those in positions of authority are able to exercise their power over others at the workplace. Years of conditioning to accept as gospel truth the words or "advice" of superiors (parents, older relatives, teachers, supervisors, etc.) are not easily erased. As such, an older superior will find it easier to assign tasks because of the younger subordinates' filial devotion and attention to the "experienced and wise elder". The superior is often viewed as "the father" or "the protector" – the nurturing parent who has rank, age and, hopefully, experience, all of which reinforce his level or right of authority. The relationship between a superior and subordinate is very much like a paternal, authoritative figure and a son who relies on the former for his growth and development.

A survey on the different value groups of post-war Malaysians carried out by Universiti Malaya (TABLE 1), reflects the importance of this value of authority. There was a high level of respect for authority (Malays – 62 per cent, Indians – 58 per cent and Chinese – 52 per cent). The strong cultural influence of reverence for authority thus cuts across all the three major races. The fact that it is easier to delegate to those who are younger reinforces this observation. This will hold true as long as the superior is not totally incompetent.

TABLE 1: Analysis of personalities and values of post-war Malaysians

An extract of Universiti Malaya's survey findings based on the analysis of personalities and values of post-war Malaysians. The survey was conducted by Professor Charles Y Yang of the International University of Japan.

Personalities and Values	% of Malaysians		
	Malays	Chinese	Indians
1. Important to conform to social norms	31	26.3	38.7
2. Important to feel part of group	54	58	64
3. Social status is an important part of life	44.1	51.1	59.3
4. Respect for authority is important	61.6	52.3	58.3
5. Listen to the advice of elders	61.8	44.5	66
6. Perceive achievement in education as important to one's future	80	79.5	82.3
7. Would work smart rather than work hard	56	63.7	53.7
8. Want to get ahead financially	57.3	65.6	69.7
9. Regard most people as trustworthy and honest	10	6.0	14.3

(Source: *The Star*, 2 July 1990)

• **Control**

Many managers perceive the need to be in control as a reflection of their capability to manage. The delegator feels a great sense of insecurity when he is not seen to be "in charge". As a result, Malaysian superiors may want to manage their subordinates in order to avoid feeling insecure and powerless. They want to be in control in order to convey to others the impression that they are capable. At times, this sense of inadequacy can make the manager under-delegate, over-react to mistakes or generally become abusive when things go wrong. An observed practice of this dilemma is the manager's assigning a task without giving enough authority to get the job done. When the delegator is younger, less qualified or less experienced than his subordinates, the tendency to want to be in charge is usually greater.

The desire to "hold on to control" can deter managers from applying the more soft-spoken or *halus* approach of communicating with subordinates.

- **Trust**

As suggested by Charles Handy, trust – as in believing or accepting the judgment of or about another person – is related to control. A superior will not delegate if he does not believe in the capability of a subordinate. This lack of trust will lead to not delegating adequate authority to make independent decisions. At the same time, a subordinate who does not trust his superior will accept the assigned tasks but feel insecure and resentful. A subordinate must have enough trust in his superior's judgment to prevent him from questioning the wisdom of the superior's decision. Malaysian subordinates will quite often withhold trust when their sensitivities have been ignored.

- **Harmony**

It is observed that there is a high reluctance on the part of Malaysian subordinates to seek clarification or help from the superior. Subordinates often accept tasks even if they lack the skill, knowledge or authority to complete them. Rather than "bare their chests" to the superior voluntarily, subordinates would rather suffer in silence for the sake of harmony and peace. However, managers can bring out the best in subordinates by patient probing and reading non-verbal signs rather than "brow-beating" them to open up.

- **Teamwork**

Malaysian subordinates prefer solving problems and making decisions in groups, especially when dealing with new issues or projects. This helps to overcome the problem of being reluctant to ask the superior for guidance, since in this case, the individuals working in groups are not exposing their weaknesses to close scrutiny.

- **Fairness**

Being unprejudiced and just are perceived to be important values by subordinates. One of the findings of the Intercultural Management survey (1990 - 1992) carried out by the Malaysian Institute of Management identified "fairness" as a value looked for in superiors.

The manager must be seen to be fair in the process of delegating tasks as well as in evaluating the performance of those tasks.

• Face

The concept of *maruah* or "face" has been discussed widely by management experts as being an important influence on how to interact and interface with Asians.

In his paper entitled, "Management in the Context of the Malaysian Culture", Tan Sri Abdul Aziz bin Abdul Rahman (1991) stated:

> Mutual respect between the leader and the subordinates is very important. The *maruah* or "face" concept applies to all races. Everyone, no matter how high he may be in the hierarchy, has to behave and observe the concept of *maruah*. It is believed that if you hold a high position and you are humble and respect those under you by words and deeds and avoid hurting their *maruah*, you will go very far in your endeavours as the support of the subordinates will come almost naturally.

In practising the concept of "face", Malaysian managers will try to avoid open confrontation or being aggressive, especially in public, as it can reduce the subordinate's self-esteem. Condescension and making remarks verging on racialism will also cause subordinates to "lose face". On the other hand, subordinates will know they have been "given face" when their superiors have not torn them apart when errors have been committed.

• Femininity

With the large and increasing number of women in the workforce, there is the attendant situation of more women in managerial positions. Overtly, women delegate tasks not differently from men. But do employees accept directives as easily from women superiors? On the surface, they appear amenable to having women bosses as long as the bosses are sensitive to their needs. But generally, most subordinates and even colleagues want the woman "boss" to prove her worth. Over time, the gender barrier is normally relegated less importance unless other issues arise to cause new interest to be cast in that direction. Subordinates who have worked mostly for men bosses are more likely to attribute causes of problems to the gender difference.

• Security

The concept of security influences both the delegator and the delegatee. It pervades many of the decisions that are made because most Malaysians value security – in the workplace, in the home and family and in society. In a survey of 2,000 Malaysians between the ages of 15 and 40 in Peninsular Malaysia carried out by Professor Sieh Mei Ling of Universiti Malaya, 60 per cent ranked secure life, a sense of belonging and warm relationships with others as the most important set of values, followed by 18 per cent for self-respect, and 14 per cent for advancement and self-fulfilment (*The Star*, 2 July 1990).

Most Malaysians relate security with well-paid jobs and also a cohesive workplace. When responsibilities become too difficult to handle, the subordinates can become unravelled, affecting work standards.

GUIDELINES FOR DELEGATING

Both the manager and the subordinate have their own perceptions of their roles. In the Malaysian workplace, managers must be sensitive not only to the needs of subordinates but also to their backgrounds. Over time, managers will have an adequate grasp of individual differences among staff and it is usually in new and changing situations that problems of delegation require a more structured effort to limit unnecessary delays in getting the job done.

While one cannot provide an ideal prescription, it is worthwhile for managers to consider the following guidelines when structuring delegation:

* **Understand local cultural nuances**

Understand the cultural scenario of the workplace and the subordinates and members in the team. Look for the local nuances before making a de facto application of what works "elsewhere". It may be prudent to say that even an approach that works in a Kuala Lumpur office may not work in a Kota Bharu office because of the differences in cultural nuances, even at the level of intracultural relationships.

* **Promote growth and development**

At all times, managers need to convey a desire to assist in the growth and development of subordinates. Identify as much as possible their strengths so as to reinforce them. Be fair in evaluating their capabilities by also focusing on areas for improvement and any plans to help them.

* **Plan and clarify responsibilities**

Decide on the tasks to be delegated and responsibilities to be given. Match the task with the subordinate's abilities as fairly as possible (consider training to upgrade skills and knowledge if required). Allocate time and select a suitable place to plan with the subordinate. Convey trust in his capabilities and encourage him to seek clarification, if need be. Invite him to provide input. Brief him on the assigned tasks, the importance of the tasks to achieving overall objectives, his level of authority in decision making and the results expected, and run through the steps necessary for the completion of the jobs.

- **Outline steps**

Give the subordinate an opportunity to outline the steps he would take to complete the job. Should the steps be different or unacceptable, allow time for discussion.

(The above steps are particularly useful for first-time delegators or when delegating fairly difficult tasks.)

- **Obtain feedback**

Obtain the subordinate's commitment to meet and give feedback on his progress. Be firm in the standards of measuring performance although a degree of flexibility would be useful, depending on the situation.

- **Involve group**

When the task is new to the subordinates, consider delegating it to a team of subordinates. The team members may need some careful selection so that they can work as a cohesive group. As in the case of briefing individual subordinates, the team should also be thoroughly briefed on the task or project, its importance, the authority level and the results expected. Alternatively, encourage the team members to consult each other when facing difficulties.

- **Provide recognition**

Give verbal appreciation when a job is done well, not only to the individual subordinate but also to those who assisted indirectly. Subordinates will feel encouraged if superiors give positive reinforcement on work completion. It will give them confidence to pursue the next task. If there is a need to give constructive feedback, be sensitive to subordinates' value system. Reprimand privately rather than publicly.

- **Display good manners**

Make it a point, when giving instructions, to communicate in a pleasant tone of voice and show good manners.

A matter-of-fact tone can be considered *kasar* or ill-mannered. This type of behaviour may have a repercussion on subordinates' behaviour and cause them to avoid doing the assigned tasks.

A manager who is pleasant and friendly is better able to relate with his staff. This disposition can often help him delegate work and be assured that it is done well. He will be respected not only for his competence but also for his humble ways. Without resorting to forceful commands, managers can make subordinates do the work willingly.

- **Promote group efforts**

Because of the collectivist nature of Malaysians, managers need to reduce the power distance that exists between subordinates and superiors. This can be achieved through social and group activities like *malam mesra*, luncheon get-togethers, and other professional activities like educational talks and sharing of ideas over lunch. All these activities can promote a sense of belonging and strengthen the relationship between the manager and the staff. Superiors who are able to code switch from English to Bahasa Malaysia will also help build rapport and relationships with their subordinates.

CONCLUSION

Delegation involves two parties and a relationship between them. Mutual trust and confidence have to be patiently built up in relationships for delegation to work. Therefore, the Malaysian workplace requires managers to understand the values of trust, harmony, face and the need to use a contingent approach to delegation. The perceived values are usually the tip of the cultural iceberg and managers must have a continual interest in the development of their subordinates. They must also be sensitive to their subordinates' needs, capabilities and values in order to prevent these from taking precedence over the main objective of getting the job done. Successful managers do make mistakes, but with adequate communication skills they can increase subordinates' understanding of the desired objectives.

SUMMARY OF KEY MALAYSIAN VALUES IN DELEGATING

FACE	○ Give praise whenever the opportunity arises ○ Reprimand in private
HARMONY	○ Allow the subordinate to work with a colleague ○ Encourage subordinates to ask questions – use prompts ○ Be sensitive to cultural nuances ○ Avoid racialism
RELATIONSHIPS	○ Show confidence in the delegatee by telling his friends how good he is ○ Recognize and respect age and social hierarchy

REFERENCES

Handy, Charles (1985). *Understanding Organizations.* London: Penguin Books.

Abdul Aziz, A Rahman (1991). Management in the Context of the Malaysian Culture, *Malaysian Management Review,* Vol. 26 No. 1. Kuala Lumpur: Malaysian Institute of Management.

8

COUNSELLING ON THE JOB

ASMA ABDULLAH and ONG ENG ENG

INTRODUCTION

Counselling is part and parcel of managing people. Most organizations today realize the need for managers to focus on the personal development of their employees. From the role of a caretaker and controller, managers now have to spend time and energy to develop their people.

In the broadest sense, counselling is any form of contact between a manager and a subordinate for the purpose of developing the subordinate. It is one of the most challenging tasks of a manager because it involves face-to-face discussions regarding a problem which is affecting the overall productivity of the work group. Very often, managers see the counselling session as an avenue to bring their perception of the problem to their subordinates' attention. A discussion is considered necessary before any action is taken.

Regular counselling sessions enable managers to monitor the performance of their subordinates and help develop in subordinates positive work attitudes and appropriate job skills for increased productivity. Effective counselling gives a subordinate relevant information and helps him to enhance or modify his behaviour to meet the objectives of the work group. But if the counselling session is poorly conducted, the subordinate may get upset and become dissatisfied with the manager. When this happens, the subordinate's performance at work suffers and this may adversely affect the productivity of the work group.

OBJECTIVES OF THIS CHAPTER

This chapter examines how counselling is approached at the Malaysian workplace, with due consideration for the cultural values of the recipient. It also focuses on the key challenges at the Malaysian workplace and the need for managers to understand the hidden dimensions of culture and its values prior to doing any form of performance counselling on the job. Some key observations of how counselling is normally perceived are highlighted. The chapter concludes with some general guidelines on how to conduct on-the-job counselling.

ISSUES AND CHALLENGES

Based on experiences with numerous clients and participants from diverse backgrounds in terms of gender, age, experience, management levels, outlooks, behaviours, attitudes, ethnic groups, beliefs and nationalities, there are a number of challenges in conducting counselling sessions at the Malaysian workplace:

- **Diverse backgrounds**

The issue of culture becomes more apparent when both manager, who is the counsellor, and subordinate have diverse backgrounds. A male counsellor must be aware that his presence may have a negative impact on his female subordinate. He has to be sensitive to the needs and expectations of his staff and avoid a patronizing attitude. Among Muslims, gender could be an issue which may not be understood by managers from other religions. For example, a female manager may have some difficulties in handling an elderly male subordinate.

- **Handling poor performers**

There is a general reluctance among Malaysian managers to conduct counselling sessions for poor performers. It can be a discomforting activity as most Malaysians find it difficult to have a face-to-face discussion with their subordinates under such circumstances. The values of face saving and harmony have to be handled with great care.

In the Malaysian context, counselling has a negative connotation, as it is often associated with those who are not performing according to expectations. Because of face saving, people tend to avoid being seen to receive counselling by their supervisors. This stigma is detrimental to the value of harmony, which is an important element for social cohesion at the workplace.

- **Lack of training**

There is a general fear among Malaysians that those who receive counselling are seen to be problematic. This fear is made worse when the manager is not trained in counselling to detach the performance problem from the person. When a subordinate is reprimanded, he will feel ashamed and shy away or merely close up. He goes away feeling bad, defensive and may even show a lack of interest and motivation towards his work.

- **Counselling orientation**

There are some managers, particularly the younger and Western trained, who perceive that it is not professional to probe into the feelings or the private matters of their subordinates. Apparently, they do not see the relevance of this "private world" to that of the workplace. It takes a trained counsellor to be able to regard counselling as a professional relationship and not a personal one. In the case of the Malaysian manager cum counsellor, he may even be expected to show care and concern towards his subordinates by taking their total welfare into consideration when counselling.

- **Listening skills**

Most managers are not trained in the skills of empathetic listening (as opposed to sympathetic listening). There is a tendency for them to quickly move to suggestions on how to rectify the performance problem. In fact, the true purpose of listening is to understand and not to judge. Good listening will encourage comfortable sharing, thereby facilitating the process of identifying what the real problem is. To be effective listeners, managers have to manifest a non-judgemental attitude and acquire the skills of listening with their "ears, body, eyes and heart."

DEFINING PERFORMANCE COUNSELLING

Counselling is a process that is initiated by the manager to help the subordinate (often referred to as a "client" or a "counsellee") to gain knowledge, understanding and insight into a performance concern. During the process, a supervisor has to assist his subordinate to reflect on his performance and attitude towards work in order to improve his work output, develop a more positive orientation towards work, and polish his interpersonal skills to relate with others.

Effective counselling can lead to optimal results for the organization and optimal development for the subordinate. It helps to improve the subordinate's performance and attitudes – contributing to increased productivity.

Counselling is therefore a continuous process of monitoring an employee's performance, identifying problems and determining a course of action. Managers have to be observant and be able to recognize situations which need counselling, such as the following:

- The subordinate has problems in performing his task at the workplace, for example, not being able to balance process with task, and people with production.
- The subordinate is not aware of his own potential for self-growth.
- The subordinate is manifesting symptoms of a potential problem.
- There are conflicting viewpoints which need to be bridged.
- The subordinate refuses to do a job because of an attitude problem.
- The subordinate is not pulling his weight in completing an assigned task.
- There are perceptual differences between manager and subordinate over work priorities and the subordinate takes a defiant stance.
- There are hidden strengths in the subordinate that need to be developed.

Consequently, a manager can look out for signs that a subordinate is in need of counselling. The most obvious is a decline in the employee's performance – perhaps caused by constant complaining, difficulty in establishing good working relationships, being unresponsive to attempts to help others in their workload and loss of interest or motivation on the job.

The goal of counselling is to help subordinates recognize that they have a problem and to take positive steps to overcome it. Subordinates should be made to realize the impact of their behaviour on the group and the need to overcome any adverse consequences on work output.

Once subordinates are persuaded to own up to having a problem, the focus should then be shifted to solving or managing the problem and the issue at hand. It is critical that the subordinates themselves, not their managers, make the commitment to change for the better (Buzzota, Lefton and Sherberg, 1983).

Effective formal counselling is, therefore, based on a job description, standards of performance and a plan of action, all of which have been mutually agreed upon by the manager and the subordinate. When performance falls below the agreed standards, the manager should make this clear to the subordinate. Together, they should examine why the job was below expected standards and how to improve the situation by focusing on time, training, tools, effort, work climate, authority and job specifications.

The key elements as emphasized in the counselling process are performance and rewards. Managers who conduct counselling are expected to define and communicate objectives, issue clear work goals and reward subordinates based on results. These actions must be consistent with the belief that counselling is worthwhile and necessary for managers in order to help their non-performing subordinates fulfil their job expectations.

There are three types of counselling: remedial counselling, preventive counselling and developmental counselling, which are further elaborated as follows:

- **Remedial counselling**

Remedial counselling is a process of helping the person resolve his grievances or problems. However, there is a negative connotation to this form of counselling as the counsellee may shy away from seeking help for fear of being labelled as problematic.

- **Preventive counselling**

Preventive counselling is used primarily to nip a potential issue in its bud before it erupts into a problem. In the workplace, there are subgroups such as new employees or the relatively long-serving staff or those who are single parents or even the newly promoted ones, who are more often at risk in encountering or creating problems. Therefore, preventive counselling helps to prepare them for such challenges. It can make a positive difference in turning a potential problem around rather than allowing it to contaminate the climate at work. The result is that employees are able to perform and maintain their productivity levels.

- **Developmental counselling**

Developmental counselling is to prevent poor performance and to maintain productivity. Everyone needs this particular dimension of counselling, for it informs and trains people in the normal developmental tasks of living. The issue at hand is not necessarily a problem but a tool to explore more ways to attain a subordinate's highest possibilities and capacities. Subordinates' potentials are fully released when they do the tasks befitting their abilities, challenging them to rise to heights yet unachieved. Developmental counselling even has its role in educating the employees of a company's vision and mission, paving the way for a more synergistic team and thereby creating the right culture so as to translate that vision into reality.

Developmental counselling activities include seminars and workshops using primarily the counselling skills of active listening, asking the right questions, interpreting body language, avoiding costly communication mistakes, avoiding giving advice but rather giving encouragement to the counsellee or client to become more resourceful, creative and independent. Other tasks involving developmental counselling are in conducting effective interviews, coaching to perform a job expectation, bridging conflicting views, creating a mentoring programme and increasing commitment and interest to work tasks or projects.

KEY OBSERVATIONS RELATING TO COUNSELLING

Most Malaysian managers find it difficult to counsel a subordinate regarding his poor performance. Such face-to-face discussions run counter to the issues of face and the importance placed on maintaining harmonious relationships. In addition, a counselling session may result in a "win-lose" situation where the subordinate feels compelled to do what the manager prescribes.

Sometimes, instead of a problem-solving exercise, a counselling session may become a "tell and sell" session where the subordinate does nothing except "listen and sulk". He does not challenge the manager because it would undermine harmonious relations, and the manager himself may not expect him to do so! The subordinate, therefore, may end up feeling that "the boss is not always right, but he is still the boss".

Below are some typical observations made on counselling by both local Malaysian and foreign managers.

• **Loss of face**

Frankness and open confrontation are not valued because they contradict the concept of face, or loss of face. *Jaga maruah* means maintaining a person's dignity by not embarrassing him. If face is preserved, then relationship is enhanced. Hence, it may not be a norm for a Malaysian to receive frank and negative feedback. A non-Malaysian manager should be aware of the value of *jaga maruah* so as not to create misunderstanding.

Most managers feel uneasy about counselling because it requires them to have a face-to-face discussion with their subordinates. In addition, communicating negative feedback can be awkward as indirectness is more the norm in communication than directness in day-to-day behaviour.

Counselling becomes even more difficult when it involves a long-serving subordinate who has his own set ways of doing things and will not change no matter how much counselling is done. Some managers may even avoid counselling their subordinates and will tolerate their poor performance for the sake of maintaining harmonious relationships and face saving.

- **Hierarchy**

When a younger counsellor deals with an older client, that counsellor has to be sensitive to the inter-generational value of respect for elders. As the Malaysian society is generally hierarchical, subordinates are expected to abide by the decisions of those who are in power, rather than bring disagreements out in the open.

- **Data versus feelings**

The counselling process is more likely to focus more on data and behaviour than consideration for feelings. Malaysians on the other hand believe that a task may not be properly done if relationships and feelings are neglected. As a result, focusing only on performance during the counselling process may hinder efforts in building harmonious work relationships.

Managers often find that in rebuking a subordinate, they run the risk of severing relationships. It may even lead to a lack of cooperation and general apathy in the subordinate towards work.

- **Personal attack**

Malaysians find it difficult to separate personal from professional relationships. There is a tendency to look at any form of negative feedback during the counselling session as a personal attack. Very often, a manager does not want to cause shame to his subordinate because it affects the name of his family and the ethnic group he belongs to.

A manager who gives direct feedback or confronts a "failed" employee may be considered tactless and not refined in his ways. He may even be regarded as "without heart", *ta' ada hati perut.*

- **Defamation of character**

Evaluating employees merely on their performance and competencies can be demoralizing because their potential remains very much in their ability to function in the group. Employees prefer their managers to take into consideration their total character as well as their ability to perform the task. To fairly assess an individual, the manager should not only look at his skills and performance, but also his ability to work harmoniously with members of the team and obtain their respect and admiration. His commitment and loyalty to the group should carry more weight than his ability to perform assigned tasks as stipulated in his job description.

- **Tendency to generalize**

Malaysians are not very precise in identifying areas for improvement because of the need to save face. When alluding to a subordinate's weakness, they tend to approach the subject by making some generalizations about how the subordinate comes across to others. To avoid hurting the subordinate's feelings, some managers even use analogies or metaphors to communicate their concern about the subordinate's performance. It is expected that the subordinate will read between the lines and change his behaviour accordingly.

- **"Sensed" rather than verbalized**

Among Malaysians, a lot of meaning has to be "sensed" rather than verbalized – which means a person cannot be taken at face value. A manager has to be able to interpret what a subordinate is thinking and doing but not saying. As a result, a manager may find it difficult to be direct or forthright in reprimanding or expressing his views. Similarly, the subordinate will not be forthcoming in putting across his opinions to his superiors. Hence, many times what is seen is usually not what is perceived, felt or thought, and what is said is not what is meant. In fact, it is often stated that such non-verbal communication constitutes 60 per cent of our interactive message (Elashmawi, 1996).

It is not uncommon, therefore, to see employees speaking on behalf of their colleagues who are uncomfortable in verbalizing their personal needs to their superiors.

- **Handling elderly subordinates**

It is often difficult for a younger manager to counsel a subordinate who is older and has been in the organization for a longer period of time. While the manager may be technically competent, his behaviour and character may not be exemplary if he is rude, brash and outspoken. As a result, he may find it difficult to engage in any face-to-face discussion with the latter. The younger manager must first gain the respect, trust and support of the older subordinate before any work problems can be discussed.

- **Fear of incrimination**

A subordinate is not likely to challenge, disagree or question his superior's perception of his performance as it can cause the latter to lose face. Rebutting a superior is akin to not respecting him as one who has more influence, authority and knowledge about what needs to be done. There is also the possibility that the superior may make life unpleasant for his subordinate.

GUIDELINES FOR CONDUCTING COUNSELLING

Managers, as leaders, are expected to be role models who are not only knowledgeable in their area of work but are also able to provide guidance and advice *tunjuk ajar* to their subordinates. Managers who regard their team members as an extended family and show genuine care and concern for them are often well-regarded. To enable the organization to serve its customers more effectively, managers may be expected to play familial roles – i.e. "big brother", or a parental figure to subordinates.

As a general guide, managers who undertake performance counselling with their subordinates have to keep the following in mind:
- Focus on actual observed actions and avoid giving opinions.
- Make employees realize their own shortcomings rather than being lectured to.
- Use observations rather than inferences.
- Agree on standards to be achieved and explain with examples.
- Provide information to help subordinates perform their jobs.
- Gain subordinates' commitment rather than compliance.

Below are some specific guidelines on counselling, including what to do before and during counselling.

1. Before Counselling

• Be a "nurturing" parent

Managers have to be prepared to play multiple roles as they are expected to be role models for their subordinates. Not only are they expected to be technically competent, they should also be sensitive to their needs, aspirations, welfare and development. Managers who demonstrate a benevolent and caring attitude in speech and action, use culturally appropriate non-verbal expressions and project a fatherly figure of wisdom and experience are better perceived by their inexperienced as well as their seasoned elderly subordinates.

On the other hand, managers who are task-oriented, impersonal and have a matter-of-fact approach in their interactions with subordinates may find it difficult to have "heart-to-heart" discussions. Rather than using an adult-to-adult approach, a manager would be better received by subordinates if he can offer advice and guidance in a caring manner. This approach is in line with the hierarchical nature of the society where the relationship between managers and subordinates is unequal.

For older subordinates, it may be wise to use a different approach where they can be given the task to serve as mentors to junior members. Being sensitive to their feelings and encouraging them to contribute ideas to the work group can help create an open climate where they feel that they are given recognition and respect.

- **Build rapport**

Make an attempt to build rapport and establish a personal relationship of trust, understanding, and familiarity with subordinates before conducting a counselling session. Subordinates tend to be more receptive to feedback from those with whom they have a mutual bond of understanding and are genuinely interested in their development and growth. In the counselling relationship, the counsellor, regardless of age, should be humble and courteous in order to gain the trust and respect of his subordinate. He must at all costs avoid using a confrontational mode of interaction.

Once a familial relationship of trust and understanding has been cultivated, it will be easier for the manager to convey negative feedback. By sharing stories and exchanging information on an informal basis with subordinates, supervisors can help and pave the way for more effective counselling sessions in future.

- **Seek training**

Like information technology or crisis management, counselling management is a specialized field. It has its own ethics, principles, a structured system and a repertoire of skills. With training, managers will become aware of the skills and competencies to conduct effective counselling and deal with people from diverse cultural backgrounds. In addition, managers also need to be aware of non-verbals as they have an indirect impact on the counselling session. They need to be sensitive to body language and other hidden subtletics, like the tone of voice and facial expressions, in order to encourage the client-subordinate to open up.

2. Conducting the Session

- **Focus on feelings**

Make it a point first of all to understand the feelings of the employee regarding the issue before conducting the counselling session. For the Malays, focusing on feelings *rasa* is part of the *budi*[1] complex which is embodied in the notion of the superiority of intuitive inner feelings, *rasa*.

---

[1] *Budi* requires man to be rational but sensitive and concerned for *rasa*. While rational thinking enables man to control and exploit nature, the use of *rasa* guides him to control, exploit and become part of nature and the universe. Hence a *budi* thinking man is one who is both rational in his thinking and sensitive to feelings (*rasa*).

Sometimes, being too task and time driven for changes tends to communicate to subordinates that their feelings are not important.

- **Preserve face**

Understand the need to preserve face. This is an ongoing sensitivity which is part of the social conditioning of most Asians. Face can be preserved by being sensitive, apologetic, humble and forgiving towards the counsellee. For example, a manager conducting the counselling session may like to consider the following:

  - Begin by apologizing for having to conduct the session. Say: "I am sorry to have to do this, but you know, I am really concerned about you and how you are doing. Please regard me as an elder brother who is giving you some advice ... "
  - Use appropriate analogies and metaphors to illustrate the performance concern. For example, if it is about teamwork and the subordinate is letting the group down, the following analogy may be used: "A house has four legs, and if one leg is weak, the whole house will collapse."
  - Use the concept of shame, e.g. "What will others think of us if you do not make an effort to change?" This puts some group pressure on the subordinate to improve his performance. Impress upon him that the entire work group will be affected if he does not improve, change, etc.
  - Beware of rank, status and gender differences. A female manager may have to consider the male ego when counselling male subordinates. Find out his reaction towards being counselled by a female. If need be, use a third party.
  - Be sensitive to the time and place for conducting the counselling session. The office may not be the best place to conduct a "heart-to-heart" discussion. Hard, factual data is better received when delivered in an atmosphere of informality and congeniality. The counsellor has to be someone who is caring and nurturing. The counselling session may also be conducted over a cup of coffee.

- **Use an appropriate communication style**

Develop and use a friendly and informal communication style. Learn to read non-verbal cues (manners, body language and facial expressions) to detect any form of resentment and rejection of what is happening as the counselling session progresses.

Using a soft and gentle voice is more effective than being assertive, which tends to be intimidating and directive. If intimidated, the counsellee may ignore the content of the message entirely. Open, direct criticism and outspokenness are to be avoided at all costs for the sake of harmony and face.

Avoid being condescending and be selective in the words used to convey and solicit information. Say "Let's discuss ... ", "What's your opinion?" or "Have I failed as a manager in not ... I am ashamed ... ", which some may consider a form of emotional blackmail[2].

Use appropriate physical postures – mannerisms, good manners and politeness – as these indicate respect for the counsellee. Sensitivities revolving around status differential, the grey hair syndrome, royalty, class and ascribed status versus achieved status when communicating with people from different cultures, must be understood and respected.

- **Use a third party**

Consider using a third party to convey negative feedback, sense issues and obtain possible responses from the subordinate before taking the direct approach. The third party can be someone who is respected by both the manager and his subordinate. In some organizations, the third party may be the person who recommended the employee to the organization or someone with shared common grounds such as ethnicity, age and religion.

Third parties can act as a buffer to help reduce vertical friction, explore hidden fears and preserve the relationship, face and reputation of the individual in the group. Their role is to solicit the views of the two parties before any plan of action is taken. They play an important function in minimizing the differences between the two parties from escalating into an open conflict. In a way, they can help preserve harmony at the workplace.

On the other hand, the manager has to know the limitations of using the indirect or third-party method as there may be situations where it is inappropriate – for instance, during emergencies or when dealing with a stubborn or insensitive subordinate who misinterprets the situation and the intent of using a third party. The subordinate may ask questions like: "Why can't my manager tell me himself? Why go through a third party? Is he afraid to tell me himself?"

---

2 Managers as nurturing parents have the special licence to use what seems like emotional blackmail but which is acceptable to subordinates and the young alike. This is a form of indirect reprimand and is a means to correct any unaccepted behaviour when it occurs.

3.   During Counselling

At the start of the counselling session, be aware of what you would like to achieve as a result of the discussion. Explain that your role is to help the counsellee become more effective on the job. Identify possible discomforts on the part of the subordinate in face-to-face discussions. At the same time, recognize and explore the feelings of the subordinate towards the problem. If possible, use a variety of counselling skills ranging from clarifying to empathizing and summarizing in dealing with different situations, issues and people.

4.   Alternative Approach

•   Use team approach

Consider using peer group pressure to change a subordinate's behaviour if face-to-face counselling fails. Members of the work group can be brought together to share their observations on what is happening and how to improve the situation. There may be a need for the manager to assign a colleague to work with the counsellee as the latter may be more inclined to discuss his problem with a peer rather than a superior.

The team approach can be a powerful motivational tool but care must be taken so that it does not become too intimidating and make the non-performing employee lose face.

Counselling can also be conducted on a group basis where the manager facilitates the discussion and focuses on the need to solve a performance problem collectively. The concept of shame can be used as a tool to make the non-performing employee "feel the heat" from others who are affected by his behaviour. Here, the role of the manager is to establish some ground rules to facilitate a friendly and constructive atmosphere, prevent open conflict and preserve harmony within the group.

•   Consider upward feedback

To further enhance the climate of the work group, the manager can also promote a system of upward feedback where subordinates are encouraged to convey constructive feedback to their managers through a respectable third party or coordinator. Any feedback should be regarded as contributing to productivity improvement which can provide valuable input for the manager to reflect on his own style. Feedback given anonymously is usually more candid in a culture where people are not so direct and open in their views.

CONCLUSION

Counselling at the Malaysian workplace is a challenge for managers. Western norms that are often used in the counselling process may not always be applicable in Malaysia as there are cultural barriers to be considered. As a result, managers need to put in time and effort to develop an approach to counselling that serves as a developmental review exercise, benefits the work group and establishes bonds of friendship between the manager and his subordinates. All this in the long term can contribute to teamwork and productivity.

Managers who are involved in counselling and want to do it well have to plan how they should handle the process and take into consideration the issues of face, relationship and harmony. They must be perceived by their subordinates to be both nurturing and caring individuals. They need to establish a relationship of trust and understanding, and be accepted as leaders who are respected and admired by their subordinates. Failure to lay this foundation can lead to undesired consequences of strained ties, lack of cooperation and consequently, low productivity.

SUMMARY OF KEY MALAYSIAN VALUES IN CONDUCTING PERFORMANCE COUNSELLING

FACE
- Focus on the total person and his contribution to promoting team harmony
- Be sensitive to the individual's feelings by looking at non-verbal cues
- Consider using a third party when discussion is not going well
- Use group pressure on the non-performing subordinate if he is perceived to be a problem

CARING
- Play multiple roles, i.e. leader and parent
- Be friendly and approachable (know subordinates' needs)
- Use an informal leader to sense the climate

HARMONY
- Avoid open confrontation during discussion
- Listen with the intent to understand
- Be apologetic in having to conduct the counselling session
- Consider the feelings of the subordinate
- Promote a familial work environment
- Be cautious about over-generalization of problems
- "Sense" the real meaning as it is usually not verbalized
- Consider both verbal and non-verbal aspects ("high context" communication style)

REFERENCES

Buzzota, V R, Lefton, R E and Sherberg (1983). Counselling: How You can Improve the Way It's Done, *American Training and Development Journal.*
Elashmawi, Farid (1996). Sailing Across Cultures, *Certified Management Digest,* Vol. 3, Issue 3, March 1996. Kuala Lumpur: Cedar Publications Sdn Bhd.

9

MANAGING CONFLICT

SARAN KAUR GILL

INTRODUCTION

The Malaysian workplace is made up of a diverse multicultural workforce which comprises Bumiputras, Chinese, Indians, Sikhs and others. Against such a pluralistic backdrop, managers have to understand the cultural diversity and sensitivities relating to various aspects of our daily living ranging from food preferences and linguistic differences to religious beliefs and traditions. The challenge for them is to train, develop and mobilize a workforce that is able to manage their differences and work together as a cohesive team.

Notwithstanding the cultural diversity, there is a tendency for Malaysians to perceive the work group as a family unit where harmony and understanding are goals that must be worked on and strengthened. The manager-cum-leader has to project the image of a nurturing "father" (or "elder") who takes care of "his family's needs and problems". In working with a diverse workforce, a manager often has to handle differing viewpoints as every person will bring to the work situation certain unique cultural, work and social values and perceptions. Therefore, individual and cultural differences are bound to arise and this may lead to conflict. Hence, the ability to manage or handle conflict in organizations is an essential skill for managers in Malaysia.

OBJECTIVES OF THIS CHAPTER

This chapter seeks to raise some of the issues and challenges relating to conflict at the Malaysian workplace. It will describe some of the effective ways used by Malaysians to handle conflict and explore the underlying values of their approaches. The chapter concludes with some general guidelines which managers and supervisors should consider and incorporate in their repertoire of skills for handling a multicultural workforce.

ISSUES AND CHALLENGES

Conflict when not handled properly by managers can lead to reduced job satisfaction, inability to concentrate on the job, impaired judgement, high staff turnover and absenteeism. Therefore, the role of the manager in handling conflict is to ensure that the views of all, especially the "hurt" parties, are heard and understood. He has to use culturally appropriate ways to handle the difficult situation so that the individuals or parties concerned are satisfied with the outcome.

In an intercultural workplace a manager has to take the lead in seeing that conflict or differences are not denied or mismanaged. He has to combine his power and authority to get the task done and emphasize cultural sensitivities in order to ensure that the feelings of team members are dealt with fairly and patiently. The manager has to take the responsibility of finding ways to resolve conflict situations harmoniously before they get out of hand.

There are a number of issues and challenges relating to conflict and these are:

- **The cultural context**

To understand conflict, there is a need to look at the cultural context in which it occurs. Context has become a concept for ordering, structuring and interpreting behaviour. As a result, culture defines the values and interests that are at the core of conflicts. It shapes perceptions and alternatives, and defines outcomes. While a Malay is more likely to avoid or even suppress conflict, a Chinese may use an indirect method while an Indian may prefer to have a face-to-face open discussion in managing conflict. As a result, there is a need to recognize that behaviours occur within a context and this is particularly important for managers who are looking at ways to resolve differences should they occur in workgroups.

• Importance of harmony

Generally, Malaysians do not feel comfortable expressing their problems with another individual openly. Such a direct approach to conflict management is often seen as impolite and clumsy in the eyes of their peers. Also, the cultural ideal of harmony tends to make Malaysians of all ethnic origins regard conflict as an embarrassment and therefore should be avoided. In addition, the need to preserve face and relationships makes it even more difficult to confront directly and resolve differences immediately. A manager, therefore, has to be patient in finding culturally appropriate ways to address the differences amicably. Getting the two conflicting parties to talk it over may not always be the best solution for a manager as conflict is more often addressed at the feeling than the thinking level. Sometimes, what is reported may not be the whole truth as there are the covert issues of face saving that must be recognized.

• Local sensitivities

There are many sensitivities that can be traced back to the issues of hierarchy, respect for elders and even religion which can lead to conflict and these are not easily communicated. Hence, a manager who would like to assume the role of the third party or mediator has to be seen to be fair and constructive in how he handles conflict. He has to be able to read the hidden nuances and make every attempt to hear what both sides are sensing but not articulating before taking an action to resolve the conflict. In fact, the grapevine, contrary to popular belief, can be a good place to start to obtain information on how both parties are reacting to the issues at hand.

• Separating task and person

It is not easy for Malaysians to separate a conflict relating to task completion from the person who is assigned to work on it. More often, the issues relating to work and behaviour are so interrelated that criticizing a person for his incomplete work can also be interpreted as an attack on his personality. However, it would be easier to manage such a situation if the individuals involved had earlier established a long-standing relationship of give and take.

• Latent disagreements

When conflicts and interpersonal arguments are minimized and well-managed, employees will find the workplace conducive to work in. The environment will also be one where relationships, trust and respect prevail. Team spirit is enhanced and productivity increases. If they are mismanaged, opposing viewpoints may become irreconcilable, a competitive spirit emerges and team spirit weakens. When conflicts are not resolved, the ignored differences will deepen, members polarize, distrust sets in, and productivity and morale drop. This form of latent disagreement can manifest itself in less overt actions such as tardiness, lack of commitment, putting in minimum effort, poor service, resistance to change, avoidance of face-to-face interaction, sabotage, withdrawal, etc. Over time, these symptoms of dissatisfaction may surface in the form of open frustration in the affected subordinates and resentment towards the leadership of the team.

DEFINING CONFLICT

Conflict occurs when the interests of two or more parties or individuals are incompatible. The key elements of perceptions, behaviour and understanding are viewed differently by the involved parties. Within an organization, a conflict can occur between colleagues of similar (intracultural) or different (intercultural) ethnic groups, between a subordinate and his boss (interpersonal), between two or more departments or between a labour union and management (inter-group). It could take the form of purposeful interference by one party to frustrate the aims of the other.

There are many sources of conflict. Some could be due to differences between one's personal or individual values and those of the organization, a lack of role clarity on the job, competition among individuals or groups for limited resources, strained relationships arising from work norms, role perceptions, work ethics and ethnic values and unequitable rewards.

Managers who are able to resolve conflict effectively within the workplace can bring about positive outcomes when they are aware of "brewing" problems between individuals and groups. By being sensitive to the issues related to conflict, managers can deal with problems at the initial stage and promote a work milieu that can generate new ideas and solutions.

For the purpose of this chapter, the focus will be on what managers need to know about the underlying values and assumptions in handling difficult situations which can cause conflict between individuals or groups among Malaysians.

KEY OBSERVATIONS RELATING TO MANAGING CONFLICTS

Below are some observations typifying the Malaysian way of expressing differences and managing conflict:

- **"Give and take" approach**

There is a tendency for Malaysians to handle conflicts either by reaching a compromise or avoiding it altogether. Conflict is seen as deleterious to team spirit, harmony and racial tolerance. Conflict situations are often worked out on the basis of compromise - "This time I give in to you, next time you give in to me." There is a strong preference for a "give-and-take" approach *bertolak ansur*, which may be perceived as a watered down solution or a "lose-lose" approach. But, in Malaysia this is considered a "win-win" approach, as the main purpose is to avoid embarrassment. Open conflict can be volatile and harmful to a multicultural work environment.

- **Importance of hierarchy**

Hierarchy is important and forms the basis of relationships; therefore, vertical friction is often avoided to facilitate group performance. Malaysians are not assertive and generally do not confront bosses unless provoked. Subordinates tend to demonstrate deference to their superiors by not challenging or even clarifying their judgements. As such, a "win-lose" approach is acceptable in a manager-subordinate relationship. The tendency towards groupthink[1] can also deter members from being too articulate in voicing aloud their differing viewpoints. Most feel that "though the boss is not always right, he is still the boss".

- **Personal feelings**

Most Malaysians find it difficult to draw the line between task and relationship issues. While the Western approach tends to focus on tasks by having direct, clear and frank discussions and dealing with conflict out in the open, Malaysians tend to bring their personal feelings and self-esteem into the conflict. To ignore this dimension will upset the affected party. That is why it is uncommon to see two good friends arguing or openly sharing conflicting viewpoints at a meeting. Disagreements are seldom discussed in a frank manner because of the importance placed on group loyalty, cohesiveness and face.

As expressed by Theodora Ting Chau (1986):

> To attain the goals of the collectivity, interpersonal conflicts had to be avoided at all costs. This resulted in highly regulated patterns of interpersonal relationships – deference to authority, responsibility in leadership, self-abnegation, emotional restraint and cooperativeness.

---

[1] Groupthink occurs when the group avoids critical thinking and does not want to challenge the decision made due to the need to preserve group harmony ("Don't rock the boat").

131

- **"Poison pen letters"**

Malaysians, in general, are not direct, open, clear and frank in working out their problems face to face because of the values of face and harmony. Hence, there is a tendency to express their anger and conflict indirectly. Differing viewpoints are then more likely to be conveyed anonymously and collectively. The instances of poison pen letters or appealing for an influential third party to intervene to resolve a conflict indicate the parties' preference for a more indirect and less confrontational approach. Often, the third party will act as a conveyor of negative information, feelings and innuendos from one party to another and may even play the role of a mediator of the conflict.

- **Avoidance of verbal encounter**

Malaysians, especially Malays, do not like to engage in verbal encounters that are outright confrontational and direct. They are not comfortable in asserting their views too strongly and directly and tend to offer proposals rather than arguments. If demands are made in a direct manner, they will often react to them indirectly. To be direct is tantamount to being impolite and unrefined (against the *halus* behaviour), and it affects their self-esteem.

- **Negative channelling**

Conflict can turn into or be negatively channelled into gossiping, name-calling, backbiting, character assassination, gestures and silence of contempt. Resorting to "black magic" is not uncommon where dire revenge is contemplated. These forms of covert behaviour are harmful because they can damage self-esteem and destroy what little trust and respect that exists between the conflicting parties.

GUIDELINES FOR MANAGING CONFLICTS

Both managers and employees in a multicultural work setting have to recognize that their own values and perceptions can influence the way they manage conflict. Keeping this in mind, managers must be able to maintain a balance between focusing on the task at hand and preserving harmonious interpersonal relationships and face. Politeness, patience and showing care are essential when dealing with the conflicting parties' feelings and emotions.

- **Build relationship**

Take time to establish relationships with subordinates as this can help create a work environment which can facilitate mutual understanding and problem solving. While the Chinese and Indians prefer to maintain the superior-subordinate distance, the Malays prefer a friendly relationship with their superiors. Hence, spending time together during lunch or tea break with different groups of subordinates is one way of discovering potential problems and difficulties. These informal interactions can be a means of sensing the working climate and enabling subordinates to raise their problems and difficulties with their managers. By being open and allowing subordinates to share their feelings, managers will be able to nip any potential conflict in the bud before it gets out of control.

In addition, once relationships are strengthened and maintained, it would be easier for managers to deal with conflicts on a face-to-face basis as subordinates have already seen them to be caring and concerned.

• Read non-verbal language

Learn to read the non-verbal cues – gestures, facial expressions and tonal variety – of the parties in conflict, as what is observed may not be what is being felt. As open anger and true emotions are not usually expressed, there is a tendency to suppress them and suffer in silence. Managers would therefore need to be able to read these forms of covert behaviour. A lot of anger may be hidden and so the manager must be constantly "in touch" with the feelings of his subordinates.

In a conflict situation, managers should prioritize the work tasks and create minimum opportunities for the parties in conflict to work together face to face. If open conflict ensues, it will be difficult for the two parties to work in the same place and effectively contribute to the common task.

But, if the opportunities for direct interaction are minimized, then with time, the chances of conflict recurring will be minimized and relationships reconciled at least on the surface level. It is hoped that during this phase, the stress and tension caused by interpersonal conflict will "simmer" down and time will take its course to heal the relationship.

Rushing in to end the conflict may be a hasty move which the conflicting parties may not fully accept and may even suspect any good intentions meant. Latent conflict may still exist and resurface at a later stage, sometimes in a more harmful form.

• Use third-party intervention

In minor conflicts, seek the assistance of a third party who is of the same ethnic group, race or religion, or have some other common ground with the parties in conflict. Given the various ethnic groups' difficulties over cultural differences, conflicts can be better handled by someone who is from the same ethnic group and one who is more elderly or senior and is trusted and respected by all.

- **Avoid being confrontational**

Avoid being confrontational when angry, so as not to be seen as quarrelsome, argumentative and insensitive to preserving group harmony. These behaviours tend to spell disaster for any attempt to resolve the conflict. Always remember that an open argument over a conflict may create an atmosphere of tension and helplessness. Any negative feedback – even if it is constructive, is often regarded as a "personal attack" on an individual's character. The party which loses the argument may harbour resentment, which over time, may either be healed (which maintains group harmony) or be manifested in unproductive ways (which can be destructive for the group). Every effort should therefore be made to bring a conflict to a "win-win" conclusion or a "lose-lose" compromise. The latter, applied as a last resort, normally uses the concept of shame - "What will others say or think?"

- **Be "feeling"-oriented**

Be approachable by encouraging and inviting subordinates to share their feelings and viewpoints in discussions. Be aware of the negative consequences of groupthink, as total compliance with the manager's viewpoints may not necessarily promote quality decision making. Encourage a work environment where differences are not seen as threats but instead as different perspectives of looking at an issue, which is important for building synergy at the workplace. Personal differences are better handled when the parties in conflict know that their feelings are being considered by their manager. If the manager only focuses on the task, work may get done, but it will be at the cost of the subordinates' morale and self-esteem.

- **Build inner strength**

Be prepared mentally and spiritually when handling a conflict situation. Understand the situation first and be flexible when interacting with different team members. A flexible manager is one who is able to adopt or improvise on certain cultural elements from each of the various ethnic groups to his advantage. Doing this can cement relationships between the various ethnic groups that make up the Malaysian race. *Budi bahasa* (good manners in language) expressed through proper choice of words and appropriate body gestures will be appreciated by all ethnic groups. Managers who are too task-oriented and confrontational in resolving issues may cause the affected parties discomfort and to withdraw from evolving a "win-win" solution.

- **Focus on generalities**

Be general about commitments and try not to be too specific about how the conflicting parties should settle their differences. Give them time to simmer down and to resolve the conflict among themselves. In this way, the manager may be able to conserve time and energy. In some cases, when time is specified and conflicts are forced to a superficial resolution, underlying currents may still exist, causing tension and discomfort between the affected parties.

- **"Patch up" the heart**

Avoid asking the conflicting parties to shake hands (or make a public apology) as an indication that the conflict has been resolved. A solution is not merely a physical manifestation of the parties coming together as it has to originate from the "heart". Thus, forcing the individuals involved to "patch up" their differences should be avoided at all costs.

CONCLUSION

What is most important at the workplace is the smooth and uninterrupted flow of work and cooperation among the people that make up the organization. As organizations are living organisms of interpersonal relations, it is critical that managers allocate time and energy to coordinate, inspire and channel employees' activities in the interests of the common goal. In the process, equal emphasis must be given to promoting harmonious relationships at all times – just like in a family unit. If there is stress and tension, the manager as the "father" should step in to offer his "wisdom" and judgement to the issue and draw effectively upon the superordinate goal to promote harmony and peace.

There is no one remedy for all problem situations. But whatever method is chosen, there is a need to be calm and patient. In addition, the ability to "style flex", i.e. to put forward one's ideas succinctly and yet be respectful and polite in the manner of approach, is an essential quality for Malaysian managers. Even so, it may be well to heed the wise words of Lao Tze: "Even if harsh interventions succeed brilliantly, there is no cause for celebrations. There has been injury; someone's process has been violated."

SUMMARY OF KEY MALAYSIAN VALUES IN MANAGING CONFLICT

NON-CONFRONTATIONAL	○ Acknowledge that conflict exists and that you as manager need to do something about it ○ Use third party/indirect method when things get tough
HARMONY	○ Develop the ability to "style flex" ○ "Give and take" – be accommodating and flexible ○ Develop relationships with all parties ○ Look out for signals of groupthink as it can be negative
RESPECT FOR OTHERS/ELDERS	○ Invite subordinates to share their views ○ Have someone elderly to resolve conflict between individuals ○ Look for signs of resentment towards decisions communicated through body language and informal discussions
FACE	○ Avoid specifics and describe how the conflict is "damaging" the team's morale by using analogies ○ Allow time for the two parties to resolve the conflict among themselves or else use the concept of shame - "What will others say?"

REFERENCES

Chau, Theodora T (1986). Managing Conflict in Asian Organizations, *World Executive's Digest,* October.

10

MANAGING MEETINGS

SURJIT SINGH

INTRODUCTION

Meetings are an important vehicle for making management decisions, sharing information, learning about something new and solving problems because they allow members to interact face-to-face about the issues at hand. However, meetings can be a waste of time if they do not meet everyone's expectations, or when they are dominated by a few personalities. This can also happen when meetings are swayed by influential individuals and cliques resulting in groupthink or when the emphasis is more towards the form rather than the goal, to the point that it overshadows the spirit of the meeting.

It has been estimated that a manager in the office spends between 35 per cent and 55 per cent of working time in meetings while organizations spend between 7 per cent and 15 per cent of their personnel budgets on meetings (Doyle and Straus, 1976). This means that a manager is likely to spend about 9,000 hours (i.e. at the rate of four hours a week) or 365 days of his lifetime at meetings!

The various types of meetings include staff meetings at regular intervals for information update, problem-solving, fact finding, planning, decision making, introducing change in the organization, task force/special committees, project implementation, performance appraisal, training and counselling.

OBJECTIVES OF THIS CHAPTER

This chapter looks at the typical management and non-management meetings which are often held or attended by Malaysian managers in their day-to-day work. Some common observations of how Malaysians conduct meetings will be made and the chapter will conclude with some guidelines on values and practices which managers need to observe when organizing meetings.

ISSUES AND CHALLENGES

Since meetings are a form of interaction among people, they are highly predisposed to patterns of behaviour which are culture specific. What is considered a norm in one culture may not be acceptable in another culture. It is therefore not surprising that the way attendees behave at meetings largely affects the outcome. When these meetings are attended by members who come from different ethnic groups and nationalities, it is critical for the manager-cum-chairman of the meeting to be aware of his own values as well as those of others. This can help prevent any misinterpretations and misunderstandings that may arise at these meetings.

In an article entitled "In Search of Euroman" (*World Executive's Digest*, 1992), some observations were made on the British management style by European managers working in the United Kingdom. The writer quotes the incident where a Frenchman, posted to England, relates his experience of the first meeting he chaired in his new post:

> The meeting was in the afternoon, and it got to about 3.30 p.m. and everyone started looking at their watches. I didn't know what was going on. I turned to my secretary (who was English) and she said, "I think they want to break for tea." I couldn't understand it. In France, we just carry on until we have finished ....

Talking about "Doing business in Japanese style", the *Management News* (1992) of the British Institute of Management warns:

... Never expect, for instance, a quick deal. In Japan, an average of eight meetings must be held before any real business can transpire. The Japanese will want to establish that a manager is trustworthy and can think long-term.

Hence, for Malaysians originating from different ethnic groups and being exposed to both local and Western work-related values, there are a number of issues and challenges related to meetings in terms of how and when they are held.

The issues and challenges are:

- **Food and ceremony**

   It should not surprise foreigners in Malaysia when our meetings start with tea and coffee, since "food and ceremony" is a way of life – an extension of the value of hospitality. It would be considered inhospitable for the organization calling the meeting not to provide this essential prerequisite for a meeting! Malaysians may even ask jokingly, "Hey! No coffee? Didn't have breakfast-lah!" A meeting in Malaysia can be viewed as a social gathering to enhance relationships as well as getting some business done; whereas in the West, a meeting is held for making some business decisions and building relationships is secondary.

- **Punctuality and timeliness**

   There is a tendency for Malaysians to regard time as diffused – where things happen when people are ready. This is in sharp contrast to cultures where time is displaced and things happen one after the other (turn taking) and in a sequential manner. As a result, Malaysians tend to be rather accommodating in the use of their time and are not likely to be too specific with meeting times, for fear of being labelled as too task driven. For instance, while the introduction of the punch card system has made Malaysians become more particular about being on time to the office, the need to build relationships over morning *kopi* and *makan* prior to work is still the norm in some places.

- **Active participation**

   Some meetings are called because the chairperson, who is the most senior person, wants to give his point of view. In this context, it is unlikely that members will raise questions or concerns that will counter what the chairperson says. Malaysians, in general, are more likely to remain quiet at formal meetings even when they disagree with the viewpoints being put across by those who are more senior in age and position. However, dissension may be solicited in an informal way during coffee breaks or small informal discussions.

Some of the current practices and norms may have taken root over the years and have never been questioned. However, in the context of the present environment, some of these practices may have to be reviewed by those who are the most senior persons in the group. If changes are required, it is important that the senior manager-cum-leader initiate the move and set the pace, timing and agenda of the meeting as juniors are not likely to challenge the status quo.

DEFINING MEETINGS

A meeting is a gathering or assembly of persons convened for the purpose of conducting a business in accordance with the relevant statutory provisions. In Malaysia such statutory provisions would be the Companies Act 1965 and the Societies Act 1966. Therefore, a meeting is held for a specific purpose, usually with an agenda and some structure such as timing, roles, rules, norms, procedures and an agreed upon process.

Meetings can be formal (board or committee meetings), semi-formal (quality circles) or informal (briefings), but an effective meeting is one which accomplishes its purpose in the minimum time and involves full participation of the attendees. Most meetings would have a common purpose or objective, involve two or more people interacting to achieve the purpose agreed upon, follow a number of predetermined conventions and a discussion leader or chairman to steer the meeting.

According to Shaw and Smith (1976), meetings can be classified into:

1. Public meetings, which are lawfully held to discuss a matter of public interest and where the general public has open or restricted access, e.g. political rallies
2. Private meetings, which may or may not be conducted in accordance with statutory requirements, and where members have the exclusive right to attend, e.g. company or society meetings

For the purpose of this chapter, management meetings fall under the classification of private meetings, which do not need to adhere to specific statutory requirements, although the process usually follows the pattern prescribed for statutory meetings.

Private meetings can be further divided into:

*   Formal meetings, which are conducted according to specific statutory requirements
*   Informal meetings, which are not bound by any statutory constraints

As for informal meetings, generally they have three basic objectives, namely:

- Giving information – to share knowledge among members of the organization
- Receiving information or data – to enable management to make decisions or plan a strategy
- Solving operational problems – at departmental or organizational level

KEY OBSERVATIONS RELATING TO MEETINGS

As mentioned earlier, meetings in Malaysia are greatly influenced by the values and practices of its group members. Since Malaysians come from different ethnic groups, a number of cultural values, meeting practices and traditions will be manifested in the conduct of the meetings.

The following common observations have been made of Malaysian meetings:

- **Meeting procedures**

There are meetings which follow parliamentary procedures or standing orders according to the Robert's Rules of Order (Doyle and Straus, 1976). These meetings, therefore, have a leader or chairperson, meeting conventions, agenda, finished business, new business, minutes of meeting, agreements/disagreements/ decisions and follow-up action, etc.

The above process is closely related to Parliamentary Standing Orders or the rules for the constitution of societies promulgated under Schedule 1 of the Societies Act 1966 or other similar Acts like the Companies Act, Trade Union Act, etc.

However, it must be stressed that we are only making this relationship to the extent of the basis for the process practised in management meetings. We do not suggest that any written procedure is required. The management meetings are, therefore, basically conducted based on similar lines as the conventions of formal meetings without strictly adhering to any written rules and procedures as such.

This form of meetings is likely to be practised in departmental or interdepartmental meetings in both the private and public sectors.

- **Extent of formalities**

The extent of formality or informality at management meetings is influenced by various factors, such as the purpose for which the meeting is called, the level of education of attendees, the number of attendees, the venue of meetings, the racial mix of attendees, and the chairperson's organizational status, gender, academic qualifications, educational background, family status and social connections.

Since the outcome of meetings is the result of the attendees' values and attitudes, the "mood" of any meeting will invariably be dictated by the organizational culture and personal values of the attendees and the chairperson. For example, one would find a meeting with members of the civil service to be more formal than a meeting in an American multinational organization based in Malaysia.

- **Meeting style**

The conduct of meetings is a matter of the chairperson's individual style and organizational culture. The process can range from a very formal business-like approach to a rather *laissez-faire* easy-going approach; from a cut-and-dry, time-conscious, bottom-line orientation to a collegiate, meandering or even "chaotic" style. Malaysians in general can be rather non-linear in their approach to agenda items. At times, therefore, it is not unusual to see discussions going back and forth on a single topic.

- **Greetings**

Malaysians by nature display a friendly disposition at meetings and tend to promote an atmosphere of warmth and cordiality. Besides having a perpetual smile, they may also offer a handshake or *salam* when introduced in public (Hamzah-Sendut, Madsen and Thong, 1989). Although the varied versions of *salam* are culture-bound, the common handshake – a Western adaptation – is the norm. The Indian and Chinese handshake is generally the strong clasp of the Westerner whereas the seemingly "soft" Malay handshake is "from the heart", as it is a meeting of outstretched hands lightly held and then withdrawn to touch the heart.

The women are expected to offer their right hand first as a gesture of approval for the handshake. This is even more so in the case of Muslim women and especially those who are less urbanized or are deeply religious and follow the *dakwah*. A gentle "Hi" with a smile is more common with the younger generation.

- **Agenda**

Business meetings generally have an agenda while ad hoc meetings may be called at short notice by the "boss". Some of the routine meetings like the "monthly-briefings" or "Monday-prayers" may even take on the ritual of a "meditation" or a "kangaroo-court" for the attendees since they are so used to the routine. Unless adequately notified of the purpose, there is often a tendency to go unprepared or only partially prepared. The propensity for such meetings has increased to such an extent that they are not infrequently considered a waste of time.

- **Attendance and punctuality**

Formal meetings may require the marking of attendance while the more informal meetings do not register the attendees. Generally, punctuality is attempted rather than being strictly observed. This, too, is dependent on the purpose of the meeting and the person chairing the meeting.

It is not uncommon to have some people arriving late and apologetically taking a seat. The chairperson generally does not make a fuss of it but may admonish the latecomer non-verbally through a cynical smile or a look of disapproval. This, too, will depend on the status of the chairperson. It is common, however, for the chairperson to wait for the key people to turn up before commencing the meeting.

On the other hand, there are also occasions when the chairman will strictly observe punctuality. As one executive puts it: "Our boss is the no-nonsense type. Everybody is there before time. The boss arrives on the dot and gets down to the order of the day. Latecomers are not allowed in. That's it! I don't know whether you call it Western or Malaysian style but we know that we have to be punctual for meetings with the boss."

- **Scheduling meetings**

While Malaysians do not mind whether the meetings are held during the mornings or the afternoons, those working in the city prefer to have meetings during working hours. Rather than a value, this preference is more a practical solution to the hazards of working in the city, having to catch transport home, pick up children from school, etc. In short, scheduling meetings after office-hours can be a difficult task as it may not be at everyone's convenience.

It is important to note that on Fridays, the Muslims expect meetings held in the morning to conclude by mid-day and those in the afternoon not to commence earlier than 2:30 p.m. to enable them to fulfil their religious congregational prayers at the nearest mosque. For this reason, government establishments close between 12:00 noon to 2:45 p.m. on Fridays.

As a good practice, meetings if held in the evenings and going on into the night, should provide breaks for dinner and prayer times for Muslims.

• Chairing the meeting

It is a general practice that a meeting is often chaired by a person of the highest rank, status or expertise among the attendees. This is important among Malaysians as they accord high value for hierarchy, education and age among equals.

Some years ago, it would have been very rare to see a lady chairing or conducting a meeting. The scenario has changed and women are "accepted" to chair or conduct meetings. While the change has given an equal standing in form, the acceptance is not received very enthusiastically especially among those of the "old order". Hence, women chairpersons have to be very sensitive and diplomatic in "manoeuvring" themselves through this change in order to be more widely accepted. The resistance to change is certainly decreasing with the emergence of very capable women managers who have proven their competence and ability.

• Commencement of meetings

The chairperson normally commences the meeting with a preamble usually in the form of a general salutation to the attendees, some discussion on a current event or just an invitation to "help yourselves to a drink" where drinks are already available before the start of the meeting.

On a more serious note, the chairperson would thank those present and draw the attention of the attendees to the agenda for the day's business and proceed.

• Meeting mood

Once the stage is set, the proceedings of the day would begin. The conduct of the meeting would then be very much in the charge of the chairperson.

One of the managers in a large organization said: "The mood depends on who is chairing. It really does not matter whether he is Chinese, Malay, Indian, Iban or Kadazan. At our meetings chaired by the CEO himself, what matters is the bottom line. He is not interested in the goodie-goodies. But then it also depends on his own mood on that day. If he is in a good mood, then he is more tolerant. When things are not good, we can foresee disaster."

For the public sector, it can be said that the mood at meetings is more leisurely as survival does not necessarily depend on the bottom line and decisions made may have to go through a number of stages for scrutiny before they are implemented.

• Minutes of meetings

Most formal meetings maintain a record of the proceedings in the form of minutes. It is not unusual to find the attendees at the meeting reading the minutes for the first time and that may also go for the chairperson. To avoid any embarrassment, the chairperson would normally refer to the minutes and allow time "to refresh everyone's mind" while at the same time checking through for any recording errors.

- **Protocol and *feng shui***

Generally, the public sector meetings are more fastidious about protocol than the private sector. Protocol is observed both in the seating arrangement as well as during the interaction, especially when attendees are of high standing in their official capacity or social status, or have been bestowed titles (for example, *Haji, Datuk, Datin, Tan Sri* or *Tun)* or are royalty (*Raja, Tuanku, Tengku, Tunku, Putra, Puteri*).

While protocol may be considered a formality accorded to status as a gesture of respect and honour from the cultural aspect, individual preferences may be dictated by superstitions and beliefs. If, to a Chinese, geomancy or *feng shui* (Lip, 1991) – literally translated as "wind-water" – is a very important consideration for the orientation of business-building designs, signboards, office-layouts, lighting, colour-scheme and even the colour of furniture and settings to match the horoscope of the manager, then the overall setting and layout of the boardroom or meeting place as well as the position for the seating of the "big boss" is a matter of high priority.

- **Hospitality**

As was mentioned earlier, the organizer of meetings is expected to provide refreshments at meetings. Depending on the culture and practice in the organization, this can range from the provision of a vending machine to formal service of tea during the proceedings of the meeting. While it is common practice to serve tea or coffee with some *kuih-muih* (local cakes) at most public sector meetings as a matter of courtesy and hospitality, the practice in the private sector, according to one manager, "...is usually over a round of tea or coffee and a second round of it should the meeting continue for a couple of hours. In my company, *nasi bungkus* ("packed" meal) may be provided should the meeting continue into the lunch hour in order to complete the agenda for the day."

In some organizations, attendees may be invited to lunch should the meeting end about mid-day. Whatever the extent of hospitality, some basic religious sensitivities over food have to be observed by the organizers. For instance, Muslims should not be served any pork or alcohol, Buddhists and Hindus will not take beef and the same goes for the Sikhs, and no food or drinks should be served at meetings with Muslims during the fasting month of Ramadhan.

This religious tolerance has to be safeguarded as the country's Constitution provides for the practice of the various religions, while Islam is the official religion of the country.

There are several ways to deal with the situation – either go vegetarian or have an acceptable seafood, or non-pork, non-beef meals. While it is taboo to serve any pork to Muslim guests, the need to observe similar considerations to non-beef eaters is often overlooked. The oversight is, however, tolerated owing to the ignorance of many fellow Malaysians.

- **Trust and one-to-one meetings**

There are occasions when one-to-one meetings are held between superiors and subordinates for counselling, appraisal, interview and coaching. These meetings are held at the personal level and require building of trust and confidence in the subordinate. Unless the subordinate has an informal relationship in which he regards his superior as his mentor, the subordinate will remain cautious about what he says. In such cases, the superior has to make a greater effort to gain the trust and confidence of the subordinate before there can be open communication. This type of meetings takes on a formal cordial character most of the time and maintains a "power distance" between the two parties.

- **Informal meetings**

Meetings or discussions among peers take on a more informal character. At such informal meetings, the experienced, the more highly educated, the elderly and the expert are often given "face" even if they may not be quite right in their opinions or ideas. When all things are equal, members of a mixed group may tend to provide support that could be racially or culturally biased. The myth or reality of "unity in diversity" still exists here.

GUIDELINES FOR MANAGING MEETINGS

As members who attend a meeting are expected to participate and the chairman to steer and lead the discussion, it is critical that the latter create a conducive climate for members to offer their ideas as well as constructive criticisms. Unless the chairperson can elicit necessary data that can contribute to effective decision making, a meeting may not be able to meet its objective.

Therefore, to ensure that meetings are in line with the values of the Malaysian workforce, the following guidelines are suggested:

- **Respect the Creator of man**

Observe the fact that Malaysians, irrespective of their religious background, share a common attribute of respect to the Creator of man – the Almighty, and hence to man or humanity itself. All cultures in Malaysia disapprove of any egotistic behaviour, for in the eyes of God, all men are equal. Reference to oneness of humanity and the humankind is made in most of the religions practised by Malaysians. This value is interwoven in all interactions and quite visible during meetings.

• **Understand local values**

Understand the importance placed on local values of respect for seniority, face, social status, educational status and humility, as they are factors which contribute to the promotion of respectful behaviour among members for those in high places. A show of individual and racial-group arrogance and self-promotion are often discouraged and therefore should be played down. Pride and overt display of one's intellectual prowess are often viewed with suspect and may not earn support and commitment from others. It may be advisable to remember the words of Lao Tze, a Chinese philosopher, who once said: "He who knows does not speak; he who speaks does not know."

• **Promote mutual respect**

Be seen to promote and maintain mutual respect for the others in the group, as understanding, tolerance and interracial harmony are constantly emphasized by the government as the pillars of multiracial survival in the country. This would mean that one has to be very tactful in expressing dissent and criticisms towards an idea or suggestion for fear of being labelled as "not one of us".

• **Acknowledge attendees appropriately**

Create a favourable climate at the beginning of meetings by acknowledging attendees correctly. There may be those who carry the title of *Datuk,* *Datin* or Dr and so on. Showing your knowledge in using proper salutations and acceptable ways of addressing individuals is an indication of your understanding of the respect Malaysians have and the value they place on honour and titles.

• **Invite participation**

Make an attempt to control any monopolistic participation by attendees. It has often been noted that the Malaysian Indian is more "expressive" in discussions than the "secretive" Chinese and the "coy" Malay. The chairman must therefore master the skill of quietening the more vocal participants without causing them to "lose face" and extracting information from the less articulate members to share their ideas without causing them stress or embarrassment.

• **Use the "we" approach**

Make members feel comfortable and get them involved in discussions by using the "we" approach rather than the individualistic "I" approach. Malaysians tend to be more group-oriented and would be responsive to decisions made based on a collective effort.

- **Encourage maximum contribution**

Create an environment that is conducive to maximum contribution and participation in the spirit of *mesyuarah* and *gotong-royong* or consensus seeking and cooperation by:
- asking open questions to provide an opportunity for voluntary responses
- directing specific questions to "experts" for advice
- inviting ideas from specific individuals by name
- acknowledging any ideas and opinions by thanking each individual politely in front of his peers

It is often noted that Malaysians are more likely to contribute when they are invited to do so. "Volunteering" oneself may be interpreted as a form of self-promotion and personal arrogance and is contrary to the Malay saying *"Kian berisi, kian tunduk"* – the more knowledgeable one is, the more humble. Malaysians are more likely to feel valued if their peers were to "speak" highly of them. It promotes collectivism, encourages participation and builds confidence among fellow colleagues.

- **Be sensitive to non-verbals**

Be sensitive to the fact that attendees may not be too open with their disagreements in meetings chaired by seniors or elders. Pleasing the "boss" may be regarded as a show of loyalty and collaboration. To avoid the perils of groupthink, managers need to be aware of the tendency to discuss or have a dialogue with the "President's men" without the full commitment of the attendees. Reading non-verbals (body language) is also encouraged to detect any hidden and latent dissatisfaction towards issues discussed.

- **Be a nurturing parent**

Play the role of a nurturing parent when steering through "rough seas" by providing clarification, communicating indirectly through non-verbal cues and most importantly by using one's wit, analogies, metaphors, sayings and even *pantun* to give symbolic meanings to the issues discussed. An excuse for delays may be responded by *"Sebab tidak tahu menari, dikatakan tanah lembab"* – a bad workman blames his tools.

When conflict is evident, the chairperson must be careful not to make the reserved Malay, pragmatic Chinese and articulate Indian lose face *jatuh air muka*. At all times, preserve good manners by being polite and soft spoken in handling open and latent disagreement, keeping the discussion on track and not losing sight of the objectives of the meeting.

Since the chairperson has to be a role model, he must be neutral, firm but fair. Otherwise, the attendees may be turned off from further participation.

- **Understand character**

Learn to understand the character of attendees since their attitude is instrumental to the failure or success of any meeting. Conflicts must be managed firmly but politely by diplomatically dealing with specific behaviours (Mulligan, 1991) such as:

"the know-all": acknowledge his expertise and win him over to your side
"the interpreter": give him face to an extent and politely request him for specific input
"the insensitive": call for his cooperation to help the meeting progress
"the loud mouth": ignore him by looking elsewhere
"the arrogant": solicit his response to some difficult question
"the egoist": give him a special role
"the indifferent": invite his participation
"the fault-finder": throw his criticism for comments by others
"the jester": ignore his pranks
"the avenger": point out the irrelevancy of his argument
"the double-edged sword": seek clarification on what is said
"the rambler": rephrase his thoughts into a specific question or statement
"the time-keeper": refer to the time to show your awareness of it
"the dreamer": draw him into the discussion

There is a need to handle the above behaviours with tact and diplomacy so that attendees do not take the rebuke *teguran* to heart; otherwise, it may lead to bad-mouthing and back-stabbing. The ability to balance a focus on both task and relationships requires a manager to be able to "tune in" to indirect innuendos *sindiran*. A chairperson with this ability will be able to preserve intragroup harmony and foster good relationships among colleagues and also help build inter-organizational linkages. It is advisable to remember that the greater the variety of characters, the more challenging is the task of handling different types of behaviour.

- **Be aware of sensitivities**

Be sensitive to issues relating to religion, organizational secrets and race and try to avoid making any indirect reference to them. Periodically reminding attendees of such sensitivities may be seen as a positive gesture which may earn praise and credibility.

- **Handle latecomers tactfully**

Cultivate an attitude of tolerance and patience towards time management as Malaysians are not likely to be punctual always. The chairman may have to skilfully "impose" some indirect and face-saving forms of good time management by personally approaching the latecomers during a tea break and making a plea that they be more punctual at future meetings.

- **Recapitulate progress**

Recapitulate the progress of discussion based on the agenda of the meeting. Make sure everyone is given an opportunity to present his views. Decide in accordance with the majority view or in accordance with the predetermined decision seemingly "ratified" by the meeting. This is especially so when the meeting is chaired by the "boss" himself or a high status individual.

- **Conclude meeting**

Conclude the meeting by thanking the attendees and inviting them to another round of refreshments or even a lunch "on the house" as a gesture of goodwill, especially after a successful conclusion to an important negotiation.

CONCLUSION

It would be seen from the above discussion that the process of leading a discussion or conducting a meeting is not really different from the Western or Eastern or Japanese style. However, there are certain practices that are an overt expression of the values of the various cultural groups that exist in Malaysia. Depending on the corporate culture of the Malaysian organization and the mix of their employees, the difference is basically in the task-driven and cut-and-dry meetings among Americans and the British compared to the more people oriented, easy, indirect style adopted in the East. Malaysia, with its multiracial, multireligious, multilingual environment, is different from its other Eastern neighbours and hence the style of conducting meetings has to be adapted to suit the cultural mix.

It is not the intent of this chapter to claim that Western management does not display these values at meetings. What is attempted here is a snapshot of some typical behaviours and practices observed at local meetings to enable managers of different ethnic cultures to better comprehend the way meetings are being conducted.

While deliberations at a meeting may be attributed to culture, it would be an over-generalization to say that Malaysian meetings are different from Western management meetings. Most Malaysian managers today are Western-educated or have been educated through Western literature and hence are largely influenced by Western theories of management. What is different is that the practice of management is in an environment different from that on which the management theories are based. This creates the challenge for the managers in the Malaysian environment. While they may be influenced by Western theories of management, they are themselves Malaysian, have their roots in the Malaysian culture and have to manage a Malaysian workforce. The same applies to expatriate managers who have been posted to multinational organizations in Malaysia; they too have to appreciate the culture of the local workforce and need to adapt to the local values in conducting their business operations.

Malaysian managers, therefore, will need to consider these values and practices so that their meetings are seen as a place for getting things done in a more satisfying and productive manner by both attendees and the chairperson. It must also be accepted that "what is food for the goose is not food for the gander" and in the dynamic environment in which Malaysian businesses are operating, a good understanding of meeting principles and techniques and a judicious adoption of both the foreign and Malaysian cultural values will further enhance the quality of management meetings.

SUMMARY OF KEY MALAYSIAN VALUES IN MANAGING MEETINGS

RESPECT FOR ELDERS/ SENIORITY/OTHERS

- Acknowledge everyone at the meeting, especially the elderly, and make them feel valued
- Know how to address the senior members of the meeting
- Make everyone feel at ease and build rapport
- Be aware of ethnic sensitivities

HARMONY

- Get everyone to participate and be involved in the discussion
- Avoid being too self-centred
- Build relationships through *makan* ceremonies
- Be polite as it is a basic ingredient in Asian culture
- Show good manners through speech and actions
- Acknowledge contribution by giving recognition for ideas
- Observe "give and take" attitude
- Show tolerance for ignorance of values by others

HUMILITY	○ Be humble and offer help ○ Avoid being too arrogant or egoistic ○ Avoid showing-off ○ Admit mistakes
COLLECTIVISM	○ Invite suggestions by calling on specific individuals ○ Promote the spirit of being together sharing a task ○ Seek agreement and assess consequences of decision to organization ○ Emphasize "we-ness" rather than individualism
FACE SAVING	○ Avoid embarrassing those who deviate from the group norms ○ Acknowledge differing viewpoints and use metaphors to explain difficulties

REFERENCES

Doyle, Michael and Straus, David (1976). *How to Make Meetings Work.* New York: Jove Books.

Hamzah-Sendut, Madsen, John and Thong, Gregory Tin Sin (1989). *Managing in a Plural Society.* Singapore: Longman Singapore Publishers Pte Ltd.

Lip, Evelyn (1991). *Feng Shui for Business.* Singapore: Times Books International.

Management News (1992). "Doing business in Japànese style", September 1992, British Institute of Management.

Mulligan, John (ed) (1991). *The Personal Management Handbook.* London: Macdonald & Co.

Shaw, Sir Sebag and Smith, Judge E Denis (1976). *The Law of Meetings.* London: Macdonald & Co.

World Executive's Digest (1992). In Search of Euroman, July 1992.

11

DEALING WITH GOVERNMENT AGENCIES

SHARIFAH MARIA ALFAH and ARIC H M LOW*

INTRODUCTION

In Malaysia, government and semi-government agencies monitor and regulate numerous social and economic activities and implement projects of public concern. They also provide information to the public on what needs to be observed. This is to ensure that businesses conducted conform to set procedures and guidelines.

Managers in business related organizations need to recognize the importance of government relations and acquire appropriate knowledge and skills in interacting with government officers. This will enable them to obtain vital business information on how to go about seeking approval, obtaining licences and permits for projects and activities, seeking clarification on laws and regulations, guidelines and standards, and negotiating for government contracts, including serving as technical and managerial consultants for some government agencies.

---

* The authors acknowledge CHONG SHEAU CHING for her contribution in the original edition
   of this chapter.

More often, bigger organizations would have the support of a Government Affairs or Relations Department with the main responsibility of managing liaisons with government agencies. This includes the task of setting up face-to-face interactions with government officers at the appropriate levels with the aim of achieving more favourable outcomes.

OBJECTIVES OF THIS CHAPTER

The main objective of this chapter is to describe the significant characteristics of most government and semi-government agencies and the key issues and challenges in dealing with them. Significant values underlying the expressed behaviours of government officers will be highlighted. The chapter concludes with some specific guidelines to assist members of the public to initiate, build and maintain a cordial relationship with officers in government agencies.

ISSUES AND CHALLENGES

As Malaysia competes in the global arena in the new millennium, the call is for government agencies to undergo transformation through various modernization programmes and reforms and thereby be more responsive to the needs of their customers. This is in line with the Malaysia Incorporated policy to create an environment conducive to more effective interaction between the business community and members of the public and the government agencies.

The first milestone in creating a more productive and thinking workforce amongst government officers rather than just being *kakitangan* (staff) was the change in the closing words used for signing off correspondence from *Saya yang menurut perintah* (Your obedient servant) to *Berkhidmat untuk Negara* (To perform for the nation). Subsequently, privatized government agencies have become more customer-focused in their modus operandi.

Some noticeable examples in this effort are the following:

- Pos Malaysia has created a one-stop centre for the payment of most household bills, including the renewal of vehicle road tax at its various post offices.

- The Inland Revenue Board has gone to shopping complexes to set up temporary counters to enable individual members of the public to handle queries and help people to complete personal income tax forms. Even their counter services are now more efficient and customer friendly.

- The Employee Provident Fund (EPF) has come a long way in providing fast and efficient service for contributors, specifically in cases of withdrawals.

However, the challenges faced by organizations still abound when dealing with certain government ministries and agencies especially when seeking approvals or needing a more pragmatic interpretation of various laws, byelaws and regulations. One example is the frustration of developers in obtaining the certificate of occupancy, which leaves house buyers in the lurge and with additional costs.

Therefore, the biggest challenge facing government agencies is their ability to change with the times and the needs of the people – to be able to provide effective and efficient services to the public. Managers of business enterprises, on the other hand, will likewise have to understand the functions and workings of the various government bodies and agencies and the interplay of the administrators and decision makers.

KEY OBSERVATIONS RELATING TO DEALING WITH GOVERNMENT AGENCIES

To be able to interact effectively with government bodies and agencies, managers need to understand the entire system and the unique way that it operates, i.e. how work gets done, by whom and at what level of customer's satisfaction. Like in any large bureaucratic system, there are set rules and procedures which members of the public and business enterprises will have to adhere to, especially in relation to compliance of the laws of the country and in the conduct of business activities.

The following characteristics are often associated with the leadership and managerial styles and service delivery of government bodies and agencies as seen from the eyes of the public:

- **Hierarchical**

The government system is hierarchical. It is made up of Ministries *Kementerian*. At the helm of each ministry is a Minister *Menteri*. He/She is the politically empowered figure and is often assisted by Deputy Ministers, the Secretary General, etc. (see FIGURE 1).

At the non-political level, the implementation body is the civil service, which is headed by the Secretary General *Ketua Setiausaha*. Immediately below him are numerous Directors General *Ketua Pengarah*. Each ministry is further divided into divisions *Bahagian*. Each division is headed by a Director *Pengarah Bahagian*. Then finally, the divisions are further sub-divided into departments *Jabatan*.

The policies adopted by the various ministries are formulated by the Cabinet, which consists of Ministers and Deputy Ministers and headed by the Prime Minister. Decisions arrived at the ministerial levels are translated into written

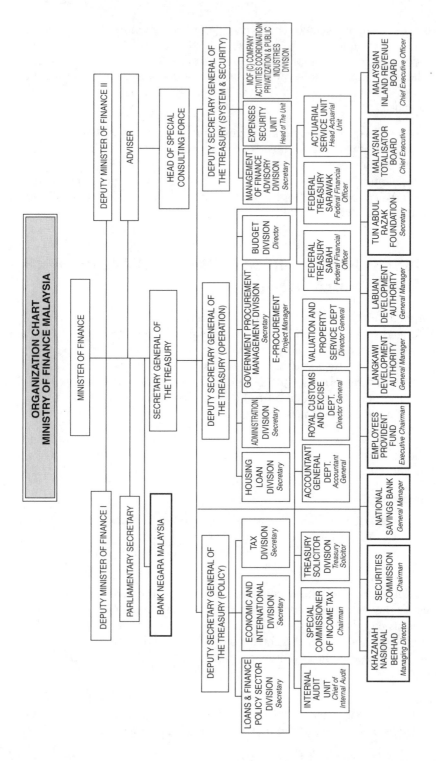

**ORGANIZATION CHART
MINISTRY OF FINANCE MALAYSIA**

Source: Ministry of Finance, Malaysia (25.07.2000)

orders and directives, sometimes referred to as General Orders, for implementation by the officers.

Senior officers are, however, given some latitude in interpreting the General Orders while those at the lower levels are the administrators who have to implement the directives. The junior officers carry out orders which are delegated to them by the senior officers. Hence, junior officers, whom the public deals with, have no or limited authority that allows for deviation from the set rules and guidelines; they will have to refer any such issues upward.

- **Information accessibility**

The system is one that seeks and dispenses information upon request. The Government printers are the ones who normally make available publications of new enactments, standing orders and other gazetted information to members of the public. Certain information can only be made available through this channel. Other publications aimed at acquainting businessmen and professionals with government services – such as *Dealing with the Malaysian Civil Service* (produced by MAMPU, 1993) – provide helpful information.

Some professional bodies and individual writers have published books to help members of the public understand the various laws and regulations better. Examples are books on the various labour laws and court precedents. The Housing Developers Authority also published a number of text materials for their members on the relevant government building rules and regulations.

As stated earlier, every government department is guided by written laws, directives and procedures which are commonly referred to as General/Standing Orders. Non-adherence to such General Orders or directives may place the officer in a vulnerable position for public inquiry, parliamentary questioning and appearing before the Public Accounts Committee.

In the wake of increasing use of the Internet and the growth of e-commerce and e-Government in Malaysia, information on various government agencies is now easily available and accessible on a global basis via their homepages or websites – an example is the homepage of the Ministry of Finance, Malaysia at http://www.treasury.gov.my.

- **Decision making**

Because of the hierarchical nature of government organizations, decision making can be a rather long-drawn tedious task. The deliberative process of collective decision making, which is the norm, can take a long time, especially with regard to key issues. On the other hand, major issues, especially those outside the guidelines of the directives or General Orders, are usually reviewed by the relevant ministers or agencies who meet and discuss, and when necessary, present memoranda to the Cabinet for consideration and approval.

However, the governmental decision-making system can be considered flexible as it allows time for members of the public to react and give input prior to its becoming law or being gazetted. On a number of occasions, top-down decisions made at Cabinet level and announced by the relevant Minister were reviewed and even changed in response to public feedback or outcry. Some observers may interpret this as an unnecessary step in the process of decision making because it tends to convey the message that the government is hasty or indecisive. However, seen from another perspective, it may be a necessary step to "test the waters" before a law gets implemented.

The government's planned actions on bank mergers, highway toll fees, seat belts, helmets, religion on identity cards, etc, are examples of issues of public interest that have undergone such treatment. The government has responded to feedback from the public by making the necessary changes.

- **Emphasis on stability and consistency**

The system is also designed to promote stability and consistency in the interpretation and implementation of government policies and regulations. As a result, the way things get done are not likely to change too drastically in the short term to accommodate new demands, unless the need to do so is initiated from the top to comply with laws promulgated by Parliament and ministerial directives.

GUIDELINES FOR INTERACTING WITH GOVERNMENT OFFICERS

At one point or another, organizations will need to deal with government offices on matters directly related to their business needs. It is, therefore, important for managers to know the right procedures and systems and the appropriate skills to work with the personnel who provide the services or information. Following are some guidelines to help explain the existing cultural scenario and the "art" of interacting with government officers, the majority of whom are Malays.

- **Use covering letters**

For any application or request for information, the importance of a good covering letter cannot be taken lightly for it can open doors, build relationships and create a positive impact on the matter at hand.

The letter must be properly addressed, generally to the Director-General *Ketua Pengarah*, with correct salutations, and written in Bahasa Malaysia. Compared with the Western style of writing, the Malaysian style is less direct and precise. The language must flow with politeness yet concise, stating the need of the organization and yet allowing for the understanding of the system. Words and phrases which have direct and negative connotations should be avoided as this may come across as demanding and impolite in the Malay culture. It is also best to provide as much information as necessary to support the application and maybe expedite its approval.

To create the right impact, the tone of the letter has to convey a real need and urgency to the government officer-in-charge. It is also important that a person of the right level in the organization signs the letter to give it credence and maintain the required protocol. This is crucial when the letter is addressed directly to a Minister or Deputy Minister.

However, if the signatory is from that of a foreigner, it is acceptable for the main text to be in English, but the address, salutations and closing should be in Bahasa Malaysia. Even then, the English text must show the same level of politeness. An expatriate may require some advice to appreciate the local indirectness and politeness in official letter writing, and not to consider it as unnecessary or as an indication of subjugation.

Follow-up telephone calls or making personal face-to-face representation will be the next step in ensuring a speedy as well as the needed outcome.

• Observe protocol

For Malaysians, the correct approach is to use Bahasa Malaysia as much as possible in face-to-face interactions with government officers as it shows respect for the national language. However, the English language may be used should the officer start speaking in English. If the conversation continues in Bahasa Malaysia and there is a need to explain better in English, it is advisable and polite to seek permission to do so, i.e. *minta izin*. Do not assume government officers do not understand English if they choose to speak in Bahasa Malaysia; the majority of them can communicate in English, and well too.

When greeting government officers, it would be preferable to use Bahasa Malaysia. For Muslims, use *Assalamualaikum*, while non-Muslims can use *Selamat pagi* or *Selamat petang*. A handshake or *salam* is acceptable with an officer of the same gender but be careful in offering one's hand with an officer of the opposite sex. A polite bow or nod of the head will suffice if the officer is female unless she offers her hand for a shake or *salam*. Some officers prefer a soft handshake or *salam* to indicate showing politeness in not grasping another person's hand. Contrary to Western summation, this form of hand gesture is not a portrayal of one's low self-esteem or lack of warmth or sincerity.

- ### Show proper decorum in communication

Meetings with senior government officers must be attended by similar, if not higher, ranking officers in the organization. Such persons, especially foreigners, must be advised on the proper decorum of meetings where the most senior officer handles the meeting, whilst his staff attend as observers to answer unexpected questions. In order to provide balance, it is advisable for the visitors to come as a team rather than be represented by an individual.

When asking or replying to questions during meetings, always refer to the chairperson and ensure that due respect is given to his/her title and position. For example, use honorifics: "It will be helpful if *Tuan/Puan/Datuk/Tan Sri/Tun* could provide me with information on..." or "With *Datuk's* permission I would like to explain the issue just raised by *Datuk's* officer, *Encik/Cik...*" It is not polite to personally address an officer at the table directly even if the officer is actually in charge of the project. This mode of communication is aligned with the Malay value of respecting senior officers and recognizing the hierarchical structure.

During the discussion, managers may want to be less direct "*berlapik*" rather than direct, especially when they sense an atmosphere of uncertainty or discomfort on the part of the officer-in-charge to provide a definitive answer or commitment. Issues should not be pressed if, like the *"silat"* or *"tai chi"*, they have been fended off. Avoid imposing deadlines at all costs; do not press the officer for a verbal response or commitment. It would be wise to watch for non-verbal cues for the next probable action. Offering to call back at a later date may be appropriate, as then the officer will have time to consult with his/her superior.

It is always advisable to summarize the discussion and decision taken by following up with a polite thank you note or letter upon return to the office. It must also be emphasized that trust is built with government officers when their help or assistance is never used to cause embarrassment to them especially with the press. The position and face *air muka* of those who are willing to help must always be protected.

- ### Dress appropriately

Equally important is to dress appropriately – in proper business outfit – as Malays consider this a sign of respect for the officer that you are meeting. While the conventional long-sleeved shirt, long pants and tie are recommended for men, women should wear clothes with sleeves and hemlines that fall below the knees when meeting senior government officers. When in doubt, the rule of thumb is to expose as little as possible one's skin. Being Muslims, Malays consider proper dressing as a sign of respect for their religion.

- ### Respect Official Secrets Act (OSA)

The OSA stipulates that any documents which are not passed by the Parliament are under the OSA. As such, the OSA is opened to wide interpretation. Some published information may be considered confidential.

Avoid insisting on obtaining information under the OSA unless directed or given permission by the highest-ranking officer in the hierarchy. The permission must be granted in writing and addressed to the head of the agency who possesses the information. Possession of unauthorized information can lead to embarrassment and even legal prosecution.

- ### Know the right person to contact

For simple and routine transactions, like paying bills, ascertain the officer responsible and bring his/her attention to the matter. If the matter requires the attention of the head of the Department, it is best to call for an appointment through his secretary or personal assistant , followed by a letter to confirm the date and issues to be discussed. At the same time, an introduction by a colleague or friend of the officer may help to pave the way for quick rapport and response.

Also, find out whether the issue being discussed is within the jurisdiction of a federal agency or a state agency. If an agency does not have the authority to make the decision, find out which agency facilitates the decision-making process such as making comments, providing relevant information and preparing the platform for decision making, etc.

- ### Observe religious practices

When entertaining Malay government officers, select restaurants catered by Muslims or outlets that display the *halal* sign. When inviting government officers for lunch or dinner, it is best to invite more than one officer in the department to avoid accusations of corruption of seeking favours. Invitation for dinner should be after 8:00 p.m. to allow the Muslim officers to say their evening prayers *maghrib*. In fact, there is a directive to government officers not to accept invitations which clash with the evening prayer time, which starts at about 7:15 p.m.

Be sensitive to Muslim officers during the fasting month, by not eating, drinking or smoking in their presence.

Generally, it would be advisable to finish any business meeting before lunchtime or Friday prayer time and before 4:00 p.m. when office is about to close. Afternoon meetings on Fridays should also be scheduled after 2:45 p.m. If possible, avoid Fridays as they are not good days for meetings and appointments, because Muslim males need to perform the noon congregational prayers.

- **Speak humbly**

Speak with a voice clear enough to be heard by others. It is considered impolite to be loud and assertive when requesting service from government officers. Malays consider a soft and well-modulated voice as a sign of good breeding.

It may even be appropriate to be apologetic at the point of contact and departure for having to seek the help of the officer. Being humble can be seen as a form of compensation for the large power distance that normally exists between government officers and the public. This is also the appropriate local cultural behaviour often demonstrated by a guest for "imposing" on the host.

- **Be polite**

Always appear cordial, soft-spoken and non-aggressive when asking questions. Avoid being so direct that it puts a high ranking officer in a dilemma when he has to respond to difficult questions, especially when he does not have all the answers.

When providing answers, use a conciliatory tone and explain things subtly, e.g. "Am I right in saying...?", "Do you mean...?", or "I am sorry that I don't understand the matter very well. I think it deals with..."

It may even be advisable to sound "needy" and convey the message that the officer's assistance is crucial for success.

The following points are worth remembering when in the presence of government officers:

- Avoid making demands and challenging the officer's beliefs and knowledge in front of his peers and supervisors as this may cause him to lose face.

- Show support of the nation's stance on political issues.

- Sympathize with the officer's complaints about his job and problems.

- Share problems and establish a sense of "we are in the same boat" or "we are all working for a living" *Kita cari makan saja*, so that one is not seen as socially or financially better off than the officer.

- **Observe non-verbal cues**

There are a number of non-verbal gestures relating to the local polite system which should be observed by those who interact with government servants. Examples are pointing with the thumb rather than with the second finger, ensuring that one is seated before talking to an officer who is seated, having the senior officer rather than yourself end the meeting, and touching food or sipping the drink only when offered or invited to.

It would be best to discuss the expected body postures with a local colleague prior to any interface with the government officer, such as the proper way to greet, talk and bid farewell. A loud, assertive and brash manner may leave a negative impression on the government officer in attendance.

CONCLUSION

Every organization has its own unique cultural characteristics of getting things done. In the case of a large bureaucracy like the government here, members of the public need to acquire skills of good interpersonal relationships coupled with the ability to build rapport with officers at all levels. An effective face-to-face interaction with all levels of the hierarchy can pave the way for a smooth verbal and written exchange. Hence, knowing what to do and what not to do is often the key to getting things done through government agencies in Malaysia.

SUMMARY OF KEY MALAYSIAN VALUES IN DEALING WITH GOVERNMENT AGENCIES

RELATIONSHIPS
- ○ Know the right people to contact for help
- ○ Build relationships or rapport with government officers

HARMONY
- ○ At meetings, make suggestions which are beneficial to all parties
- ○ Avoid giving negative feedback to officers because it may upset feelings

PATIENCE
- ○ Learn to wait for requests, approvals and decisions to be made by the right level of officers

HUMILITY
- ○ Be polite, cordial and soft-spoken
- ○ Downplay one's status and power
- ○ Apologize for imposing on the officer's time
- ○ Prepare data, facts and figures before formal meetings

RESPECT FOR OTHERS
- ○ Acknowledge position titles of agency head
- ○ Be courteous at all times
- ○ Know protocol and proper behaviour towards the officers at the different levels of the government hierarchy
- ○ Submit proposal or request to the highest level agency
- ○ Dress appropriately, especially when meeting senior government officers
- ○ Be sensitive to religious practices, e.g. prayer times and fasting
- ○ Never cause the officer to be embarrassed or to be reprimanded by his superior

LOYALTY AND CONFIDENTIALITY
- ○ Observe confidentiality by knowing legislations pertaining to one's business
- ○ Know the Anti-Corruption Act and Official Secrets Act
- ○ Show deference to political ministers of the various agencies
- ○ Use the national language as often as possible, especially during discussions

12

EXPATS WORKING WITH MALAYSIANS

PETER SHEPHARD

INTRODUCTION

Malaysia has been exposed to foreign influence beginning with the Portuguese in the 16th and 17th centuries, Dutch in the 18th century, British in the 19th century and Japanese during the Second World War. Now, foreign influence comes in the shape of large multinationals with headquarters in USA, United Kingdom, Europe, Australia, Japan, Korea, India and countries all over the world.

With the increase in foreign investment and the government's efforts to industrialize the country through various national development policies, the number of expatriates (*expats* in short) working in both the private and public sectors of the Malaysian economy is likely to rise in the next 10 – 20 years. These expatriates bring along with them a more "professionalized" and state-of-the-art management technology, systems thinking and a business culture which would enhance Malaysian managerial practices and work methods.

With Malaysia's vision to become a developed nation by the year 2020, and a Newly Industrialized Country (NIC) even earlier, the rate of industrialization

165

will require an increasing number of resources and expertise to transfer both technical and management technology.

In the process of becoming more "global" and striving to become "world class", Malaysians will have to interact with foreigner investors, technologists and customers – many of whom will visit Malaysia for both short and longer term periods.

Thus, learning to work with expatriates, or even becoming one, and working with those from other cultures will require both Malaysians and expatriates to be able to work cohesively and move the country ahead to achieve its vision of being a developed country by the year 2020.

OBJECTIVES OF THIS CHAPTER[1]

This chapter will focus on the role of expatriates in Malaysia and some of the knowledge and skills that they need to acquire in order to make their stay and working assignment an enriching experience for themselves as well as for those who work with them. It will offer foreign expats in the country some guidelines to help them in their interactions with Malaysians in both work and non-work settings.

ISSUES AND CHALLENGES

Expats in Malaysia have come mainly from Anglo-Saxon and European-American contexts where the way of life can be remarkably different from the Malaysian way of life. These expats are likely to bring into the local based organizations, work methods and procedures which have originated in another foreign setting. In attempting to "force fit" some of the foreign ways into the local context, adjustments are inevitable. As a result, expats who are working in Malaysia are expected to understand the local norms and sensitivities.

Some of the key challenges for expats who are working in Malaysia are as follows:

---

[1] For the purpose of this chapter, we are largely excluding the Diplomatic Corps amd focusing mainly on the private sector multinational corporations (MNCs) and international companies (which include airlines, hotels, retail chains, restaurants, management consultants, engineering consultants and property and golf course development projects).

• Dual role

Expats are often seen to play a dual role of which the first is to represent the financial interests of their enterprise while the secondary role is to transfer technology. The first role is often played by the CEO, or the Financial Controller, while the second role is that of the Technologist or Technocrat who plays a key role in ensuring a smooth transfer of technology and that sufficient locals are being trained. This role – while sometimes managerial – is often developmental, acting in an advisory, training or consulting capacity.

Very often, expats perceive their role as a "change" agent and, due to their experience and qualifications, may convey an attitude reminiscent of the "colonial master" *tuan besar* to their Malaysian colleagues. If this "superior" status is very evident, it could lead to resentment or antagonism on the part of Malaysians.

• Malaysianization

The role of the expat is "to work himself out of the job" and empower the Malaysian to take over his job. Rather than being a "controller" or "administrative manager", an expat is more often appreciated if he takes the role of an "inspirational" leader, with responsibility for the motivation, morale and development of human resources.

To be seen both as an expert and an inspirational leader, an expat manager needs to understand how his own culture differs from his host country's culture. It is also important for him to learn more of the cultural values, norms and ethos of his fellow colleagues (in this case, Malaysians). Otherwise, expats may be seen as impersonal or even intimidating task masters who are only interested in getting things done without considering the feelings and views of their Malaysian colleagues. Both are expected to learn from each other and be willing to work as a team where the task, rather than the expat, becomes the boss.

• Global and local

Expats have to balance an orientation for global consciousness and a conviction for local appropriateness. While their knowldege and skills are needed to enhance productivity, their managerial styles and practices may not always be well received if they are not sensitive to the local nuances. Expats also need to be always conscious that their previous successes with local people do not always guarantee that they will be accepted by the local community. A successful expat manager has to be aware that while principles of good business are universally defined, the way they are articulated differs at the local level of implementation. For example, an ethics policy derived in corporate America may have a different flavour when implemented locally (Asma, 1996).

• **Language of computers**

While the assignment increasingly calls for more technological literacy in using the universal language of Microsoft, Internet or the web sites, expats are also required to enhance their skills in cultural literacy on the job. In this work setting – when one turns away from the computer, the faces and language of local employees present a different challenge. This becomes even more challenging in Malaysia, which has a multicultural workforce with many different sets of values and practices.

DEFINING EXPATRIATES

An expatriate is anyone who is working outside (ex) his own nation. He may be sent or may have requested a posting overseas because his skills and expertise are required. Some multinational organizations or international agencies refer to expats as "International Officers".

Historically, before Independence from the British, most expats in Malaysia were either civil servants or managers and technical experts in the private sector. They "represented" their own nation's interests in trade, investment or development. However, in the last 10 years or so, they are largely found in the private sector – working for large enterprises like Shell, ICI, Dunlop, Guthries, Harrison and Crosfield and British Petroleum. These made up the "First Wave" of expats in Malaysia. In the Government, there was still a large number of advisors, diplomats, academics and technical specialists – many of whom, after retirement, chose to remain in Malaysia.

The British who formed the majority of expats in Malaysia were later joined by the Dutch, French, German, Danish, Swedish, Swiss and American expatriates representing large multinationals such as Philips, Siemens, East Asiatic (now known as Hap Seng Consolidated), Volvo, Nestle and Esso. These formed the "Second Wave" of expats.

As Malaysia grew closer to Australia and the NICs in Asia, and with the introduction of the "Look East" policy by the Government in the 1980s – a "Third Wave" of expats emerged – representing the growing interests of their governments and private sector investments. They include now the largest number of expatriates – those who are Asian such as Japanese, Taiwanese or Korean. However, with the dramatic growth in the electronics industry, some Europeans and Americans joined this wave, representing such organizations as Motorola, Intel, N S Electronics, Texas Instruments, RCA and Harris – as well as Thomson.

The number of first-wave British expats – while decreasing over the last 15 to 20 years – has been more than made up for by the Japanese, Australian, American and the other Asian "tigers". Thus the white man *Orang putih* expat is no longer the norm, as the Asian expat is now more common.

In the last few years, with the advent of the Multimedia Super Corridor (MSC) and the explosion of twinning programmes between local colleges and foreign universities, a sort of "fourth" wave of expats started to occur. This new breed of expats consists of a younger group of highly computer literate technologists and investors from the "Silicon valleys" of the world with expertise in high technical areas of telecommunications, research and development in information technology as well as tertiary level education.

With the establishment of the MSC and MSC-status companies which are favoured with minimal restrictions on entry, this fourth wave of expats has in turn brought with them a new set of values, spawned by cyberspace and the Internet. They include the emphasis on speed and directness of communication, networking globally and a work orientation for instant data that fostered speed and efficiency over the "soft" interpersonal and social skills that previous expats would have needed.

In the quest for provision of tertiary education, the rapid increase of twinning and distance learning programmes has brought in the jet setting professors with their laptop computers to provide services with Malaysian organizations. While these "dons" of distance or online learning are technologically advanced and academically competent, they may not be all too familiar with the hidden nuances and local subtleties when dealing with Malaysians.

In the past, most of the expats were from the United Kingdom and the United States of America. However, with the Asian crisis and devaluation of the ringgit, there is a now a greater influx of expats from the Pacific region, namely Australian and New Zealand universities. Consequently, as more Malaysians pursue their university degrees from these antipodean cultures, they will be more exposed to a neo-colonial set of influences which tend to be different from the values of "colonialism" found in the traditional British educational system.

GETTING TO KNOW MALAYSIANS

In working with Malaysians, an expat needs to know that Malaysians, regardless of race share a common trait of being proud of their ethnic cultures. They value harmony, and are family-oriented, hospitable and religious.

Some useful insights to help expats to better understand their Malaysian colleagues are given below:

- Malaysia is a complex multi-ethnic society with each ethnic group having its own set of values and rich traditions. Some of these values such as not challenging elders, compromise and tolerance for ambiguity may seem like weaknesses to Westerners. Try to understand their values and do not force them to conform to the ways that are familiar to expats.

- Malaysians, regardless of race, value face, humility and conservatism. They are intrinsically warm, friendly and hospitable, but may appear shy and reserved initially. But once the ice is broken, they may ask questions which seem to intrude into one's privacy – but it is likely their way of making an expat "feel accepted".

- Most Malaysians view the organization as an extended family. Expats may find themselves being called "Uncle" by the children of their local colleagues. In times of crises, employees will look to the organization for support. For instance, allowing time off for employees to attend funerals is expected.

- Rituals and ceremonies are a norm, and formal speeches and food will take precedence over the task (an hour may be "lost" from the beginning of a seminar or training course, due to such rituals and ceremonies). Malaysians consider these rituals as part of their way of showing hospitality and building relationships.

- Business should not be mixed with food and refreshments. Business always comes second, and should not be at the expense of eating, drinking and socializing. Relationships must be nurtured first before Malaysians can begin to trust others. They prefer to conduct business with people they are comfortable with.

- Things may often seem to take longer than planned. Malaysians are less hurried and more easy-going. The sense of urgency is less obvious because they consider time as more of a framework for orientation than something to be mastered. (Locals are here for perpetuity – unlike the expat whose time here is limited.)

- Malaysians respect titles and status. Even if those with titles and status seem less qualified, their goodwill may be important in the long term. An expat who shows respect for titles and status demonstrates respect for local culture.

- When speaking in English (or another language) to Malaysians, speak clearly and at an even pace, always mindful of accents and avoiding slang or colloquial speech.

- When interacting with Malaysians, be aware of gender and sex role differences.

- Clarify one's role perception and check if the locals have a similar perception.

- Empathize and understand Malaysians' needs, hopes and fears. Understanding the expectations of the Government is an added bonus to building rapport with locals. If married, the expat should encourage his spouse to interact and learn the local culture as well.

KEY OBSERVATIONS RELATING TO WORKING TOGETHER

There are a number of potential problems when expats interact with Malaysians. Some of these may be attributed to misconceptions by both parties due to differences in values and underlying assumptions.

TABLES 1, 2 and 3 show some observations made at the Intercultural Management Study workshops (1990-1992) conducted by the Malaysian Institute of Management.

TABLE 1: Observations of Malaysians by expatriates working as senior managers in Malaysia

• Some characteristics of Malaysians:
  – slow-moving compared to Westerners
  – very proud of their ethnic subcultures (ethnocentric), to the extent that racial issues take precedence over work issues
  – have difficulty saying "No" and are non-confrontational
  – indirect and ambiguous
  – loyal to authority
  – gracious and friendly
• Malaysians need to be more open, global and should have a more long-term perspective
• Malaysians tend to value traditions, so it is not easy to introduce change
• Malaysians dislike face-to-face communication, so it is difficult to give them feedback. Criticism may be taken seriously and lead to loss of face
• Lack of technical expertise
• A "laid-back" attitude towards deadlines – "rubber time"
• Suffer form "Guidelines Syndrome" – want things to be put in writing expecially with regard to instructions for filling in forms from government agencies
• A predominant involvement of government policies vis-à-vis human resource development sytems
• A need for "brutal" follow-up after assigning tasks to Malaysians
• The educational system accentuates differences more than common grounds
• Not used to making demands and so are seen as unassertive and servile

TABLE 2: Comparing Malaysian and American values by 100 managers and supervisors working in multinational companies in Malaysia

Malaysians	Americans
Have difficulty saying "No"	Assertive
Face saving	Not so concerned about face
Informal	Formal structure
Flexible	Compliant (go by the book)
Generalities	Specifics, analytical
Patient	Less patient
Indirect	Direct and to the point
Family-oriented at work	Less family-oriented at work
Respect for seniors	Equal treatment, fairness
Non-confrontational	Open, challenging

The following are some common observations made by Malaysians and expats of one another:

- **Cultural superiority (ethnocentrism)**

There is a tendency for expats (whether deliberate or intentional) to adopt a "superior" attitude due to their formal, legitimate or expert power bases. While expats may not be conscious of this, most Malaysians look to their *orang putih* superiors to speak for them and represent them.

- **Emphasis on results ahead of relationships**

Due to the nature of an expat's foreign assignment, which is often short term, his career and future may depend on the results he produces during his tenure. As he does not have to live with the local people for long, he may not want to concern himself too much with developing long-term rewarding relationships.

- **Different expectations**

Expats often find that they have to work with a group of people who do not have the same value orientation towards work. They often perceive Malaysians as unassertive, too humble, conservative and even subservient because they are not likely to challenge or question them. There are expats who want the Malaysians to be just like them – open, decisive and forthright in their dealings with others.

On the other hand, Malaysians tend to perceive expats as trying to overshadow their local counterparts. Their values of humility, face-saving, respect for elders and harmony are often overlooked, misunderstood and seldom affirmed or used to strengthen and even reinforce managerial practices. Local values may

TABLE 3: Comparing Malaysian and American expectations by 100 managers and supervisors working in multinational companies in Malaysia

Expectations by Malaysians of Americans	• Show respect for hierarachy • Give face – not putting the person in a tight spot • Avoid conflict • Show you can be trusted by word and action • Listen more • Do not use "slang" when speaking • Seek a "win-win" outcome • Be more patient • Do not brag • Treat us as equals • Establish informal relationships • Show you care • Speak from the heart
Expectations by Americans of Malaysians	• Be more verbal/open with feelings • Be direct and concise • Be punctual • If a task is not completed on time, do not make excuses. Deliver what has been done • Be specific. Give data and facts • Do your homework • Do not be shy to confront • Speak up and share views and ideas • Build credibility • Be more persistent • Update expats with status reports, etc. • Admit problems or mistakes • Assume nothing – check everything out • Ask questions to clarify matters • Treat women as equals • Do not pull rank • Maintain eye contact – look at us when speaking • Do not take criticism personally • Be more informal – use first name • Avoid showing emotions • Indulge in "small" talk • Get financial details nailed down

even be perceived as weaknesses and impediments to greater productivity and efficiency as they are regarded as not appealing to logic, systems thinking and the rational mind.

- **Sex role differences**

Expats have to understand that the perception towards working women may differ from what they are used to. Those who come from more egalitarian cultures (like the US or Australia) will be used to "Women's Liberation" values, and professional women especially, who may be more assertive in demanding equal rights, rewards and treatment. On the other hand, the Japanese expat male for instance, may view the role of women in business or management very differently. These differences in expectations may create some misunderstanding when expats – Americans and Japanese – relate with the female workforce in Malaysia.

GUIDELINES FOR EXPATS WORKING IN MALAYSIA

There are a number of skills that can be developed in cross-cultural communication, whether written or verbal. They are in essence human relations skills which include knowing something about one's own culture as well as that of the host country.

These skills are critical for anyone who works across cultures in attempting to bridge the cultural gap and achieve synergy with the strengths of the different ethnic groups that make up the workforce:

- **Understand each other's culture**

Be aware of one's own culture and how one is being perceived by others. The expat needs to understand the different underlying assumptions about his own culture as well as those of the host culture. Only then will he be able to adjust his style according to the situation and learn to accommodate those from another culture.

- **Show empathy**

Learn to look at things from the eyes of others. Avoid imposing work methods (which may have been successful "back home") without first of all attempting to understand the local people and their work values. Empathy is a powerful tool because people prefer to work with managers who try to see things from their viewpoints.

- **Respect others**

Show respect and tolerance for differences as it is a *sine qua non* – a condition for effective cross-cultural interactions. Malaysians value those who show respect for them in speech and in action. Good manners are important as it demonstrates respect for the other person. Although it may be difficult initially, the expat should find out more about the core local values and use them to get things done.

• **Look out for sensitivities**

Avoid passing value judgements and making generalizations about other people because they are different. Be sensitive to cultural differences relating to social status, acquired titles, religious observations, sex and ethnicity.

• **Refine communication skills**

Communicate effectively by using basic skills such as asking open-ended questions, using silence, paraphrasing and reflecting feelings. Listen and observe the reaction of others towards one's actions. Malaysians are usually reluctant to tell expats their perceptions of them as this is considered too direct and disrespectful. Therefore, an expat has to be sensitive to indirect means of gathering this information. Learn the local language as well as read non-verbals. Double-checking the actual meaning of a message or comment is advisable.

• **Balance between task and relationships**

Relate to people in both work and social levels. Spending too much energy on the task and not enough time on understanding the needs and values of fellow Malaysian colleagues may jeopardize the entire work project.

• **Tolerate ambiguity**

Malaysians can be rather vague especially when it is something to do with bad news, deadlines and commitments. Expats should learn to tolerate ambiguities as there are times when things are better left unsaid. Always wanting things to be spelt out clearly may cause Malaysians undue tension and anxiety. However, this does not imply that issues be left unresolved. Look out for opportunities, often indirect and subtle, and after some time bring the issue to a close. Doing this requires the expat to have a lot of patience and persistence.

• **Punctuality**

If invited to an "open house", punctuality is not expected. It is generally acceptable to bring friends or children, and a simple gift or flowers, fruit or chocolates. (Avoid alcoholic drinks if with Muslims.) For a formal business function or dinner, then punctuality is important. But for weddings, guests are not expected to be early (although the practice is slowly changing in favour of punctuality, among both Malaysian hosts and guests.)

SPECIFIC GUIDELINES FOR FEMALE EXPATS (OR WIVES OF MALE EXPATS)

The following are some guidelines when interacting with locals.

- Malaysia is still largely a patriarchal or "male dominated society" and female expats or wives of expats must be prepared to be treated as a "Mrs" – as a number two, not as an equal.

- Note that not shaking hands could be an indication of respect – especially in a Muslim society, where a soft gentle handshake is more valued than the Western "macho" or hearty handshake.

- Dress conservatively and avoid "exposing too much skin" – this gesture is a mark of respect for the local values of common decency. Generally, less touching (physical contact), and covering up of shoulders and arms is recommended. For formal occasions, it is best to have long sleeves, high collar and low hemlines.

- In social interactions, men tend to mix with other men, and women with other women. Men will often be invited to eat first.

- Avoid loud or abrupt speech (especially with Malays) and do not openly contradict or confront. Frankness and directness are not values among Asians. Such behaviour may even be considered ill-mannered.

SPECIFIC GUIDELINES FOR MALE EXPATS

Male expats may find the following guidelines useful when mixing with Malaysians:

- Be patient with them. Malaysians have a natural curiosity for others and will often ask foreigners a lot of questions which may be interpreted as "prying". Personal questions like "Is your family with you?" or "Do you have children?" are seen as attempts to be friendly.

- Learn to engage in "small talk" initially to develop sufficient confidence or intimacy before discussing more personal matters. While Western expats expect locals to have opinions and ideas to contribute to the discussion, some locals may not want to be too vocal about what they think and feel.

- Look for non-verbal cues when extending a handshake to Muslim women who may not want to shake hands with men – especially if they have just performed their ablutions before praying.

- For social occasions, for instance, a dinner or formal functions, wear conservative dress and colours. At Malay dominated functions, men and women may not mix as freely as found in Western cultures.

- For functions held by Malaysian hosts, Western expats may have to understand the food preferences of the various ethnic groups in the country. While the Chinese and Indians may take alcohol, Muslim Malays may not expect you to drink in their homes. And while gift-giving or bringing a bottle of wine is quite acceptable for Chinese and Indian hosts, the Malay host will be more open to receiving indigenous artifacts or local crafts. They become decorative or utilitarian souvenirs as well as memories of friendship.

- Alternative to a gift is a reciprocal invitation to dinner, either at one's home, a club or a specially favoured local restaurant of the local host. But check out their food preferences and dietary habits.

ASIAN EXPATS

This chapter has so far emphasized the interactions involving Western expats rather than Eastern expats. As Malaysia is in the East, most Malaysians should be more familiar with the cultures of Eastern expats. However, the Japanese, while similar in many ways to other Asians, are unique in several aspects.

When interacting with the Japanese, it is worth learning some aspects of their culture. For example, they respect strict punctuality and status differences. Group harmony, cohesion and face are very important, and there is a whole range of protocol and formalities that are adhered to quite strictly. Women especially, are rare in the business or professional field, and wives of Japanese male expats will rarely be included in business and social events. Japanese wives may also not speak English very well. Japanese businessmen may find it hard to deal with local or foreign women in business.

CONCLUSION

If the values and norms of politeness, courtesy, sincere empathy, clear and even-paced speech, patience, careful listening and conservative behaviour are all adhered to, then interactions between Malaysians and expats should generally be smooth and productive.

For the first-time expat visiting Malaysia or a Malaysian being posted overseas, some form of cultural orientation and training in cross-cultural communication would be beneficial. More important is the need to focus on the values and underlying assumptions of the host culture.

While it is important for the expat to know Malaysian values and norms of harmony, respect and face, it is equally important that Malaysians working with expats be sensitive to their values and norms. Similarly, Malaysians who go overseas and become expats will also need to learn about their new host culture and how they may be perceived by that culture.

As Malaysia becomes "more global", "more technological" and more competitive, it is likely that interactions between expats may become increasingly common.

SUMMARY OF KEY VALUES IN WORKING WITH MALAYSIANS

RESPECT FOR OTHERS

- Appreciate local values and norms. Get rid of the notion of "I am more superior than them", even if technically more competent or senior in authority
- Maintain face

HARMONY

- Build and cultivate a circle of local friends who can offer advice
- Be seen to work and socialize with locals
- Attempt to learn the national language
- Use words, vocal tone and body gestures that come across as "local"
- Be empathetic

REFERENCE

Asma Abdullah (1996). *Going Glocal: Cultural Dimensions in Malaysian Management.* Kuala Lumpur: Malaysian Institute of Management.

13

WORKING WITH FOREIGNERS

EZHAR TAMAM

INTRODUCTION

The process of industrialization and liberalization of the economy has brought about an increasing number of cross-national joint ventures and collaboration in technology transfer. Along with several workforce trends which include the need for organizations to compete in the global market, there is now an increase in the frequency and intensity of local-expatriate interfaces at the Malaysian workplace. These foreigners, either in the private or public sector of the Malaysian business community, in multinationals, joint ventures or local conglomerates, come from various countries, notably the United States of America, the United Kingdom, Japan, Singapore, Taiwan, Korea, Germany, Hong Kong, Australia, Switzerland and Sweden.

Recent reports show that in the manufacturing sector, the number of projects approved with foreign participation has increased from 45 per cent in 1996 to 88 per cent in 1997 (MIDA, 1998). With the setting up of the Multimedia Super Corridor (MSC) and increasing business globalization, more and more foreign companies and personnel are visiting Malaysia and doing business with Malaysians.

Through foreign joint ventures and subsidiaries of multinationals, Malaysians are now interfacing with working foreigners and expatriates or visiting professionals on short-term work assignments, including consultants, engineers and academics. This face-to-face encounter requires Malaysians to develop the knowledge and appropriate skills to be able to effectively relate with their foreign counterparts. As foreigners bring with them technology and management expertise from their own countries, Malaysians will have to adapt and learn as much as they can in order to hasten the process of transfer of technology.

OBJECTIVES OF THIS CHAPTER

The purpose of this chapter is to sensitize locals, particularly Malaysian managers, to the potential problems and challenges inherent in cross-cultural interfaces and how they can be adequately addressed at the Malaysian workplace. It will highlight a number of issues and challenges faced by both Malaysians and foreigners who bring in the expertise and management technology.

This chapter will document a number of observations made by foreign expatriates as they work with and supervise Malaysians and the differences in work orientation and communication behaviours that are partly due to one's earlier cultural programming. It will offer some guidelines for local managers to effectively relate with their foreign counterparts who have been employed to share their expertise with the Malaysian workforce.

ISSUES AND CHALLENGES

There are a number of issues and challenges when people of different nationalities and collective programming come together to get a job done. Because of cross-cultural differences in work-related values, attitudes, and communication patterns, the potential for misunderstanding and disagreement is high, and this can lead to a breakdown in communication. There are often misperceptions, conflicts and tensions, causing locals as well as expatriates to experience frequent disappointments and frustrations. Ultimately, this can affect productivity and workplace harmony.

More observations reported later in this chapter underscore the difficulties faced by foreigners when they interface with Malaysians who come from different ethnic groups as well as at different levels of the organizational hierarchy. Both locals and foreigners sometimes feel alienated and exasperated because of their contrasting work norms and interaction styles. Nevertheless, these cross-cultural challenges can be managed through various cognitive, affective and behavioural coping strategies.

Some of these issues and challenges are:

- **"Cultural baggage"**

Expatriates in Malaysia – if they are professionals in their fields – tend to bring with them their own unconscious "cultural baggage" of values, norms and ways of getting things done along with their technical know-how and expertise. This is more pronounced among expatriates from provincialistic cultures such as Germany, as noted by Kopper (1993). He believed that Germans take their "behaviour" with them on their overseas trips, and this can affect their effectiveness in cross-cultural communication and work collaboration. Similarly, American managers and Japanese managers are likely to bring along their own cultural values, which may be different from those observed by the local Malaysian workforce.

- **National and organizational culture**

A local-expatriate interface is a challenging encounter as the interface process is affected by values inherent in both national and organizational cultures. At the national level, culture is a collection of behaviour patterns relating to thoughts, manners and actions which members of a society have shared and learned. Within an organization, as defined by Lorsch (1986), culture refers to the shared beliefs senior managers in a company have about how they should manage themselves and other employees, and how they should conduct their business(es).

Hence, if the organization is managed by foreigners, the work culture will tend to take selected national characteristics and is an added dimension that influences communication and work processes. Nevertheless, while organizational cultures influence the way employees behave in the workplace, they do not erase the effect of the cultural background on the behaviour of employees at work (Gudykunst, 1991). As an example, a Malaysian who works for an American company will have to be able to compare and contrast two behavioural styles that are contextually appropriate. What an expatriate American manager values may be perceived differently by a senior Malaysian manager.

- **Emerging influence of the parent company**

The work setting of a multinational corporation requires Malaysians to conform to the values and practices of its main headquarter-organization (i.e. the parent company) located overseas. The way multinational firms in Malaysia run their businesses in many instances tends to mirror the way it is done in the parent company.

Although most multinational corporations today are more responsive to the values and aspirations of its overseas affiliates and therefore strive to blend into the culture and social structure of the country in which they are located, Asma (1996) has noted that in many foreign-based organizations, their business-oriented values are still derived from the values of its founding fathers, shareholders and key players. A Malaysian working with Motorola, for example, is expected to accommodate its corporate culture in terms of shared rituals and practices which are based on the values and underlying assumptions of an Anglo-American culture.

- **Hybrid management style**

Today, a joint-venture company is more likely to adopt a hybrid management style, either more of Malaysian style or more of a foreign style depending on who is in charge of managing the affairs of the company. In a study of Japanese ventures in Malaysia, Smith (1993) found that in many cases the joint ventures tend to adopt the corporate culture of the parent company through the daily work practices modelled by the individual efforts of its expatriates. Even though day-to-day management is done more in the Malaysian way, foreigners working in a local conglomerate or government agency still expect local employees they supervise, regardless of national identity, to uphold the values of timeliness, speed, accuracy, promptness, cost efficiency, completeness, and up-to-date information in order to be competitive in the global arena.

- **The "foreigner" stigma**

The locals' perceptions and attitudes toward foreigners have implications on the nature and consequences of cross-cultural communication and collaboration. The word "foreign" is central and signifies the notion of difference – "not like one of us" – with accompanying conflicts and potential discomforts, real or perceived, and they do need to be addressed. How different (or similar) are the foreigners? Are they viewed as partners or strangers? Do they understand our culture? The degree of the level of interculturalness, perceived cultural distance and inter-group posturing are pertinent here. A perception of greater differences and an unfavourable attitude towards the foreigners would certainly complicate the process and impede efforts towards effective cross-cultural communication and collaboration.

DEFINING CROSS-CULTURAL INTERFACE

Cultural differences between employees in a particular organization are often felt when Malaysians and their foreign counterparts relate across the table on an equal footing. The situation becomes even more apparent when problems and decisions are interpreted by managers who are being programmed with different sets of cultural lenses. Conflicts that emerged are often based on the differences between the values and assumptions that managers take with them to the meeting place to influence the way they perceive problems, make business decisions and implement an action.

With increasing business globalization and internet connections, more and more managers are beginning to recognize that cultural literacy will now become part of a manager's repertoire of skills. It should be treated up front and on centre stage. The more diverse the cultural elements, the greater the impact culture would have – through the values of the manager – on managerial effectiveness. Additionally, the increasing local-expatriate interfaces have placed a premium on the ability to deal with cultural differences and difficulties within the workforce. In fact, an ability to work with people of a different culture and to balance the conflicting demands of global integration versus local responsiveness is among the core competencies needed by 21st-century managers, as identified and attested to by Tung (1997).

There are two salient issues that will have to be considered in discussing the topic of Malaysians working with foreigners. First is the context in which the Malaysian-foreigner interfaces take place. When Malaysians work with foreigners abroad, they are more likely to follow or are expected to accommodate the foreigners' way of doing things. But this is not necessarily so when foreigners come here to work with Malaysians. This chapter focuses on the latter setting – especially when foreigners are brought into the country because of their special expertise, whether technological, financial or managerial.

The second issue involves the type of organization – in addition to location – which is also a contextual factor that influences how Malaysians should relate to foreigners as well as local colleagues. The way Malaysians perform and carry themselves at the workplace depends on whether they are working with a multinational corporation, a joint-venture firm, a local conglomerate, or in a government agency. In the case of a multinational corporation, Malaysians may even have to learn two sets of work behaviours: one when they relate with their foreign counterparts and another when they relate with fellow Malaysians who come from many different ethnic groups.

KEY OBSERVATIONS AND SURVEY FINDINGS

The following observations are based on research (FIGURE 1) that was done by those involved in cross-cultural management as well as by the author at the Malaysian workplace of foreigners when they interact with Malaysian employees.

Malaysia is culturally distant and different from some selected countries based on four dimensions of cultural variability, namely:
- collectivism-individualism
- contextualization of communication
- power distance
- uncertainty avoidance
- time handling behaviour

Using Hall's dimensions of the low and high context continuum and two of the four values from Hofstede's typology of cultural variability, Asma and Gallagher (1995) clustered culture into two types: Type A and Type B. Type A refers to industrialized western and northern European countries and are identified as low-context, medium to small power distance with an individualistic orientation while Type B includes Eastern, Mediterranean and Latin American countries which are identified as high-context, with a collectivist orientation and high power distance. Malaysia is considered Type B, as it is high on context, collectivism and power distance, and described as polychronic-oriented with high tolerance for ambiguity.

Type A is task-centred and values self-reliance, freedom, privacy, equality, self-actualization, structure and order, directness, specificity, clarity, openness, confrontation, quality, reliability, scheduling, and timeliness. Type B is relationship-oriented and values culture, group harmony, conformity, cooperation, respect for hierarchy, face saving, indirectness and flexibility. One must also bear in mind that countries in the same cluster, whether they are from a collectivist culture or an individualistic culture, also differ significantly in many ways. For example, although the Germans and Americans share a significant part of each other's culture, they clash on communication needs and patterns. Some differences may appear subtle and of minor importance but could be critical issues in cross-cultural interfaces.

With these analytical concepts in mind, Malaysians and foreigners do differ in the way they perceive and evaluate things. These are related to the following:

• Time orientation

There are contrasting ways in which time is handled at the workplace among polychronic locals and monochronic foreigners. The way time is treated signals attitude, evaluation of priorities, mood and status. Most Western and Northern Europe expatriates showed more pronounced observance of timeliness, importance of meeting deadlines, exact schedulings and appointments because they are compartmentalized and believe in turn taking in their approach towards work. The Germans are thought to be more compartmentalized than the British in that turn taking

FIGURE 1: Culture clustering of some selected countries

High-context culture   **Low-context culture**
   China   *Malaysia*   France   USA   Germany

<--->

Japan   Arab countries   Italy   Canada   Switzerland

Collectivism culture   **Individualism culture**
   Korea   *Malaysia*   Japan   Germany   France   UK   Australia

<--->

Taiwan   Singapore   Arab countries   Switzerland   Canada   USA

High power distance culture   **Low power distance culture**
   Arab countries   Korea   Japan   USA UK   France   Australia

<--->

Malaysia   Singapore   Taiwan   Italy   Germany   Switzerland

High uncertainty avoidance   **Low uncertainty avoidance**
Japan   Korea   Taiwan   Switzerland   *Malaysia*

<--->

   France   Italy   Germany   USA   UK   Singapore

Polychronic culture   **Monochronic culture**
   Malaysia   France   Italy   USA   Australia   Switzerland

<--->

Arab countries   Singapore   UK   Canada   Germany

Note:
1. A high-context culture focuses on the implicit messages; the meaning of messages is context dependent.
2. Low context means focusing on the explicit verbal messages.
3. An individualistic culture emphasizes individual interests and achievement, and competition.
4. A collectivist culture focuses on group interests, goals, group achievement and cooperation.
5. A high power distance culture accepts a hierarchical order and unequal distribution of power and influence.
6. A low power distance culture strives for power equalization and demands justification for power inequality.
7. High uncertainty avoidance stands for lower tolerance for uncertainty and ambiguity.
8. Low uncertainty avoidance stands for greater tolerance for uncertainty and ambiguity.
9. A polychronic culture is characterized by several things happening at once. Involvement and completion of transactions are more important than adherence to a pre-set schedule.
10. A monochronic culture emphasizes schedule, segmentation and promptness. Important things are taken up first and allotted most time; unimportant things are left last.

is more pronounced as seen in their willingness to form a queue. According to Hall (1989), monochronic promptness is even more important in Northern Europe, particularly among the Germans and Swiss, than it is in the United States.

Compared to Western and Northern Europeans, Malaysians are less compartmentalized and therefore have a more relaxed attitude towards time which could be interpreted by monochronic people as lacking a sense of urgency, weakness in planning, irresponsible, egocentric, or rude. Unlike monochronic people, who treat time commitment seriously, polychronic Malaysians, who do many things at one time, tolerate constant interruptions. They consider time commitments an objective to be achieved, if possible. Malaysians consider completing human transactions more important than adhering to schedules or appointments, delivery dates or deadlines. To monochronic people, such orientations make planning difficult. Countries that are similar to Malaysia in terms of time system include Arab countries, France and Italy.

Lack of understanding of the differences between the monochronic and polychronic time system, as well as the variation among nations of the same cluster, could cause serious work difficulties. The findings of a local-expatriate interfaces study (Tamam, 1997) are illustrative of the potential problem for locals working with monochronic expatriates. Most of the Northern European expatriates interviewed in the study expressed their frustrations working with Malaysians, as summarized by a British expat working in a national firm:

> "It's difficult to get things done through Malaysians. It's not that they don't have commitment ... perhaps they lack discipline in terms of work prioritization. They face difficulties in knowing which job needs to be done first."

A German expat working with Malaysians in a multinational organization also made a similar observation:

> "They (Malaysians) do not put much emphasis on schedule. They are less hurried and more accommodating to time change. In executing projects, they have milestones, but throughout my experience working in project teams led by Malaysians, the schedules keep on changing. They do not emphasize sticking to schedule unless they are being put to close scrutiny by their boss."

The tension attributed to the differences in time orientation is acknowledged by the locals. While they see their foreign counterparts as inflexible and rigid, expatriates, on the other hand, see locals as poor in time management and lacking in discipline.

Clearly, such cultural misperception can be a potential barrier in developing a productive work relationship between Malaysians and their foreign counterparts. For those who have adjusted to the values of on-time delivery and value-added service, the Malaysian "relaxed-time" orientation can be an irritation for those who look upon time as a resource that can be measured and saved. As a result, while Western and Northern European expatriates are particular about time, managers from Eastern, Mediterranean and Latin America countries look at time in a more polychronic way.

• Mismatched expectations

Different expectations on decision-making, problem solving and disagreement with superiors also contribute to cross-cultural workplace difficulties. In Western organizations, managers are expected to reach decisions and solve problems rationally and in a democratic and participative manner; decisions are made by focusing on results while facts, risk taking and logical reasoning are the basis of decision-making.

However, in Malaysia, participative and problem-solving approaches to decision-making are often considered a long-drawn-out process of negotiating. Managers who are fast in making decisions can be seen as impulsive and probably those who do not weigh the feelings and sensitivities of all concerned. In addition, they are also expected to maintain a greater social and professional involvement with their subordinates and even take the lead and decide for them. Malaysians believe that their managers and leaders are still those who have to be seen to take charge.

This orientation of showing reverence to their seniors and elders is the consequence of adhering to the values of harmony, conformity, modesty and greater respect for superiors. It is the passivity and the dependent and uncritical attitude of Malaysians that Western and Northern European expatriates find difficult to work with. The frustrations, tensions and disappointments the foreign managers might face when working with locals is best demonstrated in the following incident reported by a UK expatriate:

> "A typical answer was "what to do?" to my question for ideas from them on problems. It was much later, through the grapevine, that I learned that this had created the impression and the situation that the boss didn't know what to do. From my perspective, I was doing this to develop the skills of the staff. By questioning, I was getting the staff to think and evaluate and that is a coaching role."

• Group orientation

Another problem that frequently surfaced in local-expatriate decision-making exercises is the conflicting collectivist vs. individualistic approach

187

to decision making. The group factor is an important consideration for collectivist Malaysians and is less salient in individualistic societies. Thus, consultation and consensus-seeking behaviour are widely practised in Malaysia. The problem and tension attributed to different expectations and approach towards decision making is illustrated in the following critical incident reported by a United Kingdom expatriate in Tamam's (1997) study.

> "Four years ago, I tried to introduce total quality business management. It required everyone in the company to actively look at their job functions and come up with suggestions for improvement. However, some middle management personnel took the suggestion as a personal complaint against them."

In this incident, the local's reaction may be typical of a collective culture where consultatively, group decision making is valued. An implication of consensus-seeking, group-centred decision making is that it is difficult to reach a speedy decision. In addition, Malaysians also tend to take a longer time to implement the decision unless they are being requested and closely watched by their superiors. On the contrary, Gannon (1994) noted that in other consensus-seeking organizations such as German and Japanese organizations, decision-making time may be longer, but once the decision has been made, it is implemented without delay.

• Separation of private and public lives

Another important aspect of work orientation is the separation between private and work lives in some cultures. This definitely has implications on local-expatriate interfaces at the workplace. While privacy is highly valued in individualistic cultures in Germany and Switzerland, Malaysians, being collectivists, may not interpret it in the same manner – as seen by a greater tolerance among Malaysians for the level of noise, for instance.

The Germans have a strong sense of privacy and tend to view themselves as very independent while locals, who are more group oriented, are used to being interrupted and are cordial to visitors who drop in without an appointment. For the same reason, the Germans hold employees responsible for performance but do not supervise them. Kopper (1993) reported that unexpected demand of overtime and more contact within and outside the workplace violates German and Swiss "private garden".

The Japanese, on the other hand, tend to extend work into their private lives. Smith (1993) in a study found that a Malay personnel manager may appear to be lazy to the Japanese manager because he insists on leaving the office at 4:30 p.m. each day. The Japanese expect local managers to stay behind late at work and keep busy on the job. While the Japanese consider the "after-five Japanese hour" as valuable, the locals see it as not important. Most of the locals interviewed in the study by Tamam (1997), cited family commitments as the reason for the limited socialization with expatriates after office hours.

• Communication patterns

According to European expatriates, Malaysians have a tendency to be indirect, ambiguous and under communicating, and are perceived as unassertive, passive or even hypocritical. They are also reluctant to sit down and talk out the difficulties and would prefer to use a third party to tell their disagreement or to work out the problem rather than telling the person directly.

This indirect style of communication among Malaysians can often be a source of conflict and tension for expats who are used to being given more information and are not comfortable with vagueness and ambiguity. However, Malaysians may perceive this posture as aggressive, persistent and hard headed. Problems are also more likely to occur in upward communication and in conveying information as Malaysian subordinates are rather reluctant to volunteer information which may not be appreciated by their superiors. This seemingly reticent and passive outlook will result in restricted information flow, thus causing concerns in such managerial practices as performance evaluation, and feedback, group decision making, conflict resolution and delegation or empowerment.

• Homogeneity-heterogeneity

Participants in a communication event can be classified along a continuum of homogeneity-heterogeneity. Sarbaugh (1988) used this continuum to establish the level of interculturalness of a communication event. The more heterogeneous the participants' background, the higher the level of interculturalness. As such, a local manager-American expatriate interface could be conceptualized as highly intercultural when compared to a local manager-Japanese expatriate interface. This is because the Malaysian culture is "closer" to the Japanese culture than it is to the American culture. It would be much less intercultural in the case of a Malay manager with his Indonesian colleague.

The degree of foreignness conceptually can be based on various dimensions of cultural variability such as the value orientation of individualism and collectivism (Trandis, 1988), the perceptual orientation of high-context and low-context culture (Hall, 1981), time orientation (Hall, 1984), and Hofstede's (1984) four work-related values of individualism-collectivism, power distance, uncertainty avoidance, and masculinity-femininity. These are analytical concepts to be used in examining and explaining cross-cultural variations in behaviours at workplaces.

Sarbaugh (1988) contended that when participants are highly heterogeneous in their world views, normative patterns, code system, and perceived relationship and intent, communication will require great effort. According to him, communication difficulties would increase as the level of interculturalness increased. Hall (1989), likewise, argued that the greater the cultural distance, that is the greater the cultural difference in such things as time, context and space, the more difficult the interface will be.

In other words, the more the locals and foreigners differ in cultural backgrounds, the more intercultural is the interface, and in turn the greater the potential for misunderstanding and conflict. It must be emphasized, nevertheless, that the notion of difference is more in the emphasis than in kind.

- **Language proficiency**

Many believe that misunderstandings and problems in cross-cultural encounters are due to one of the individuals not being competent in the other's language. Language facility alone, however, is not enough to ensure that communication and collaboration with foreigners will progress smoothly and effectively. Misunderstanding and problems in intercultural encounters at the workplace stem from not knowing or ignoring the unstated and hidden norms, nuances and rules guiding the communication and behaviour of people from different cultures. As Stephen and Greer (1995) pointed out, although language problems complicate the communication process, far greater difficulties seem to occur because of cultural misunderstandings and unmet expectations.

SOME GUIDELINES FOR LOCAL MANAGERS

The observations reported above show that locals will encounter difficulties when working with foreigners, and more importantly the difficulties attributed to cultural differences are consequential to communication effectiveness and work process. What can local managers do to manage the difficulties and maintain a productive working relationship with their foreign counterparts?

Following are some broad recommendations, at organizational and individual levels, for working effectively with foreigners in Malaysia.

- **Create clear policies and work procedures to avoid ambiguity in interpretation**

Local managers need to create a set of clear and well defined procedures, explicit rules and policies to guide the behaviour of all employees regardless of national origins. Where possible, avoid situations where there are uncertainty and ambiguity in interpretation.

A weak organizational culture is one in which the framework for noticing, interpreting and responding to events is not commonly held; there are uncertainty and ambiguity, and the demand for a single response is open to many interpretations. Recent empirical evidence showed that cultural differences are more frequently expressed in weak organizational settings or situations and less often expressed in strong organizational settings or situations where policies and procedures are clearly laid down and cascaded to all levels in the organization (Maznevski and Peterson, 1997). In other words, cultural differences are more salient and consequential in weak organizational settings.

With the guide of clearly defined policies and procedures, employees will have a common framework and approach towards work which in turn can reduce the potential for friction in local-foreigner interfaces, thus facilitating a smooth task interaction.

This means that organizational values and work norms have to be explicitly communicated to organizational members through its mission and vision statements, philosophy and operational policies. Assumptions, values and expectations of both cultures – expatriates and locals – must be made known and clearly understood by all parties involved.

One effective strategy in attempting to create a strong situation is putting on the agenda some ground rules on how organizational members may differ in certain areas of problem solving and decision making because of the underlying values and assumptions of their key managers. Once these are expressed, pertinent questions can then be raised and discussed openly to sensitize locals and foreigners to the potential cross-cultural issues and problems.

- **Develop cross-cultural organizational socialization mechanisms**

Over a period of time, locals and expatriates have to adopt common organizational ways of thinking and doing things. This organizational strategy is imperative in building a strong organizational culture. Research findings have shown that cross-cultural organizational socialization enhances perception of organizational-individual fit and thus facilitate local-expatriate task interactions (Granrose, 1997). Granrose suggests that the contents of institutional socialization (i.e., formal training and feedback systems) and individual socialization should include the following:

(a) Focus on shared superordinate organizational goals and values

(b) Provide rewards for desired behaviour

(c) Affirm one's membership in national and organizational groupings

(d) Address areas where conflict is likely to occur because of value incongruence

In addition to sensitizing locals and expatriates of cultural influences and the potential implications of culture through formal discussions of work procedures and schedules, organizations need to conduct regular social discussion of work life and sharing of perspectives among their workforce.

One factor that inhibits locals from socializing with their foreign counterparts is language deficiency. Hence, an understanding of the language of the expat and locals will go a long way towards overcoming the communication difficulties and breakdown. This has to be adequately addressed by the management.

- **Use cultural orientation to explain and understand cross-cultural workplace difficulties**

A cognitive strategy in managing cross-cultural challenges and difficulties will be to organize a cultural orientation for both locals and expats in the organization. In addition to language facility, locals need to understand the values and underlying assumptions of the culture of the expatriate who is brought into the organization. They will have to familiarize themselves with the key cultural concepts of individualism-collectivism, time orientation, power distance index, uncertainty avoidance orientation, and low- and high-context communication, and consider their implications at the workplace. These concepts are very useful analytical tools for examining and anticipating workplace difficulties.

- **Adjust to different work styles**

Local managers and employees who interact and work with expatriate supervisors or managers need to adjust to their work styles and manage expectations realistically. They must not assume information will be shared readily when working with expatriates as the latter is more inclined to compartmentalize work and personal matters and may not be supportive of the Malaysian's interpretation of confidentiality and sharing of privileged information among ingroup members.

Malaysians may therefore have to get used to a work setting where the values of individualism, punctuality, timeliness (a monochronic orientation) task focus and outcome driven and work practices with proper planning and scheduling, adherence to schedule, providing decision-making input, and being accurate and quality conscious are vital to efficiency and effectiveness. Anything less would make their foreign counterparts label Malaysians as incompetent.

Locals, too, have to learn to talk about their personal accomplishments, to establish short-term relationships, and to pay attention to contracts when working with expatriates who come from individualistic cultures. At the same time, they also have to learn not to look over the shoulders of the expatriates who come from low power-distance cultures.

- **Avoid social attribution and do not use stereotypes of outgroup to explain communication difficulties and problems**

When working with people from another culture, it is important to keep in mind that cross-cultural misunderstanding and problem occurs when one interprets others' behaviours based on one's cultural knowledge and assumptions. Inaccurate stereotyping has to be minimized and this can be done by understanding the hidden values of the other, questioning images of stereotypes available through literature, and reflecting on one's attitudes toward the outgroup. Hence, when there is a high potential for misunderstanding, one should be mindful and conscious of what others are thinking but not saying.

- **Avoid ethnocentric attitudes**

Attitudinal arrogance or cultural ignorance is unwelcome and tends to invoke resentment. While acquiring a sound knowledge of other cultures and how they differ from one's own is encouraged, it is insufficient to overcome any negative sentiments. It would be better to focus on the cultural similarities and opportunities – perceived or otherwise – and seek to adapt accordingly as this would contribute positively to face-to-face interaction. A lower perception of cultural distance and positive intergroup attitudes should be encouraged as it can increase the perception of team membership in local-expatriate interfaces. Avoid membership based on cultural groupings to serve as the primary basis for interaction as it can lead to unhealthy competition.

- **Be aware of "normal" tendencies**

Local managers must be aware of their "normal" tendencies in order to reduce cross-cultural communication problems. Knowing one's own communicative style is crucial and is the first step towards establishing effective cross-cultural interactions. If there are substantial differences between one's own culture and that of one's corporate setting or foreign counterparts, one will have to stretch a bit. Such behavioural flexibility has been reported as one of the key requirements for effective cross-cultural interactions.

When collaborating with expatriates who are from low-context cultures with low tolerance for uncertainty, one needs to be explicit, provide details and be frank in stating a point or giving instructions.

On the other hand, when relating with expatriates from high context cultures and who are concerned about face-saving, a less direct approach is preferred.

There is also a need to be sensitive to contextual cues in ascertaining the meaning of messages. When requesting for information, look for ways to access them.

- **Use confirming behaviours when interacting with others**

A productive approach to building and sustaining relationships with different expatriates is to try to be "confirming" in one's interaction. Confirming behaviours are those that cause the other person to value himself or herself as an individual. Bantz (1993) suggests that maintaining social support by engaging in confirming communication even when disagreeing is one tactic of managing cultural differences.

- **Speak clearly**

It would be advisable for locals to speak up clearly and use simple language if it is English. Checking out and restating are some behavioural strategies that can be used in dealing with language difficulties when working with people from different national origins. English, while it is spoken in many cultures, is often laced with local nuances as well as syntax and pronunciation. In this case, "Malaysian English" is a fine example.

CONCLUSION

In working effectively with people from other cultures, Malaysians need to be aware of differences in values and expectations, understand the culture of their respective workplaces, and the work orientation of the expatriates. Most importantly, Malaysians must understand how their own "cultural filters" as well as those of their foreign partners influence their communication and work behaviours. They need to resist using their own set of assumptions to evaluate the behaviours and actions of those from another culture. In addition, they also need to make a conscious attempt to expand their repertoire of cross-cultural communication skills when relating with people who are not like them.

Synergistic work practices can only evolve when locals recognize the consequences of their cultural values on communication and work behaviours and begin to vary their styles depending on the situation they are in. They have to employ an array of tactics – cognitive, affective and behavioural – to manage the difficulties due to cultural differences. Qualities such as patience, open-mindedness, cultural empathy, sensitivity, compromise, diplomacy, flexibility and adaptability are keys to effective interfaces with foreigners.

SUMMARY OF KEY VALUES ON WORKING WITH FOREIGNERS

DIRECT AND TO THE POINT	○ Be able to speak up clearly and confidently
"I" NOT "WE"	○ Be willing to give an opinion even if it is contrary to popular/majority opinion ○ Show confidence and mastery of your knowledge and skills
TASK DRIVEN NOT RELATIONSHIP BASED	○ Focus on task objectives and deadlines ○ Be more open and less sensitive to negative feedback

REFERENCES

Asma Abdullah (1996). *Going Glocal: Cultural Dimensions in Malaysian Management.* Kuala Lumpur: Malaysian Institute of Management.

Asma Abdullah and Gallagher, E L (1995). Managing With Cultural Differences, *Malaysian Management Review,* Kuala Lumpur: Malaysian Institute of Management, Volume 30(2): 1-18.

Bantz, C R (1993). Cultural Diversity And Group Cross-Cultural Team Research, *Journal of Applied Communication,* 21(1), 1-19.

Hall, E T (1981). *Beyond Culture,* Garden City. New York: Anchor Press.

Hall, E T (1984). *The Dance of Life,* Garden City. New York: Anchor Press.

Hall, E T and Hall, M R (1989). *Understanding Cultural Differences.* Maine: Intercultural Press.

Hofstede, Geert (1984). *Culture's Consequences: International Differences In Work-Related Values.* Beverly Hills, CA: Sage.

Gannon, M J (1994). *Understanding Global Culture.* Thousand Oaks, CA: Sage.

Granrose, C S (1997). Cross-cultural Socialisation of Asian Employees in U.S. Organisations. In: *Cross-Cultural Work Groups* (C R Granrose and S Oskamp, eds.), pp. 186-211. Thousand Oaks, CA: Sage.

Gudykunst, W B (1991). *Bridging Differences. Effective Intergroup Communication.* Newbury Park, CA: Sage.

Kopper, E (1993). Swiss and Germans: Similarities and Differences in Work-Related Values, Attitudes, and Behaviour, *International Journal of Intercultural Relations,* 17(3), 167-184.

Lorsch, J (1986). Managing Culture: The Invisible Barriers to Strategic Change, *California Management Review*, 28(2), 95-124.

Malaysian Industrial Development Authority (1998). Report On The Performance Of The Manufacturing Sector 1997, Kuala Lumpur: MIDA.

Maznevski, M and Peterson, M F (1997). Societal Values, Social Interpretation, And Multinational Teams. In: *Cross-cultural work groups* (C R Granrose and S Oskamp, eds.), pp. 61-89. Thousand Oaks, CA: Sage.

Salk, J (1997). Partners and Other Strangers. Cultural Boundaries and Cross-Cultural Encounters in International Joint Ventures Teams, *International Studies of Management and Organisation*, 26(4), 48-72.

Sarbaugh, L E (1988). A Taxonomic Approach Of Intercultural Communication. In: *Theories In Intercultural Communication* (Y Y Kim and W B Gudykunst, eds.), pp. 22-40. Newbury Park, CA: Sage.

Smith, W A (1993). Japanese Management in Malaysia, *Japanese Studies Bulletin*, 13(1), 50-77.

Stephens, G and Greer, C R (1995). Doing Business in Mexico: Understanding Cultural Differences, *Organisational Dynamics*, 39-56.

Tamam, E. (1997). Communication with Expatriates: Difficulties as Voiced by Locals and Expatriates. Paper presented at the Forum on Managing the Malaysian Workforce organized by Malaysian Institute of Management on 29 December in Kuala Lumpur.

Trandis, H C (1988). Collectivism vs. Individualism: A Reconceptualization Of A Basic Concept Cross-Cultural Social Psychology. In: *Cross-Cultural Studies of Personalities, Attitudes and Cognition* (G Verma and C Bagly, eds.), pp. 60-95. London: Macmillan.

Trompenaars, Fon (1993). *Riding the Waves of Culture.* London: Nicholas Brealey Publishing Ltd.

Tung, R (1997). International And Intracultural Diversity. In: *Cross-Cultural Work Groups* (C R Granrose and S Oskamp, eds.), pp. 163-185. Thousand Oaks, CA: Sage.

14

MANAGING CHANGE IN BUSINESS ORGANIZATIONS

ASMA ABDULLAH, ARIC H M LOW and PETER SHEPHARD

INTRODUCTION

A survey of intervention models used by both local and foreign consultants in change management in the country has shown that they are often based on ideas and practices which have originated in more advanced countries in the Anglo-Saxon world. Organizations in these countries have built their business policies and strategies solely on the forces of the free market and the capitalistic ethos of individual enterprise and competition.

According to Hampden-Turner and Trompenaars (1993), authors of the book *The Seven Cultures of Capitalism,* each country has its own brand of capitalism based on a number of historical, social, economic and cultural values. For example, the Japanese, American and British ways of doing things are often governed by their own version of capitalism that has evolved in their countries based on their own values and assumptions of how businesses should be and are conducted. Therefore, how managers relate in the transaction of their business, their accountability to their shareholders and their responsibility to customers and employees are all embedded in the different ways capitalism is interpreted in their respective countries.

OBJECTIVES OF THIS CHAPTER

This chapter examines the key issues and challenges for managers who seek the professional expertise of management consultants to develop and implement change initiatives in their organizations. A number of key observations will also be described. The chapter concludes with a list of guidelines for both managers and consultants to consider when collaborating on a change effort in a Malaysian organization.

ISSUES AND CHALLENGES

A study by the renowned change strategists, John P Kotter and Leonard A Schlesinger (1979) states that to be competitive most companies or divisions of major corporations have to undertake moderate organizational changes at least once a year and major changes every four or five years. To continue to survive, managers in today's organizations need to seek and adopt a number of change strategies for greater efficiency and productivity of their workforce.

Competitive organizations are also expected to maintain stable operations to attain corporate goals. Any change effort will involve the reshaping of its internal work processes, which are culture-bound. Thus when the workforce feels that its set culture is threatened, there is a need to examine its values and practices as they can become barriers to the needed change. Harvey and Brown (1996) noted that a change effort often has an impact on the existing culture, and when it is large, there will be resistance and a low probability of success (FIGURE 1).

In managing the change process, both the external consultant and the client-manager have to be sensitive to the deep seated values of the workforce and their perceptions of how changes can bring about both positive and negative consequences for them as well as their organizations. From a cultural perspective, there are a number of issues and challenges which managers in Malaysia face when they introduce change in their organizations, and these are as follows:

- **Prevailing managerial style**

It has been found that managers, key shareholders or entrepreneurs tend to bring their own set of values into the organizations to determine work norms and practices. While the individualistic and entrepreneurial spirit is more prevalent in managing and leading organizations in most Western cultures, the relationship between Asian superiors and their direct reports is often more paternalistic due to the values of respect for elders, loyalty and relationships.

Similarly, organizations which are foreign-owned are likely to bring in values and practices which have evolved in another culture. Those who are change agents, especially from foreign consulting companies, have to recognize that the way local managers relate with their subordinates to get things done may

FIGURE 1: The Change Model

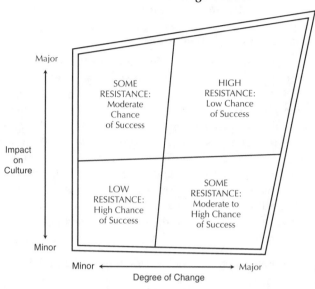

Impact on Culture (vertical axis: Minor to Major)

Degree of Change (horizontal axis: Minor to Major)

SOME RESISTANCE: Moderate Chance of Success	HIGH RESISTANCE: Low Chance of Success
LOW RESISTANCE: High Chance of Success	SOME RESISTANCE: Moderate to High Chance of Success

The larger the area, the greater the resistance

Source: Harvey and Brown (1996: 157) – "An Experiential Approach to Organization Development."

not always be similar to what they are used to in Western-based organizations. While subordinates in organizations in the West are expected to question existing work practices if they are found to be ineffective, their Asian counterparts may be less likely to do so, for the sake of harmony and face saving.

• Embedded values in imported systems

The macro capitalistic system in which a particular consulting organization is formed has an overwhelming impact and influence on how its managers and professionals do their work. Most American consultants often bring their own work styles in how work is done – the way they make an entry and exit from a change intervention project in their client organizations.

Similarly, consultants from Britain or Europe would also carry their own set of work related values and practices when providing their services to their client organizations. These "alien" values are often "transplanted" across cultures on the assumption that they are applicable and replicable. Their suitability with local work practices is not often looked into or questioned by client recipients.

In fact, most systems – human resources, financial, accounting, tax, banking, and customer service – have been conceived and designed to work in an industrial context which is more advanced than that of the recipient culture.

When these systems are "exported" to another setting, they may not necessarily have the same support structure and outcomes at the receiving end.

- **Human and technology integration**

The values accompanying the age of Information Technology (IT) are often associated with a less hierarchical mode of superior-subordinate relationship and more direct face-to-face communication. For example, an IT system in a bank is often designed to operate in a work environment where the employee is expected to make his own independent decisions. The person who is working behind a personal computer is expected to be given some amount of discretion, independence and authority to make quick decisions without having to consult his superiors. In many ways, the use of IT tends to promote a more egalitarian way of relating across the organizations and empowering people to decide and act on the spot. While this mode of relating on a one-to-one basis empowers people to decide and be responsive to market changes, there are those who would only perform tasks given by their superiors.

These values of empowerment and being direct, considered the norm in a more individualistic society, may not be received in the same way in the collectivist and more hierarchical work culture in Malaysia. In many instances, therefore, how efficiently and effectively technology is used will depend more on the culture or social system in the organization than the "spirit" of technology itself.

- **The changing ICT environment**

Most Malaysian organizations are now in a state of transition as a result of the advent of the Internet and e-commerce, which is transforming the entire business landscape in Malaysia as it is the world over.

In view of these external changes, many organizations have to rethink the impact of ICT (information and communication technology) on their organizational structures. With billions of money being transacted in a matter of minutes and seconds, most organizations around the world have yet to be equipped to manage the new wave of technology change that is having a powerful impact on how businesses are transacted across borders. As the whole range of operations in finance and banking, for instance, depends on IT-based systems, IT will have an increasing impact on how Malaysians relate with their subordinates, managers and customers at the workplace.

Therefore, the ability of organizations to continuously adapt to the rapidly changing ICT environment and thereby achieve a steady state of dynamic equilibrium will be the greatest challenge for managers in the years to come.

- **Consultant's knowledge and access to information**

A consulting organization is based on the knowledge and expertise of its key professionals. Knowledge – both the process and resource – is power and forms the main currency in shaping the appropriate interventions consultants offer to their clients. As change consultants enter their client systems, their information, ideas and thoughts will shape and form part of the deliverables. While the focus on knowledge requires consulting companies to be at the leading edge of the technology of the client industry, local-based organizations have yet to build an infrastructure to receive these innovations. Hence, consultants who design and introduce change initiatives into organizations may therefore have to consider the existing facilities and the degree of comfort local employees have with work systems and values that are externally induced.

- **Preparation for a "K-economy"**

In recent times, there has been an urgent call to Malaysian employers and employees to implement immediate measures to prepare the Malaysian workforce for a fast developing digital economy, or, more commonly known as the "K-economy". In its broadest sense, this concept is based on knowledge as an important contributor to sustainable economic growth and development.

The British Department of Trade and Industry in the United Kingdom's White Paper on the K-Economy gives a tentative working definition that "a knowledge-driven economy is one in which the generation and exploitation of knowledge play the predominant part in the creation of wealth" (Zainal, 2000).

The emerging trend has created a massive need for knowledge workers in Malaysia to form the backbone of the future of its national economy and the realization of a developed nation status by the year 2020. Changes, therefore, have to be put in place. They include an education system with greater and wider use of IT or ICT. Any obstacles – both social and cultural (such as forces that resist learning or using and disseminating information) – must be removed when embracing change and technology so that the organization can stay competitive.

Probably, the greatest challenge organizations face is to be able to achieve a harmonious balance between having "high tech and high touch" as the workforce becomes highly dependent on information and the electronic media. The bulk of management training may indeed be to focus on how to achieve that balance.

MANAGING CHANGE DEFINED

Change, as it is often described, is part of doing business today. In fact, it is a way of life in today's organizations. More than before, change is rapid, complex, less predictable and less easily managed. It is also continuous, irregular and complex. As organizational structures call for flexibility, adaptability and higher levels of tolerance of ambiguity, new competencies in how to receive, accommodate and manage change have to be acquired by managers.

A change programme would involve modifying the existing organizational systems, structure and culture. The ultimate aim of change is to enhance organizational efficiency and effectiveness or even to ensure survival.

Traditionally, the management of change has been defined as the planning, directing and controlling of events leading to a specific state of equilibrium. But as change becomes a norm or constant, managers have to be highly responsive to simultaneously collect data, analyse them and take appropriate actions. They have to be more competent in their ability to access and assimilate valid and larger volumes of information, and make accurate and timely decisions. At times, they may even be called to use intuition, hunch or gut feel in their response to change.

From another perspective, there is also a need to factor in "personality" differences as distinct from cultural differences. A left-brained person will be more inclined towards analysis of information to produce knowledge while a more right-brained personality will be inclined towards synthesis and a wholistic view of information, which includes use of intuition. The latter is more aligned to the cultural concepts of the Asian manager where harmony with nature, a high-context form of relationship, being adaptable, having a higher tolerance for ambiguity or uncertainty and ability to "go with the flow" are expected of them. Managers may have to nurture these cultural characteristics to provide that needed edge for the 21st century organization in Asia or beyond.

In introducing change, more often a client manager is expected to pay a substantial fee for the professional services of an external consultant to work on a set of deliverables within a certain time frame or deadlines. Both the client and consultant should use a set of measurements or benchmarks to monitor and evaluate the effectiveness of the change effort. They should also recognize that unless all stakeholders are enrolled in the change process, total commitment may not be achieved.

KEY OBSERVATIONS RELATING TO MANAGING CHANGE

There are a number of observations in Malaysian organizations when they seek help from external consultants to manage the change event. These are as follows:

- **From an operational mode to a critical thinking mode**

The Malaysian economy until recently has been on an operational mode where the thinking and decision-making processes are the prerogatives of those in the senior technical and management group, who are more often foreigners. Even today, most Malaysians who use the services of foreign consulting organizations still depend on "imported" management expertise and technology to bring about change. For example, multinationals like SHELL, Motorola and Nokia tend to bring into Malaysia a number of work systems conceived and designed overseas. In fact, even the building of highways and airports, etc. is still very much in the hands of foreign expatriates who have the technical expertise which is not available locally.

The recent shift of the workforce from an operating mode to a thinking mode is most evident in the manufacturing industries. However, it is also found in the service industry like in McDonald's and Kentucky Fried Chicken, where Malaysians have tended to adopt the systems and practices developed overseas and recruit Malaysian workers to operate them. As a result, Malaysians have a rather limited exposure to the conceptual and design aspects of a particular procedure and system as they are developed outside the country and only imported into the country to be locally operated.

- **Professionalism of the change consultant**

One of the challenges for consulting organizations is to equip their personnel to be creative, innovative and with the ability to make a lasting impression on their elderly clients. While they may appear to have the right credentials, they may not necessarily have the experience to communicate to their often elderly clients of the need to change. What has worked successfully in Johor Port may not work in Renong Bhd as they have different organizational priorities and cultures. To be able to convey the right message, the consultant may have to be able to understand the intricacies and the hidden dimensions of power and influence, key stakeholders and informal structures within the organizational culture of their client system.

- **Hierarchical structure**

Because of the value of respect for elders, the style of management in most Malaysian organizations is more likely to be characterized by a top down, and hierarchical structure. Compared to more egalitarian systems of working in Anglo-Saxon cultures, this managerial style tends to take a longer time to get things done because of the tendency for subordinates to "wait to be told" by the senior managers. As a result, changes may not be easily implemented without the "blessings" of their elderly seniors. Carried to the extreme, this practice may make it difficult for subordinates to initiate new and more productive ways of getting things done; it may even slow down their ability to make the appropriate response to remain competitive.

• **Consultant-client relationship**

The approach in dealing with a particular change event requires both the consultant and client manager to be explicit in their communication practices. Sometimes in data gathering and in feedback exercises, a consultant may have to adopt a rather confrontational and direct approach in pinpointing the shortcomings of their clients. However, because of the values of preserving face and relationships, a consultant may need to articulate his findings and recommend possible interventions in the most diplomatic manner to their Malaysian clients. As a result, the consultant may need to spend time and effort when communicating feedback, especially "bad" news, so that the client will receive the information without "loss of face".

GUIDELINES FOR MANAGERS

In bringing about a change event, managers and consultants need to know the values of their workforce and identify certain work habits which can either strengthen (i.e. the driving forces) or weaken (i.e. the resisting forces) any change initiatives.

Managers too have to be visible and be seen to champion the desired behavioural or cultural change, as words articulated have to be reinforced by consistent behaviours ("walking the talk"). Management must, therefore, enrol the support of their workforce to embrace change by appealing to their core values in order to gain the expected outcomes.

Below are some guidelines for managing change efforts:

• **Evolve a culture of high performance**

Managers have to build a culture that promotes the values of customer service orientation and timeliness as expected by any commercial entity, particularly those that are being corporatized,' like the ports, the airports, and telecommunications. To become competitive and remain globally connected, they have to benchmark their systems with the best practices around the world. This means managers and change consultants have to demonstrate certain work practices that are congruent with the values of the workforce and are supportive of a productive work culture like becoming highly responsive to the need of the customer, being innovative and highly conscious of quality standards. Any work practices which are counter-productive to these values will have to be downplayed while those that enhance work output must be encouraged.

- **Be innovative and move towards a creative thinking mode**

Malaysian managers have to promote creativity and innovation among their subordinates, be more open in their communication and feedback sessions and show a willingness to share information at all levels of the organization. They have to be prepared for the advances in technology that will pave the way for a more questioning workforce where the need to create intellectual capital will be a priority.

In forging ahead, they will have to promote the next phase of an innovation-driven economic structure or the "k-economy" where the biggest challenge is to equip the workforce to be knowledge workers. To achieve this, they may have to restructure the entire organization to improve its work processes, strategies and systems of governance. The work culture too, has to be redesigned from an operating to a thinking and building mode. Managers now have to build a knowledge infrastructure, a sort of learning organization where continuous learning, creativity and innovation are revered and consistently rewarded.

- **Become more competitive across cultures**

As the Malaysian workforce moves to a higher value added economy, managers need to equip their human resources with new competencies and ways of working. They have to be more competitive both locally and globally by emphasizing intellectual capital as well as harnessing the collective efforts of diversity. This will prepare their workforce to handle increasingly changing demands from their customers, who may come from different parts of the world.

- **Be flexible**

The new breed of consultants in change management has to be sensitive to the needs of their clients who may not welcome change. As each organization has its own ways of doing things which are only known to insiders, consultants therefore have to be able to "sense" these hidden dimensions and nuances within the organizational setting. This approach would require them to be equipped not only in quantitative analysis but also with the ethnographic data collection skills of a cultural anthropologist.

In addition, they need to use the traditions and values within the culture of the workforce as a tool to spearhead change. Instead of asking people to give up their traditions, which may cause resistance, it is better to acknowledge and build on them. For example, a strong traditional value of respect for one's elders can still be preserved by incorporating the views of the younger and better-qualified employees. In this context, there is a need to adopt a "both-and" thinking (Hofstede 1991; Zohar, 1997) rather than a dichotomized thinking of an "either or" in order to achieve a win-win solution.

- **Develop robust systems**

There is a need for Malaysian organizations to develop robust systems based on local best practices ranging from financial, human resource, and accounting to IT systems. Managers have to understand several aspects of local culture which may be dysfunctional for organizations to move forward. For example, the importance of getting immediate feedback would mean that there are systems that will have to be organized to solicit data without "attacking" the person. Also, the need to make fast decisions would mean that Malaysian managers have to be seen to empower their subordinates to take charge. The views of those who are in junior positions may have to be elicited, heard and included in the decision-making process.

CONCLUSION

Organizations of the future will need to make critical decisions to find people with a set of work-related values and work orientations that support international best practices. While the global workplace demands business standards that are universal in meeting the needs of the customer, the influence of local culture will remain a key challenge for consultants wanting to bring about change in their client systems. Local indigenous factors such as culture, history, religion, business practices and political ideologies will all need to be considered.

The challenge ahead for Malaysia is to move away from the operating and building mode towards a new work culture where creativity, innovation, risk-taking and competitiveness are revered and rewarded. Managers have to question their past successes and old precepts of getting things done that are no longer relevant for a more competitive and highly interconnected world. They have to be able to manage these competing forces and deal with the technology explosion of wealth creation in the new millennium. To ensure this becomes a reality, Malaysians will then have to contribute more to the next wave of investment, and not rely on foreign investment.

In preparing the future workforce, which will take on a markedly different form from the workforce of yesteryears, managers have to identify managerial practices which may impede progress in their current organizational and business systems. Only then can they design a desired future state to enable Malaysians to face the challenges of the new millennium and by so doing, help propel the nation to a developed status by the year 2020.

SUMMARY OF KEY VALUES IN MANAGING CHANGE IN BUSINESS ORGANIZATIONS IN MALAYSIA

PATERNALISTIC WORK ORIENTATION	○ Understand the relationship of care and concern held by managers, leaders, shareholders and entrepreneurs towards their subordinates
COLLECTIVISM AND HIERARCHY	○ Avoid asking Malaysians to make decisions on the spot and alone, as they work better in pairs or groups
RELATIONSHIPS	○ Learn to relate informally and on a long-term basis with subordinates
TOLERANCE	○ Tolerate more ambiguity or uncertainty

REFERENCES

Hampden-Turner, C and Trompenaars, F (1993). *The Seven Cultures of Capitalism.* New York: Currency Doubleday.

Harvey, Donald F & Brown, Donald R (1996). An Experiential Approach to Organization Development. New Jersey: Prentice Hall Inc., p. 157.

Hofstede, G 1991. Managing in a Multicultural Society: The Malaysian Experience, *Malaysian Management Review*, Vol. 26, No. 1: 3-12. Kuala Lumpur: Malaysian Institute of Management.

Kotter, John P and Schlesinger, Leonard A (1979). Choosing Strategies for Change, *Harvard Business Review*, vol. 57, no. 2 (March-April 1979), p. 106.

Zainal Aznam Yusof (2000). K-word is the new sound of power, *New Straits Times*, Business Section, March 25, 2000, p. 27.

Zohar, D (1997). *Rewiring the Corporate Brain.* San Francisco: Berrett-Koehler Publishers Inc.

15

THE FUTURE MALAYSIAN WORKFORCE – A MANAGEMENT OUTLOOK

TARCISIUS CHIN and MANO MANIAM

QUESTION: What do you see to be the key issues and challenges for the Malaysian workforce in the new millennium?

TARCISIUS CHIN:

We have been blessed. The Malaysian workforce has, generally, been a responsible partner in wealth creation. This has contributed to industrial peace and promoted a strong management-labour relationship.

The future for the country lies in how well we move towards new wealth-creating opportunities and in how strong we behave as a civil society. The way forward has already been articulated in Vision 2020.

The challenge for the future is to generate ground level action to fulfil the vision. The issues for the Malaysian workforce are associated with the willingness, ability and concern to contribute towards fulfilling Vision

2020 in the context of expected substantial change in the marketplace. On all fronts, change can be expected. Economically, Malaysia will have to compete in the international marketplace as globalization and the borderless economy will force us to be more competitive. Technologically, the digital revolution will force us to re-engineer our value chain to be more responsive to market needs. Socially, we will be more educated, more mobile and more conscious of individual rights as traditional values erode. Organizationally, the workplace will have less hierarchical rigidities and more flexible work patterns, including working from home.

The management of business enterprises will have to respond to change by seeking competitive advantage, measured against international benchmarks of performance. This will suggest increasing our productivity through raising efficiency and effectiveness. Technology can intervene to assist. But the Malaysian workforce, which normally constitutes the largest cost element in sustaining a business, has to be receptive in partnering management to seek competitive advantage. One expression of support is in subscribing to a productivity-linked wage system that rewards high performance and penalizes those who contribute least.

A wage system that is biased towards productivity rather than seniority can only work if workers fully subscribe to it and are provided all the necessary training and development to raise their performance. More rapid obsolescence of current skills demands training and retraining to develop multi- and potential skills so that the workforce can keep pace with change. As the workforce moves from manual to knowledge work, the development of employees assumes a different focus as narrow training gives way to broader education.

The prospects for much greater collaboration between management and employees in the future are indeed bright. A more educated workforce can address higher value contributions and will be less threatened by worries over redundancy. Adversarial postures will surrender to more cooperative relationships. With mutual respect, both management and employees will see complementary roles as stakeholders in the enterprise and as active players in fulfilling Vision 2020.

MANO MANIAM:

The Malaysian workforce is probably the most dynamic of all sectors of Malaysian society bearing the brunt of the incredible transformations since the second half of the 20th century. These changes, both macro-level and micro-level, have proceeded at an exponential rate into the new millennium, with the workforce responding to a host of changes. In many areas, the workforce has initiated and provided the impetus for change, with obvious ramifications on all levels of society.

The new millennium requires a huge paradigm shift in thinking, and with it a modification of social values and practices.

One old challenge which Malaysia has faced and succeeded is the shift from an agro-based economy to an industrial one; in fact, the shift continues towards a post-industrial economy where extraction industries have given way to the service and manufacturing sectors, and moving from rural areas to urban areas. This challenge will continue, at the expense to the rural hinterland and resulting in an urban-metropolitan population majority and the continuous shrinking of the rural workforce. Food shortages, ecosystem upheavals and other related problems will manifest themselves.

The swelling urbanization and middle-class values and lifestyles, are inevitable issues in characterizing the workforce of the new century. A more educated, better informed, more discerning or choosy, mobile and demanding workforce has already emerged and will be the key challenge to economic and social growth.

The knowledge worker, by replacing the preceding manual worker, will bear many qualities which will have more far-reaching consequences than most people realize. The management-labour equation will be altered, most likely towards a more equitable, just and harmonious relationship from the traditional owner-worker mindset.

The multilingual, multicultural worker has fewer inhibitions, greater versatility, more needs to satisfy, more flexibility in adapting to work environments, and is definitely more vocal in announcing his needs and wants.

Meritocracy will continue to wear down traditional arrangements based on ethnicity and neo-feudal values.

Immigrant labour at the higher (specialized) and lower levels of the workforce will continue and may pose serious challenges to the local workers; signs of this are already prevalent at the turn of the century. At the core of this immigrant labour issue are wage-levels and unavailable skills. The question of rising expectations and an upward spiral of the wage bill may cause havoc to the quality, quantity and the character of the Malaysian workforce.

Other key issues will be inter-related to the above forces and will include demands for continuous learning at both the organizational and individual levels.

The triangular relationships among management-labour-government will see more anti-podal and adversarial situations in the short run; but in the long run, the new compromises, legislation and the speed at which agreements can be reached will lead to more cooperation and harmony in the work environment.

This paradigm shift will spawn even more shifts affecting all levels of society and will require new definitions and new approaches to deal with the workforce. Not least of all will be the challenge to provide, at an increasingly relentless pace, more and more work opportunities to the generations to come, bearing in mind that we are a youthful society with the majority of the population under 25 years of age.

The biggest challenge will remain the managing of this young multi-faceted and multicultural workforce.

QUESTION: What are your wishes for the Malaysian workforce?

TARCISIUS CHIN:

Work is not only for the purpose of earning a living. It should be the opportunity for self-expression in which the workforce can sense a contribution to a purpose and feel satisfaction that he or she has done his or her best.

As the country develops, the range and diversity of occupations will enable people to move into jobs that have meaning so that performance is driven by passion as much as by financial rewards. In the wisdom of Confucius, the best job to have is one in which we do not have to work at all! In the future, it should no longer be the worker's right to a job, but the worker's right to a satisfying job.

MANO MANIAM:

The Malaysian workforce has been described in mostly positive and even flattering terms – hardworking, educated, multi-talented, versatile, generally well-behaved and loyal, among other things. No doubt, these qualities have helped in no small measure in creating a robust, progressive and envied Asian Tiger out of Malaysia.

However, with the new challenges and a burgeoning youthful population on the rise, changes and a new order of doing business have become necessary.

Multiculturalism where many socio-cultural values and practices merge to create new meanings and validity will continue to demand prudence and careful planning. The ethnic factor will have to be solved so as not to compromise other necessary virtues like harmony, cooperation, quality-driven goals, and industrial peace. The wish is, therefore, for national unity and social cohesion, which will engender continued stability and development of the nation.

Education and training (including re-training and multi-skilling) opportunities must be made available on demand. With the youthful population in mind, and the wholesale shift from an agro-based economy to a globalized borderless world economy based on information technology, the need for continuous learning, upgrading and certification of skills, mastery of other languages, acceptance of cultural variations and sheer knowledge work will leave us with no choice but to establish and excel in the learning-teaching field. The government's move to make Malaysia a regional centre of learning and to encourage foreign institutions of higher learning to re-locate here together with the establishment of more training institutes augurs well for Malaysia.

Job opportunities may not expand conveniently to cater for the increasing supply into the job market. Entrepreneurship, small business development and self-employment needs will surge. It is hoped that the wishes for increased education and training will also cater for the development of self-starters in business.

Another wish is for increased opportunities for women in the workforce. Although there has been development in this area, the actual situation today leaves much to be desired in taking advantage of the 50 per cent of the population, who are female, to bring them as equal productive workers to the workforce. Special programmes, agencies and re-examining cultural taboos against the working woman must be instituted from the highest levels of government and the private sector. The process has gained momentum in the last decade of the 1900's, and the wish is for women to rapidly take their rightful places as workers, entrepreneurs and leaders in the economy.

The workforce, like so many sectors in a newly industrialized nation, has been generally over-regulated and many restrictions curtail optimum performance. An open collaborative approach between decision-makers and workers could lead to better decisions relating to the workforce and greater transparency in the conduct of business. Transparency, at all levels, will beget greater accountability, which is the cornerstone of successful leadership and management in any organization.

QUESTION: Will we ever develop a management style that is uniquely Malaysian? If so, how would you describe it?

TARCISIUS CHIN:

There is universality in the practice of management. The science of management, viz. its tools and techniques, can be used anywhere. But for quite a while, there is the acceptance that management is also culture-bound. Therefore, it is suggested that the art of dealing with people in Japan cannot be applied in the same way when dealing with others in the United States, for instance. Hence, as an illustration, the decision-making process in Japan consumes a lot of time in reaching a decision through the *ringgi* process, but can expect speedy implementation, while Americans believe in speedy decision making, but will have to battle resistance to change after the decision is taken.

Japan was isolated for centuries and has evolved a mono-cultural pattern that has worked its way into relationships that have influenced its unique management style of consensus and harmony. The US, on the other hand, is a plural society which has been influenced by migration of people from many other parts of the world. This openness has clearly been reflected in its management style of individual rights and personal gain.

Malaysia is also a plural society. But its Asian background has biased its cultural underpinnings towards community and clan. However, we are in transition. Younger Malaysians have been exposed to Western ideas that have given birth to Generation X. Education is enormously Western oriented. There is a tidal wave of Western thinking that is seeping into the way we manage our affairs. Indeed, the management platform we are constructing is borrowed heavily from Western thinking. Globalization and digitalization will further help create a Malaysian management community that will behave very much like any other management community in the world.

It will take intentional effort to develop a uniquely Malaysian management style. We will need to identify the positive aspects of our cultural values that can support effective management practice and unwaveringly promote them as the vital ingredients of the Malaysian management identity.

Much literature has been devoted to the intelligence quotient (IQ) in management. There is also an emerging literature on emotional

213

intelligence (EQ). The missing link in developing management as a noble profession is SQ, or spiritual intelligence. If we can identify the cultural values that can describe and support the SQ component for Malaysian managers, it will be a first step towards developing a management style that will be uniquely Malaysian. The second and more important step is to educate, train and develop Malaysian managers to practise management in accordance with the SQ profile that has been structured.

MANO MANIAM:

The fact that sooner or later there will emerge an identifiable and distinct style of management unique to Malaysia cannot really be disputed. Management, besides being a science is also a culture-based human art form embodying the traits, nuances, values, attitudes, beliefs, idiosyncrasies, history, traditions and pragmatic elements, which will truly give it its unique brand.

What may diffuse this inevitable evolution of a "Malaysian-ness" will be the very technology of management which is universal. It transcends most, if not all, traits, values, history, etc. Management practice tends to "level" the situation, stripping away the "colour" and other antecedents which confuse or complicate the management issue at hand. In such a situation, the uniqueness of any style of management may be difficult to discern.

However, the "man" in management will always prevail, and unless it is a computer which does all the managing, man's value bases and his biases, follies, invaluable insight and cultural baggage will come through.

Because Malaysia is a relative newcomer in modern management, we have been able to learn from previously existing models and can mix-and-match values and practices from not only our own varied traditions but also from all over. And given the fact that Malaysians go far and wide for education, training and even employment, we have unconsciously built a vast repertoire and database of knowledge, best practices and ways of doing business and managing resources.

From this recency in our nation's development and the vast spectrum to select from, Malaysian management has evolved and continues to do so.

With Vision 2020's nine challenges to provide focus and act as parameters, the Malaysian management style is characterized by its youthfulness, robustness, progressiveness and capacity for continuous adaptation.

It also has certain managerial values based on the cultures of its people. As the survey conducted by MIM in the late 1980's would show, these common values cut across ethnic or geographical boundaries. Highest among them happen to be honesty, respect, humility, sincerity, face-saving, loyalty, spiritual underpinning, material acquisition and communal welfare. These society-sanctioned values are, not surprisingly, the same as those which influence management.

Because we are a multicultural society and have a federal structure, the core of the management style may escape detection as something really common and taken for granted. Yet, it will take another generation to be able to converge these various factors – a common destiny, integrity, etc. – into a viable management style.

The emergent management style will reflect the style of the larger society and its cultural imperatives. Whilst the Malaysian society itself is undergoing fervent changes, so will the speed and veracity of its style of getting things done. It will, however, be characterized by its give-and-take attitude, its dynamism and capacity to respond swiftly and effectively to external stimuli. It will be increasingly transparent and accountable. And its recency will allow it to be proactive rather than reactive.

It will have the one primary ingredient vital to all management: the capacity for negative entropy, or put more simply, the ability to see where things are heading and to take effective remedial steps to avert decay, obsolescence and demise.

This last aspect of Malaysian management will certainly be the strong element in its style which will allow Malaysia to get things done on time, within budget and according to specifications.

However, the process is evolutionary and Malaysia has advantages – like a talented and educated workforce and abundant natural resources – which will take time and good leadership to forge a truly recognizable and unique Malaysian management style.

SUMMARY OF FORCES OF CHANGE AND THEIR SIGNIFICANCE IN MALAYSIA

TYPES

- ○ Moving from agro to industrialized to post industrialized economies all at one time
- ○ Rural-urban migration
- ○ Youthful population
- ○ Globalization, borderless economy, Information Technology, digitalization: K-economy
- ○ Expansion of middle-class population
- ○ Management-Labour-Government relationship

THEIR SIGNIFICANCE

- ○ Organization becoming less hierarchical and more egalitarian
- ○ Focus on meritocracy
- ○ Emphasis on continuous learning, training and education
- ○ Centre of learning for the region
- ○ Increased competition; more flexible wage patterns, productivity-linked wage system
- ○ Need for retraining and multiskilling; importance of knowledge workers
- ○ Managing the young; greater collaboration between management and employees
- ○ Need for immigrant labour
- ○ Making performance a passion
- ○ National unity and social cohesion; awareness of cultures and cultural literacy
- ○ Increased opportunities for women; examination and elimination of cultural taboos
- ○ Transparency, accountability
- ○ Emotional intelligence, spiritual intelligence

INDEX